Reassessing the Heroine in Medieval French Literature

UNIVERSITY PRESS OF FLORIDA

Florida A&M University, Tallahassee
Florida Atlantic University, Boca Raton
Florida Gulf Coast University, Ft. Myers
Florida International University, Miami
Florida State University, Tallahassee
New College of Florida, Sarasota
University of Central Florida, Orlando
University of Florida, Gainesville
University of North Florida, Jacksonville
University of South Florida, Tampa
University of West Florida, Pensacola

Reassessing the Heroine
in Medieval French Literature

Edited by Kathy M. Krause

University Press of Florida

GAINESVILLE · TALLAHASSEE · TAMPA · BOCA RATON
PENSACOLA · ORLANDO · MIAMI · JACKSONVILLE · FT. MYERS · SARASOTA

First cloth printing, 2001
First paperback printing, 2019

24 23 22 21 20 19   6 5 4 3 2 1

Library of Congress Cataloging-in-Publication Data
Reassessing the heroine in medieval French literature / edited by
Kathy M. Krause.
p. cm.
Includes bibliographical references and index.
ISBN 978-0-8130-1881-2 (cloth : alk. paper)
ISBN 978-0-8130-6414-7 (pbk.)
1. French literature—To 1500—History and criticism.
2. Heroines in literature. I. Krause, Kathy M., 1962–.
PQ155.W6 R43 2001
840.9'352042'0902—DC21   00-051056

The University Press of Florida is the scholarly publishing agency for the
State University System of Florida, comprising Florida A&M University,
Florida Atlantic University, Florida Gulf Coast University, Florida
International University, Florida State University, New College of Florida,
University of Central Florida, University of Florida, University of North
Florida, University of South Florida, and University of West Florida.

University Press of Florida
2046 NE Waldo Road
Suite 2100
Gainesville, FL 32609
http://upress.ufl.edu

Contents

Acknowledgments

This collection of essays grew out of the proceedings of a panel at the 1997 Kentucky Foreign Languages Conference. Without the support and encouragement of the panelists (William Paden, Joan Grimbert, David Wrisley, and Duncan Robertson), the book would not have been possible. In addition I would like to thank the editors at the University Press of Florida who have worked with me through the various revisions, answering multiple questions on everything from copyright law to stylistics. The first reader for the Press is also to be thanked for a remarkably thorough, and helpful, critique. Finally, our thanks to Charles Penwarden for his excellent translation of Nadine Bordessoule's article and his assistance in translating Christopher Lucken's.

The following publishers have graciously granted permission to quote portions of their copyright editions of medieval texts:

Librairie Droz, Geneva, for Gautier de Coinci. *Les Miracles de Nostre Dame par Gautier de Coinci*, ed. Frédéric Koenig, 4 vols. (Geneva: Droz, 1966–78); Albert Henry, ed. *Berte as grans piés*, Textes Littéraires Français 305 (Geneva: Droz, 1982); and André Tissier, ed. *Recueil de farces (1450–1550)* (Geneva: Droz, 1986–).

Boydell and Brewer Ltd., Woodbridge, England, for Chrétien de Troyes, *Cligés*, ed. Claude Luttrell and Stewart Gregory, Arthurian Studies 27 (Cambridge: D. S. Brewer, 1993).

Editions Gallimard, Paris, for Chrétien de Troyes, *Œuvres complètes*, ed. and trans. Daniel Poirion et al., Bibliothèque de la Pléiade 408 (Paris: Gallimard, 1994).

Slatkine Reprints, Geneva, for Jean d'Arras. *Mélusine: Roman du XIVe siècle*, ed. Louis Stouff (Dijon: Publications de l'Université, 1932; rpt. Geneva: Slatkine Reprints, 1974).

Preface to the Paperback Edition

It was with great pleasure that I received the University Press of Florida's request to publish a paperback and digital edition of *Reassessing the Heroine in Medieval French Literature*. It has been nearly twenty years since the volume originally appeared, and the field of medieval French literary studies has changed considerably in that time. New ways of approaching literary texts (e.g., ecocriticism, disability studies, digital humanities, etc.) and the expansion of the range of texts studied, as well as the return (in a more nuanced fashion) of the concern for a work's historical context, have all contributed to making French medieval literary studies a field both more historically oriented and more theoretically diverse than in 2001. Indeed, many of the scholars who contributed to this volume are presently working in these new(er) areas themselves. However, we all continue to stand by the arguments we presented in our essays, and in perusing them once again, we are convinced that they remain relevant to today's scholarship and teaching. In particular, the deliberately wide net we cast at the time in terms of genre and chronology means the essays continue to speak to the broader contours of today's medieval literary corpus. Vernacular religious texts, and later medieval lyric in particular, have gained added attention in the years since the volume was published, as has Anglo-Norman literary production more broadly, all of which receive significant attention in these essays.

Approaching the question of relevance from the other direction, as it were, a keyword search for "medieval, French, and heroine" in the MLA Bibliography produces only ten hits: the nine essays and prologue of this volume. Although the MLA Bibliography search misses (at least) one important recent contribution to the study of medieval French heroines (Brooke Heidenreich Findley's *Poet Heroines in Medieval French Narrative: Gender and Fictions of Literary Creation*), the lack of other citations demonstrates that the subject of the heroine in medieval French literature is far from being exhausted. This is not to say, of course, that there has been no scholarship on "heroines" in medieval French literature since 2001; rather, the term "heroine" itself has fallen out of fashion. On the one hand, more recent scholarly work on women in medieval French literature examines extratextual figures rather than female characters: women as authors, patrons, readers, scribes, and artists. On the other, scholars have tended to avoid the term "heroine" due to its range of connotations, many of them tending toward the passive and/or the secondary.[1] When one enlarges the search parameters, the number of significant scholarly studies concerned with questions of gender throughout the entire range of medieval French literary genres suggests the degree to which the essays in this volume continue to resonate with contemporary critical concerns.

The specific topic addressed by our volume, that of heroines and discourse in medieval French literary texts, has renewed relevance in our contemporary era. Exploring "the ways in which critical discourses, both medieval and modern, define who the heroine is, how she behaves, and the way she uses discourse herself" (Krause, "Reassessing the Heroine: Discourse and Ideology," this volume, p. 1), these essays remind us that the struggle against sexual violence, against the oppression of women, passes through women's access to speech, to (authorized) discourse. Today's #metoo movement has called attention not only to the prevalence of sexual harassment of women but also to the importance of a woman's testimony, of her words.

One final note. Through the concept of intersectionality, Western feminist theory has (finally) begun to recognize its historical failure to address issues of race, ethnicity, class, sexuality, etc. Although the critical lens of these essays is neither uniformly nor universally feminist, they are all concerned with the construction of the feminine in medieval French texts, and while they demonstrate a concern for women's voices in a variety of medieval social classes, they do not engage with issues of race, ethnicity, or sexuality. Were we to redo this volume today, we would. We probably would add new essays focused on different female characters, such as Saracen princesses in the *chanson de geste*, or cross-dressing heroines found in hagiography, late epic, and romance. We would also revisit a number of our essays, with intersectionality an explicit element of our analysis. For example, I would include a consideration of race/ethnicity in my assessment of female characters in Gautier de Coinci's *Miracles de Nostre Dame*, examining such figures as the mother in the tale of the Jewish boy thrown into the furnace for taking communion. As it stands, however, we hope that our readers will see the diversity of heroines already present in this volume and use these essays as a step toward a broader and deeper understanding of the key role played by discourse in the construction and definition of the "heroine," and conversely the ways in which female discourse subverts and surpasses the constraints of ideology, and even the texts that contain it.

NOTE

1. For a useful discussion of the difficulties inherent in the term "heroine," see Jonathan Gottschall, "The Heroine with a Thousand Faces: Universal Trends in the Characterization of Female Folk Tale Protagonists," *Evolutionary Psychology* 3.1 (2005).

Reassessing the Heroine: Discourse and Ideology

Kathy M. Krause

The essays collected in this book explore the various manifestations of major female characters in medieval French literature of all periods and genres. The goal of the book is twofold: first, to demonstrate the variety and range of heroines present in this literature, which has been characterized in several recent critical works as monolithically misogynous, and second, to look at the heroine through a particular lens, that of discourse. The essays explore the ways in which critical discourses, both medieval and modern, define who the heroine is, how she behaves, and the way she uses discourse herself. By combining a wide range of texts with this particular critical focus, the book aims to avoid the scattershot character of many collections while retaining sufficient breadth of interest.

These essays are concerned with heroines, female protagonists, or female central characters, a type of character that commands an increasingly important place in medieval French literature, especially from the early thirteenth century on. Admittedly, the earliest extant Old French poem, the *Cantilène de Sainte Eulalie*, has a female protagonist, and in the mid-twelfth century, hagiography already provided the basis for a number of vernacular texts with female protagonists, notably Anglo-Norman narratives such as Clemence of Barking's *Vie de Sainte Katerine* and Wace's *Vie de Sainte Marguerite*. But the production of female saints' lives increased dramatically in the early thirteenth century;[1] in this, hagiography conforms to the larger pattern. In the second half of the twelfth century as well, Marie de France wrote *lais*, including *Milun*, with strong female figures, and Chrétien de Troyes, in romances such as

Erec et Enide and *Cligés*, created heroines who are fully developed characters—as developed as the heroes with whom they share the narrative spotlight, though they are clearly not as central as the men.

The turn of the thirteenth century saw the advent of romances drawn from non-Arthurian and nonclassical material, romances often referred to as *romans idylliques* or *romans d'aventures*. Here the heroine truly takes a central position, receiving a greater portion of narrative energy, sharing adventures with the hero, even having adventures of her own. Jean Renart's romances, *Escoufle* and the *Roman de la Rose ou de Guillaume de Dole*, are exemplary, providing striking examples of female initiative and heroism. In *Escoufle* Aelis, separated from her beloved, becomes a successful entrepreneur, making enough money to live on and engineering her elevation out of the bourgeoisie back into court life. As for the *Rose*, Lienor is the only character other than the evil seneschal and the jongleur, Jouglet, to demonstrate initiative, using her discursive prowess to provide her own happy ending.

While his romances are unique, Jean Renart is not exceptional in his depiction of strong female characters. A significant number of other Old French texts of this period feature women who are central to the narrative. Even the *Roman de la Violette* by Gerbert de Montreuil, a much more conservative work, provides its heroine with her own lyric voice, and a strong one: she sings not *chansons de toile*, traditional women's songs, as does Lienor in the *Rose*, but rather *grand chant courtois* with a normally male *je* that she adapts to her narrative situation. She also has her own adventure, an episode borrowed from what is probably the earliest full-length nonhagiographic text with a true female protagonist, the *Chanson de Florence de Rome*: Even this quite traditionalist author, resisting the innovative *Rose* at the very time he was reusing both its main plot device—the wager on a woman's chastity—and its technique of inserting lyrics into the narrative, apparently felt it necessary to link his heroine intertextually with a female protagonist.

These texts were numerous, and they had an appreciable influence on later works. Yet traditional literary criticism has relegated their female protagonists to second-rate status, often because the texts that contain them were deemed second-rate (at best) by the male philologists of the late nineteenth and early twentieth centuries who established both the canon and the critical norms for judging medieval French literary production. In recent years many of these texts have been reevaluated, among them *Mélusine* and Jean Renart's *Rose*,[2] but such a reevaluation has most often occurred in isolation. The larger question of female protagonists and their emergence in medieval literature has only begun to be studied.

This book tries to address that larger question by looking at major female figures across the range of medieval French literature. The deliberate inclusion of essays that cover a broad spectrum of texts aims to demonstrate the importance of female protagonists in medieval French literature. The essays span the Middle Ages both chronologically, with work on texts by authors from Chrétien de Troyes to Christine de Pizan, and generically, including essays on romance, epic, lyric, farce, and religious literature. They look at female protagonists from a number of perspectives, but are all informed by questions of discourse about and by these figures. The choice of discourse as a common focus arises equally from the critical interests of the participants in the original panel at the Kentucky Foreign Languages Conference in April 1997, which served as the initial impetus for the collection, and from the important role discourse has played in both medieval and theoretical studies, particularly in feminist and poststructuralist theory. Such a choice of perspective provides a connecting thread for the collection that allows these essays to engage not only with their respective texts but with each other. While the book is arranged by genre, there are key pairs of essays across genre lines: those of William Paden and Joan Grimbert, although concerned in the one case with lyric and in the other with romance, both discuss how modern critical discourse has served to define their subjects, the lyric *dame* and Chrétien's Fenice respectively. I shall return to this point later.

To paraphrase Althusser, "Discourse constitutes concrete individuals as subjects." Such a paraphrase is possible, and logical, because discourse and ideology, as conceived by Althusser himself but also by Foucault and the poststructuralists, are so imbricated one within the other that to ask which came first is to repeat the question of the chicken and the egg. Ideology without discourse could constitute no one; discourse without ideology is not discourse, for words cannot signify without a system of signification, which is socially determined and thus ideological. While early formulations tended to speak of ideology as essentially monologic, one-voiced, theorists have elaborated upon that position and have suggested rather that at any given time there are a number of competing yet coexistent ideologies. The question then becomes how such a multiplicity of ideologies plays itself out—in terms both of discourse and of the constitution of the subject.

In a parallel development, feminist scholars have complicated the question of ideology (and discourse) through their examination of the ways in which gender is constructed—is, in fact, ideology. As Theresa DeLauretis sums it up, "Gender is not sex, a state of nature, but the representation of each individual in terms of a particular social relation. . . . The sex-gender system is both a socio-cultural construct and a semiotic apparatus, a system of representation which assigns meaning . . . to individuals within the society." She goes on to suggest, following the work of a number of feminists in Britain and elsewhere, not only that "gender [is] indeed a primary instance of ideology, and obviously not only for women" but also that "to assert that the social representation of gender affects its subjective construction and that, vice versa, the subjective representation of gender—or self-representation—affects its social construction, leaves open a possibility of agency and self-determination at the subjective and even individual level of micropolitical and everyday practices."[3] In other words, not only are individuals variously interpellated by the different ideologies functioning at any given moment, but the same discourse can and does affect different individuals in different ways; while all individuals are always already constituted as subjects, those subjects are not uniform in their constitution. And indeed, according to DeLauretis, the choices made by those subjects influence the very ideologies that constitute them.

This understanding of gender, as sociocultural system and as semiotic apparatus reciprocally influenced by subjective representation, has opened up new ways of looking at gender in literature in general (as well as film and history) and medieval literature specifically. It has proven particularly fruitful for feminist scholars of French medieval literature—to name just two, Jane Burns in her book *Bodytalk* and, more recently, Helen Solterer in *Disputing Women*.[4] Studies such as these have found what DeLauretis calls the "space off"[5] from which we can find women speaking within or through the dominant patriarchal discourses of medieval texts.

This movement in feminist criticism contrasts with studies that do not consider gender at all and with earlier feminist work that focused on patriarchal representations of women. In those earlier approaches, as Jane Burns puts it, "Feminist medievalists . . . made a convincing case that many of the literary productions we study are more about men than about women, about textual relations between men, homosocial bonding, male desire and imagination."[6] Such arguments denounced the patriarchal ideology that they believed underlay such subjects as "courtly love," which had been seen by others as a reflection of an elevation of women's status in society. In doing so, however, they also reduced the role of female characters in medieval texts to a cipher, a sign standing for a hidden male-male relationship. With similar results, but from a different perspective, poststructuralist readings of medieval literature have read woman not as a symptom of homosocial bonding but rather as a metaphor for male literary creation.[7] Both readings, feminist and poststructuralist, despite their strong theoretical differences and significantly different theoretical aims, result in the erasure of woman from the text.

In order to counter this erasure, more recent feminist scholarship has concentrated on women's voices, whether intratextual, such as the "other voices" of medieval heroines in male-authored texts which Burns articulates, or extratextual, such as the female-authored responses to male authority or authoritative arguments studied by Solterer. Such studies fruitfully complicate our understanding of the gender ideology of the Middle Ages and open up possibilities for reading women's discourse in medieval texts. We cannot, however, forget that the figure of the female protagonist is defined by a multiplicity of (male) societal, and thus ideological, discourses; in reading for her voice we should not erase the discourses of the sociocultural constructs and the semiotic apparatus that surround and construct her. The essays in this book, in their variety and range, allow for all these discourses, allow us to explore that multiplicity. We look at the medieval French heroine in relationship to her own discourse (from within the text and from within medieval patriarchy), to the discourse of the narrator and author (as well as, potentially, that of the scribe), and to that of the scholar who comments upon, and in some cases edits, the texts.

In sum, by considering a broad range of texts through the unifying theme of discourse, these nine essays not only speak to a wide variety of medieval French texts and issues, they also speak to each other, articulating the various facets of a common problematic.

The essays are grouped roughly by genre, both for simplicity's sake and because there are clear connections between, for example, the woman's voice studied by Sally Tartline Carden in the *Cent Ballades* and the figure of the "discourtoise" as analyzed by Nadine Bordessoule.[8] However, as I mentioned, the connections between essays often cross genre boundaries, and the overall order was set so as to maximize these connections, allowing for the consideration of a similar theme in two generically and/

or chronologically disparate works, such as the role of history in *Berthe aux grands pieds* and the *Roman de Mélusine*, the subjects of the third and fourth essays of the collection, or the articulation across genre boundaries of the role that early (male) critical discourse played in our perceptions of female characters.

We begin with a consideration of women in religious narratives: hagiography, miracle tale, and a hagio-epic poem. The three studies, while they are concerned with quite disparate aspects of Old French religious discourse and call on very different theoretical paradigms, share a common focus on the articulation of "official" religious discourse by and/or through female voices. The collection opens with Duncan Robertson's study of the central role of women in Anglo-Norman hagiography, particularly that associated with the Abbey of Barking. In exploring the variety of roles and discourses available to women in hagiographic literature, Robertson demonstrates the possible relationships which can form between legendary heroines and women writers and readers. He argues that a true female *communitas* was established, and reads not just the texts but also the historical situation of their production as indicative of women "speaking directly to each other, in the present tense, in their own vernacular language, on their own behalf."

The second essay, my consideration of the various female protagonists in Gautier de Coinci's *Miracles de Nostre Dame*, continues the discussion on women in "authorized" religious narratives as well as Robertson's concern with the presentation of exemplary women. I focus on three "types" of women in the *Miracles:* the Virgin Mary, female sinners as protagonists of the separate miracle tales, and the one saintly female protagonist of a miracle, the empress of Rome. In each case I highlight the contradictions in Gautier's presentation of these women; they are caught (as is Gautier) in the official theological double-bind that presents woman simultaneously as the equal of man in Christ and as equatable with the flesh, and therefore with sin (sexual in particular) and deceit. I demonstrate that, despite the female protagonists' overt characterization as worthy of the Virgin's intervention—as worthy as the male characters and in the empress's case significantly more worthy—the assumption that women are sinful and deceitful underlies the discourse both of the characters in the miracles and of Gautier's narrator.

The final essay to consider "religious" literature, David Wrisley's examination of *Berthe aux grands pieds*, looks at the role played by the discourse of prayer as it is spoken by the protagonist, Berthe, and her mother, Blanchefleur. He argues that the repeated invocations of the female protagonists—given God's concomitant responses—assure the continuity both of their family and of the "French" nation. In addition the prayers provide an opportunity for the author of the text, Adenet le Roi, to display his poetic prowess through their elaborate, literary language. While Berthe and her mother express their service to family and to God, borrowing a pious, quasi-saintly language, these "voiced" portraits also function as a mirror, and a canvas, for both the expression and the forging of Adenet's own poetic subjectivity.

The second section of the collection considers various aspects of female characters and characterization in romance. Ana Pairet's article on the *Roman de Mélusine* comes first, disturbing the rough chronological arrangement of the collection in order to facilitate a dialogue with David Wrisley's preceding article; both consider questions of familial and historical lineage (re)written on or through the female protagonist. Where Berthe's and Blanchefleur's voices raised in prayer ensure the continuation and legitimacy of the French royal house, Melusine's body is the site not only of the foundation of the house of Lusignan but of its transgression. Pairet argues that Melusine's hybrid nature, her representation as an ambivalent figure, is central to the project of genealogical legitimation undertaken by Jean d'Arras because it serves as antithesis to and yet foundation for a stable male (lineal) identity.

Another woman who transgresses cultural boundaries lies at the heart of Chrétien de Troyes's romance *Cligés*. In a reconsideration of Fenice, and to a lesser extent her mother, Soredamor, Joan Grimbert challenges the dominant contention of Jean Frappier that Chrétien's romance was written as an anti-*Tristan*. In close readings of key passages, Grimbert effectively counters the prevailing *idées reçues* about Fenice and *Cligés*, arguing that Fenice's own discourse, and Chrétien's, belie her presentation as anti-Iseut, and that despite her and her mother's determination to take control of their love lives and to reject the fatality of love in *Tristan*, what is shown most clearly by Chrétien is the extent of their delusions about that control.

In his discussion of the lyric lady in Old French narrative, William Paden also challenges traditional views of "courtly love," elaborated in particular by Gaston Paris, which see *fin'amor* as exclusively extramarital and necessarily involving a socially superior woman. Paden examines lyric insertions in Jean Renart's *Roman de la Rose* and Gerbert de Montreuil's *Roman de la Violette* that describe the protagonists' progress toward mutual love and then marriage, and argues that since such lyrics were considered suitable to depict love between an unmarried man and woman, then *fin'amor* in these narratives may be identified purely as desire, without any determinant relation, whether consonant or dissonant, to marriage.

Both Paden and Grimbert demonstrate the degree to which standard ideas about medieval literature, and about medieval literary "love" more specifically, reflect late nineteenth-century assumptions about women, and about gender, more than medieval ones. Both argue that our views of medieval literary women were, and are still, defined by the discourse of (male) critics who projected their own social constructs back onto the Middle Ages. If we no longer live in the same world as Gaston Paris, or those early twentieth-century critics who drew upon him, and if in particular we have rejected most, if not all, of their assumptions about gender, then we need to rework a critical consideration of *fin'amor*, of "love" in the Middle Ages, that, while never entirely free of their contributions, reflects our own synthesis of modern and medieval.

The last section of the book focuses on essentially nonnarrative genres. While the essays concern different forms—lyric collection, lyric allegory, farce—all three look at texts from the end of the Middle Ages (fourteenth and fifteenth centuries) where the female voice provides a discordant note in a dialogue. Nadine Bordessoule's essay links the second and third sections of the collection, bridging the gap between genres and centuries as she provides an overview of the female figure she labels "la discourtoise"—the woman who, from Jean de Meun's *Vieille* to Alain Chartier's *Belle dame sans merci* or Antoine de la Salle's *Dame de Belle Cousines*, speaks a discourse deliberately counter to the prevailing courtly code. While not, of course, devoid of misogyny (certainly *la Vieille* has been read, correctly I feel, as a misogynist construction), these female voices, as Bordessoule analyzes them, articulate both a refusal of traditional courtly love discourse and a desire to "love" on their own female terms.

Sally Carden considers a particular manifestation of this discourteous lady in her analysis of la Guignarde in the *Livre des Cent Ballades*, a lyric collection with multiple authors. She argues, counter to traditional views of the collection as a "victory" for the courtly, male voice, that the anticourtly, female voice of la Guignarde triumphs by calling into question the very foundations of courtly discourse. When la Guignarde's arguments for a man loving multiple women and using deceptive language do not succeed in persuading the author/protagonist to reject the courtly code espoused by the corresponding male figure, Hutin de Vermeilles, she proposes a judgment of the debate by others. Analyzing the responses—the espousal of deceptive language even by supposed supporters of courtliness, the placement of critical responses at key points of the compilation, the use of literary examples by the historically male respondents who authored the responses favorable to la Guignarde— Carden concludes that "the dialogic dynamic and the poetics of compilation amplify the voice of dissent embodied by la Guignarde [so that] ultimately she . . . has the last word."

With the last essay, Christopher Lucken's "Woman's Cry: Broken Language, Marital Disputes, and the Poetics of Medieval Farce," the collection both considers a new genre—for farce, although it shares its dialogue form, is clearly far removed from a lyric collection such as the *Cent Ballades*—and comes full circle, as Lucken, in his analysis of woman's voice as "noise," looks at that voice through the lens of medieval, and Patristic, theological discourse on woman. He first discusses the association in theological discourse of woman with excessive, unintelligible language and demonstrates how such assumptions play out in Old French farce. Analyzing the poetics of the farce, how it uses woman's excessive, discordant language, he then contends that the quarrelsome shrew depicted in these dramas "rules the stage and proves to be the foundation and the emblem of a poetics that plays on her *noise*—on the sounds and discordances sparked by her excessively loose tongue—in order to deploy a form of language that is severed from intelligibility or any logic of communication."

In a sense, the beginning and the end of the collection represent the opposite poles of medieval literary women's discourse. Both are enveloped in and informed by theological discourse, but where the nuns of Barking used that discourse to affirm woman's value and to build *communitas*, farce exploits the misogynist tradition for comic purposes of destabilization and discord. The middle essays of the collection—mirroring medieval textual architectures—also demonstrate the degree to which medieval women are the product of male discourse, but this time they are shown as the products of "modern" male critical discourse. Yet despite her status as always already inscribed within (male) discourse, medieval woman's literary voice, whether raised in prayer or in criticism of courtly ideology, remains present and remains a "woman's voice."

NOTES

1. For a discussion of the evolution of female saints' lives, see the introduction to Brigitte Cazelles, *The Lady as Saint: A Collection of French Hagiographic*

Romances of the Thirteenth Century (Philadelphia: University of Pennsylvania Press, 1991).

2. See, for example, the recent collection of essays, Nancy Vine Durling, ed., *Jean Renart and the Art of Romance: Essays on* Guillaume de Dole (Gainesville: University Press of Florida, 1997).

3. Theresa DeLauretis, *Technologies of Gender: Essays on Theory, Film and Fiction* (Bloomington: Indiana University Press, 1987), 5, 9.

4. E. Jane Burns, *Bodytalk: When Women Speak in Old French Literature* (Philadelphia: University of Pennsylvania Press, 1993); Helen Solterer, *The Master and Minerva: Disputing Women in French Medieval Culture* (Berkeley and Los Angeles: University of California Press, 1995). Others that might be mentioned are Roberta L. Krueger, *Women Readers and the Ideology of Gender in Old French Verse Romance* (Cambridge: Cambridge University Press, 1993), and Sarah Kay, *The* Chansons de geste *in the Age of Romance: Political Fictions* (Oxford: Clarendon, 1995), particularly chaps. 1, 3, and 7.

5. "What I mean . . . is a movement from the space represented by/in a representation, by/in a discourse, by/in a sex-gender system, to the space not represented yet implied (unseen) in them" (DeLauretis, *Technologies of Gender*, 26).

6. Burns, *Bodytalk*, 6–7.

7. The standard reference here is R. Howard Bloch, *Medieval Misogyny and the Invention of Western Romantic Love* (Chicago: University of Chicago Press, 1991), but see also Jean-Charles Huchet, "Nom de femme et écriture féminine au Moyen Age: Les Lais de Marie de France," *Poétique* 12 (1981): 407–30; Charles Méla, *La Reine et le Graal: La Conjointure dans les romans du Graal de Chrétien de Troyes au "Livre de Lancelot"* (Paris: Éditions du Seuil, 1984); and Alexandre Leupin, *Barbarolexis: Medieval Writing and Sexuality* (Cambridge: Harvard University Press, 1989).

8. The essays are also arranged, very broadly and with a couple of exceptions, in chronological order of subject.

Part 1

Saintly Women

Hagiography, Miracle, and Epic

1

"Cume lur cumpaine et lur veisine"

Women's Roles in Anglo-Norman Hagiography

Duncan Robertson

The young St. Catherine has defeated fifty professors of philosophy in a disputation. She has resisted the emperor's blandishments, and triumphantly survived his tortures; she has made many converts, including the queen herself. Finally, after all this, she is led out to be beheaded. Women standing alongside her route marvel at her beauty and youth and nobility: "Plaint la bele Cateline / Cume lur cumpaine et lur veisine" [vv. 2527–28] [They weep for beautiful Catherine, as for their own companion and neighbor].[1]

This life of the virgin martyr was written by Clemence, a nun of Barking Abbey, a little east of London, toward the end of the twelfth century. From her immediate Latin source, Clemence retains a vision of the heroine as a proud, undefeated spiritual and intellectual warrior, the personification of Christian Wisdom.[2] The poet proceeds to interpret the legend in terms of the nuns' vocation, as a call to her convent sisters to refuse earthly marriage, and the servitude imposed by merely earthly husbands, in favor of espousal to the Divine Bridegroom. Following Catherine's lead, the Barking nuns will eventually take their places in the heavenly *compaignie* with the Virgin Mary, the original patron of the abbey, now their queen:

Iloc est la grant *compaignie*
Des angles et la melodie.

La est li duz festival chant
Ki tut tens est uelement grant.
La est la grant bachelerie
E la noble chevalerie
De seinz martyrs ki mort venquirent,
Ki pur amur Deu la suffrirent.
Li apostle e li bon doctur
I sunt, e li bon cunfessur.
Le coer i est des dameiseles,
Des virges e des chastes pulceles
Ki les mortels amanz despistrent
E la chaste amur Deu elistrent.
Trestuit loent *cumunalment*
Le nun al rei omnipotent. (vv. 1769–84, italics mine)

[The great company of angels is there with their singing, the sweet festive song, which is unvaryingly magnificent. There also are the young men and the noble knights who, as holy martyrs, conquered death and suffered it for the love of God. The apostles and the good doctors of the church are there, as well as the good confessors. There too is the choir of young women, virgins and chaste maidens who despised mortal lovers, choosing instead the chaste love of God. All praise in unison the name of the all-powerful king.]

The poem celebrates the close, companionable, neighborly relationships formed among the women within the narrative, and extended to those located just outside its frame, that is to say, to the narrator, the poet, and her once and future readers. Appropriately, the *St. Catherine* has attracted modern critics concerned with women's roles, especially in England.[3] This work typifies the personal involvement of medieval women in vernacular hagiography. Indeed, wherever they appear in the genre—in great or small roles, as characters in the legend, or as writers or patrons or scribes or audience—we sense the intensity of their commitment. In this normally conventionalized form, we find women speaking directly to each other, in the present tense, in their own vernacular language, on their own behalf.[4]

The poem thus reflects the idealism of the female monastic movement, which brought about an exponential increase in the number of women's houses through the twelfth century that would end in the thirteenth as abruptly as it had begun.[5] Not all the women involved were saints. In a royal convent like Barking one might find, alongside pro-

fessed nuns, unmarried women of very high social rank who were tem-
porarily or permanently housed there but who remained in close touch
with their families and with the Plantagenet court. These aristocratic
women may not have had the access to Latinity that was available to
men in monasteries at the time; the women's investment in the vernacular would then have been correspondingly higher. The poet-transla-
tor Clemence, fully Latin-literate herself, was also remarkably well versed
in courtly romance, notably the *Tristan* by Thomas, whose rhetoric she
adapts to her hagiographic project. She and other English convent writers of this time appear to have embraced Anglo-Norman verse hagiography as a literary vehicle that could express women's spiritual needs,
and convey their special contribution to the developing insular culture.

In the *St. Catherine* we find a complex, theologically literate treatment of Christian doctrine; we find an authentic spirituality expressed
in high poetic art; and we find developed characters, whose motivations
are explored in depth, as in the courtly romances. The female protagonist is a notably eloquent, strong-minded figure, by no means the passive object of the male gaze, nor even the victim of the tortures she
survives. She is presented as closely in touch with the concerns of the
writer and the readers, who are encouraged not only to venerate her but
to identify themselves with her, to meditate on her example, and to follow through in action.

Does this poem typify female literary culture in Anglo-Norman hagiography? Or is it rather an exception to the rule, in a genre that tended to
reduce female sanctity to the sole attribute of (defended) virginity? Simon
Gaunt, following Kathryn Gravdal and other academic critics, takes the
latter view:

> That hagiographical texts about female virgins were written pri-
> marily in the interests of men, and not of women, is also evident
> from the overt denigration of female sexuality and femininity inher-
> ent in the view of virginity they perpetrate.... The universal subtext
> of saints' lives about women is forced sex, in other words rape, as is
> evident when virgin martyrs like Foi or Marguerite, or more fortu-
> nate virgins like Enimie, pray to God to save their virginity.[6]

Saintly women are a much more varied lot than Gaunt's commentary
might lead one to suppose. And their vocational chastity can take on a
variety of individual meanings. Many of them are martyrs, of course.
There are also notable abbesses, especially in England, such as Audree,
Osith, and Modwenna; there is Genevieve, the patron of Paris, who de-

fended the city against the Huns; there are penitents, such as Thaïs and Mary the Egyptian; and finally, there is the very important category of wives of male saints, including Alexis's bride and those of Edward the Confessor, Eustace, Guillaume d'Angleterre, and Julian the Hospitaller. These women are all autonomous, active figures—not victims or objects but subjects of religious experiences, who invoke the reader's interest, concern, sympathy, admiration, empathy, and eventual imitation.

Edith, the wife of the saint and king Edward the Confessor, offers an interesting case in point. The Anglo-Norman life of Edward[7] was written by a nun of Barking Abbey, possibly Clemence herself, during the 1160s, a decade or two before the *St. Catherine*. The young king, as we recall, was obliged by his position to marry, but feared to lose the "treasure" of chastity. Edith appears as the answer to his prayer. She is the daughter of the earl Godwin, who had been implicated in treachery against Edward's family, but she herself is "a rose issued from thorns"— that is to say, a type of the Virgin Mary, who was said to have issued in like manner from the Jewish people.

Following the wedding ceremony, there takes place a scene from high hagiographical lore, one that could not fail to remind readers of the *Vie de saint Alexis*.[8] Edward withdraws to a "secret place" and summons Edith; when she arrives, he delivers a little sermon, requesting that she maintain true chastity, sovereign among virtues, which admits one to the intimacy of God as a participant in a divine *fin amurs*. She responds in direct discourse, on her own behalf: What Edward asks of her, she says, is what she herself has always desired; she further asks that he maintain for himself the same continence that he expects of her; and she concludes the conversation with a prayer that God may give him the moral power (*poer*) as well as the desire (*voler*) to carry out this design.

As Jocelyn Wogan-Browne notes, "the Barking Life is the only version [of Edward's legend] to give Edith a point of view."[9] Her consent is actively sought and valued, in a development that reflected the changes taking place in the institution of marriage during the twelfth century. Edith's intervention, as dramatized by the Barking nun, resembles also that of Lesigne, the wife of saint Alexis, in the amplified twelfth-century *Rouman de saint Alessin* derived from the eleventh-century poem.[10]

In what follows, the Barking nun celebrates the ideal conjugality described in her immediate source, the *Vita s. Edwardi Regis*, by Aelred of Rievaux.[11] She explains that Edward and Edith were spouses in name, but without the deed, or the desire for the deed, that defines the marriage relationship. Edith was Edward's wife in public, but a sister or a daughter to him in private. The result of this arrangement was True Love: freed from the business of begetting offspring, they experienced joy, affection, charity, complicity—*fin amurs* indeed, as the clerical mind conceived it.

Their relationship had implications for the community, beginning of course with the Norman invasion of 1066, prompted by Edward's death without issue. His biographers further insist that his chastity had led to his receiving a prophetic, visionary power. He had in fact foreseen (vv. 4811–48), in an allegorical dream vision of a split tree, the disruption of the royal succession, and its eventual restoration under Henry I. The restored tree now bears fruit in the reign of Henry II, to whom the Barking nun dedicates her translation of the saint's life.

Edward was canonized, as we recall, in 1161, following several different publicity campaigns. The sanctification was finally obtained by a collaboration between Westminster Abbey and King Henry II. Both parties had an interest in Edward's cause. For Henry the issue would have been none other than establishing his own legitimacy, which he traced through his mother and grandmother, i.e., through the female line. Such is the agenda that underlies Aelred's *Vita* and the Barking nun's translation.

The nun herself contributes a modest, paradoxically assertive point of view to the events she describes. She apologizes at the outset for possible grammar mistakes, since all she knows is a "faus franceis d'Angletere" (v. 7) [false French of England]. Her readers, she believes, may well have learned theirs "ailurs" [elsewhere], presumably on the Continent (vv. 8–9). She expresses hope that the book will not be scorned because she, a woman, translated it; she declines, finally, to name herself, protesting that she is not *yet* worthy to be named alongside the saintly hero, Edward.

No such hesitancy clouds her praise of Henry II, "Ki de ceo saint lignage eissi / Et ore Engletere a franchie / Et religïun enrichie (vv. 108–10) [who has issued from this sacred lineage, and now has liberated England, and enriched religion]. There is no reference to the murder of the archbishop Thomas Becket in 1170, for which Henry would be held responsible. Writing in the 1160s, in a spirit of seemingly untroubled optimism, the Barking nun associates herself and her convent sisters with the king, and as she recounts the marriage of Edith to Edward, we glimpse an allegory of the union to be effected between the convent and the royal court. Together, what could they could not create? They would forge a finally reconciled Anglo-Norman society, one that would be both politically successful and spiritually informed, and in which women could play a significant cultural role.

It was not to be. The Plantagenet rulers proved less interested in cultural collaboration than in getting control of the convent and its revenues. But in the 1160s it may still have been possible to entertain the vision that appears on the horizon, as it were, in the Barking nun's life of Edward the Confessor. To her, the political is the personal. She focuses intently on individual experiences, where the root causes of events and their true meanings are to be found: in the king's piety and chastity, and especially in his love-match with Queen Edith. Their virginity ultimately engenders, and redeems, the new nation. And in this perspective, the author as female narrator inscribes herself into a close, empathetic relationship with the female protagonist, her companion, her neighbor and historical ally.

In both of the Barking saints' lives we find an inscribed intimacy between the female protagonist and the female narrator, who act together to create a wider "textual community."[12] That is, of course, ultimately located in heaven. The nun's final prayer, in her life of St. Edward, is that the *sainte cumpaignie* at Barking Abbey might be eventually admitted to the heavenly *cumpaignie* where the Confessor now dwells. It is recognizably the same assembly visualized by Clemence in the *St. Catherine,* including angels, apostles, doctors of the church, the noble *chevalerie* of martyrs, and the Virgin Mary herself.

Closer to home, the textual community created by the saint's life locates itself as a forum for exchanges between intratextual and extratextual participants. Thus the narrators frequently digress from the narrative and depart from the translation in order to open spaces where dialogues might take place. Readers are invited to refer the narrative to personal experience and their own observations. We are drawn into the discussion, into devotion, and into frank celebration of female heroism, but always in the companionable, neighborly key. The poem creates a kind of chain linking the reader to the narrator, to the saint, to the Virgin Mary, and ultimately to Christ: a chain extending upwards in a line, perhaps, or else gathered together into a center, into the common presence of all its members.

The sense of community, and the anxiety of exclusion from it, preoccupy the twelfth-century French life of St. Mary the Egyptian.[13] This legend would seem far removed from Barking Abbey and its cœnobitic or political concerns. Its heroine is a famous courtesan of Alexandria;

following her conversion, she goes out into the desert, where she spends the remaining forty-seven years of her life in solitude. Strangely enough, in this poem derived from the eremitic tradition of the *Vitae patrum*, the word *compaignie* reverberates with insistence: I count thirteen occurrences in its fifteen hundred lines, always in the rhyme position, plus three occurrences of *compagnon*. The theme is dramatized at the moment of crisis, as Mary is prevented from joining a crowd of pilgrims entering a church in Jerusalem:

> Mais quant les aperchut Marie
> Mist soi en cele *compeignie*.
> Mist soi en le procession
> Nient par bone entention.
> Le pelerin qui le veoient
> Se malvaistié ne savoient,
> Car se il seüssent se vie,
> Ja o iaus n'eüst *compaingnie*.
> Sor les degrés en sont monté,
> Dedens le temple en sont entré.
> Dedens entra le *compeignie*,
> Mais ainc n'i pot entrer Marie. (vv. 363–74, italics mine)

[But when Mary saw them, she placed herself in their company. She placed herself in the procession, not at all with good intentions. The pilgrims who saw her did not know her sinfulness, for if they had known of her life, she would never have had companionship with them. They went up the stairs; into the church they went; inside went the company, but Mary could never gain entrance.]

This incident triggers Mary's *crise de conscience* and prompts her to turn to the Virgin Mary, who alone has the power to reconcile the outcast. Up to this point in the poem, her experience as a prostitute, however spectacularly successful, has been one of deepening solitude as a pariah in the midst of urban society. For this reason (in essence) she flees Alexandria for Jerusalem (vv. 217–86), only to find herself even more isolated than before, in a strange city where she has no acquaintances: "Dolante fu et esgaree / Souspire et pleure a le rive, / Ne seit que faire le caitive. / El n'i connoist home ne feme, / Molt li sambla estrange regne" (vv. 332–36) [She was woeful and lost; she sighs and weeps on the shore. The wretch does not know what to do. She knows no man or woman there; it seemed to her a wholly foreign country]. At the moment of contrition and conversion, she turns to the Virgin Mary, who commands her to exchange her estrangement in society for actual solitude in the desert. There indeed she will no longer be alone, for the Virgin will accompany her at every turn; there also she will experience True Love (let us add, once again, "as the clerical mind conceives it") in a communion with the monk Zosimas; and finally she will be admitted into the heavenly *compaignie*:

> Prie en ten Fil, Virge Marie,
> Que me mete en se *compaignie*;
> Se une fois estoie o toi,
> N'en partiroie mais, je croi;
> Le canteroie o tes anceles
> En tes cambres qui tant sont beles
> Le cant nouvel o le douç son
> Que canta li rois Salemon. (vv. 1237–44, italics mine)

[Pray to your Son, Virgin Mary, that he place me in his company; if once I were with you, I would not ever leave, I think. There would I sing with your handmaidens, in your chambers which are so beautiful, the new song with the sweet sound that King Solomon sang.]

The vision of heaven in this poem is essentially identical to that of the two Barking saints' lives. It is the same ultimate community, the anagogical type and final form of the convent institution on earth. The purpose of all three poems, patently, is to draw the reader into association. The narrative, in each case, creates a chain of identifications linking the reader to the narrator, to the heroine—Catherine, Edith, Mary—to the Virgin Mary, and ultimately to Christ. The participating, accepting reader becomes, through the mediation of the story, a *subject* of religious experience in her or his own right, a member of the literary-spiritual *compaignie*.

Simon Gaunt argues, on the contrary, that the communal sense in these texts, especially in the *St. Mary the Egyptian*, is illusory, broken in reality by differences in class and especially gender, which separate the reader from the narrator:

> This symbiosis of the implied audience with the narrator is by no means innocent. On the contrary it is a highly manipulative rhetorical strategy used to create the fiction of a united textual community. It also proves to be another means of enhancing the value

of *clergie,* since it is the clerkly narrator who gives the community access to the saint and to the sacred story.[14]

For Gaunt, as we have noted, the legends of virgin martyrs seem to have been written primarily by and for men, and the same would be true a fortiori for the *St. Mary the Egyptian.* The latter poem is overdetermined, in his view, by "prurient" male eroticism; for women readers, then, it would be a highly alienating text, fostering the "internalization of an extremely contemptuous and negative view of the female body."[15] I have argued elsewhere a more positive view, that the eroticism of the poem, and its use of courtly-romance discourse, serve to draw the reader, female or male, into identification with Mary's experience of sin, and thereby into her redemption.[16]

Rather than returning to this matter, which resides in the (unrecoverable?) reception of the text by medieval readers, I would like to focus here on the question of "textual community" in these works, and on a traditional meaning conveyed by the Old French word *compaignie.*

The beginning of the First Letter of John reads as follows:

> Quod fuit ab initio, quod audivimus, quod vidimus oculis nostris, quod perspeximus et manus nostrae contrectaverunt de verbo vitae . . . quod vidimus et audivimus adnuntiamus vobis, ut et vos societatem habeatis nobiscum, et societas nostra sit cum Patre et cum Filio eius Iesu Christo. Et haec scribimus vobis ut gaudeatis, et gaudium vestrum sit plenum.[17] [That which was from the beginning, which we have heard, which we have seen with our eyes, which we have looked upon and touched with our hands, concerning the word of life . . . that which we have seen and heard we proclaim also to you, so that you may have fellowship with us; and our fellowship is with the Father and with his Son Jesus Christ. And we are writing this that your joy may be complete.]

The third-century passion of Perpetua and Felicitas, attributed to Tertullian, alludes to this text and applies it to the communication in writing of "recent examples" of divine power, manifested in the heroism of the martyrs. The passage stands as a *locus classicus* authorizing saints' lives in general:

> Et nos itaque *quod audivimus et contrectavimus, annuntiamus et vobis,* fratres et filioli, *ut et vos* qui interfuistis rememoremini gloriae domini et qui nunc cognoscitis per auditum *communi-*

onem habeatis cum sanctis martyribus, et per illos cum domino nostro *Iesu Christo.* [And so, my brethren and little children, *that which we have heard and have touched with our hands we proclaim also to you, so that* those of *you* that were witnesses may recall the glory of the Lord and those who now learn of it through hearing *may have fellowship with* the holy martyrs and, through them, with the Lord *Christ Jesus.*][18]

The word *communionem* (*societatem* in the current edition of the Vulgate) is translated by the English word "fellowship." This term today has a redolence of church socials and vestry meetings; in a more limited usage, it is restricted to those who may partake of the Eucharist within a given denomination, e.g., the Anglican Communion. Such would be the meaning of the word *compaignie* in our Old French texts. Mary the Egyptian, as we have seen, is excluded from the fellowship of the pilgrims entering the church, but she is finally included in that of heaven. Fellowship, or communion, indissolubly links the saints—Catherine, Edward, Mary the Egyptian, and even the uncanonized but saintly Edith—as "members" of the body of Christ. What is concretized in the sharing of the sacrament is the linkage of the parishioners with the saints and with each other in the same bond.

For the modern literary critic, the great interest of Tertullian's reading (if indeed it is his) of 1 John:1–3 is that it emphasizes the capability of writing to convey experience in immediacy: "what we have heard, what we have looked upon and touched with our hands." The implication is that writing can assume indeed a virtually eucharistic function, as a means or element capable of transmitting communion. This sense has been at all times implicit in the practice of *lectio divina*, the mode of prayer based on reading of the Scriptures. Thus Bernard of Clairvaux, in the first of his *Sermons on the Song of Songs*, refers metaphorically to the Song as a loaf of bread to be broken (i.e., interpreted) in the hands of the priest, by the power of the Holy Spirit, prior to distribution to the faithful.[19] Tertullian's reading specifically authorizes us to consider the recital of a written passion of a martyr as analogous to a Scriptural reading, through which fellowship is extended to readers/auditors as partakers in a quasi-sacramental experience.

The twelfth-century French poet-translators claim the same function for the lives and passions of saints rendered into vernacular verse. Moreover, they concretely realize the fellowship among the saints, in the form of a close-knit network of textual echoes, doctrinal affirmations, references, and allusions which make up what we now call an intertextuality. The women saints we have surveyed, among many others, form a particularly close literary association. They are heroic figures, who convey powerfully the *presence* of the saint to the narrator and to the readers, from whom they demand an active intellectual and emotional response. They propose to break the barriers that normally separate the human world from the divine, and also those that separate men from women, and clerics from laity. The women saints, in short, illustrate and confirm the writers' faith in the text as a instrument capable of conveying the fullness of religious experience to auditors, who are included within it as fully qualified communicants. They speak to the readers, and pray with them, in their own language, in a poetic yet "neighborly" discourse, stripped of grammatical protocol, but ornamented with rhyme and rhetoric: an idiom in which female spirituality could be validated, and rendered new.

NOTES

1. MacBain, *Life of St. Catherine*. All verse references are to this edition. Translations are from Wogan-Browne and Burgess, *Virgin Lives*.

2. Clemence's source, known as the *Vulgata* text, is provided in William MacBain, ed., *De Sainte Katerine: An Anonymous Picard Version of the Life of St. Catherine of Alexandria* (Fairfax, Va.: George Mason University Press, 1987), 177–216.

3. For recent commentary, see the introduction to Wogan-Browne and Burgess, *Virgin Lives*, xi–xxxv; see also Gaunt, *Gender and Genre*, 228–33, and Robertson, "Writing."

4. Jocelyn Wogan-Browne surveys the field in "'Clerc u lai.'" She finds that of some sixty saints' lives written in the Anglo-Norman dialect and/or circulated widely in England during the twelfth, thirteenth, and fourteenth centuries, three can certainly be attributed to women authors, five are dedicated to women patrons, and sixteen concern female saints. These are minimal numbers, but they include some of the most influential works in the collection, e.g., the Barking lives of Catherine and of Edward the Confessor, the twelfth-century *St. Mary the Egyptian*, Wace's *St. Margaret*, and Guernes de Pont-Sainte-Maxence's life of Thomas Becket.

5. Elkins, *Holy Women*, 106–24.

6. Gaunt, *Gender and Genre*, 196–97.

7. Södergård, *Vie d'Edouard le Confesseur*. Verse references in the next ten paragraphs are to this edition.

8. The tradition is summarized by Baudouin de Gaiffier, "Intactam sponsam relinquens: à propos de la *Vie de saint Alexis*," *Analecta Bollandiana* 65 (1947): 157–95.

9. Wogan-Browne, "'Clerc u lai,'" 69–70.

10. Alison Goddard Elliott, ed., *The* Vie de saint Alexis *in the Twelfth and Thirteenth Centuries: An Edition and Commentary* (Chapel Hill: University of North Carolina Department of Romance Languages, 1983).

11. *Patrologia Latina* 195, 739–90. Very similar to the legend of Edward and Edith is that of the emperor Henry II and Kunigund, especially in the thirteenth-century rendering attributed to Adelbold of Utrecht (*PL* 140, 187–98). See also Dyan Elliott, *Spiritual Marriage: Sexual Abstinence in Medieval Wedlock* (Princeton: Princeton University Press, 1993).

12. Concerning "textual communities," see Brian Stock, *The Implications of Literacy: Written Language and Models of Interpretation in the Eleventh and Twelfth Centuries* (Princeton: Princeton University Press, 1983).

13. Dembowski, *La Vie de sainte Marie l'Egyptienne.* All verse references are to this edition. Concerning the manuscript tradition of the poem, and its links to Anglo-Norman writings, see Robertson, "Anglo-Norman Verse Life."

14. Gaunt, *Gender and Genre*, 183, 213.

15. Ibid., 228.

16. For a discussion of eroticism and spirituality in this version of the life of Mary the Egyptian, see Robertson, *Medieval Saints' Lives*, 106–18.

17. *Bibliorum Sacrorum iuxta vulgatam clementinam nova editio* (Rome: Typis Polyglottis Vaticanis, 1959). The translation is from *The New Oxford Annotated Bible, Revised Standard Version* (New York: Oxford University Press, 1973).

18. Herbert Musurillo, ed. and trans., *The Acts of the Christian Martyrs* (Oxford: Clarendon Press, 1972) 106–8; the quotations from 1 John:1–3 are in italics.

19. Bernard of Clairvaux, *Sermones super Cantica Canticorum*, in *Sancti Bernardi opera*, ed. Jean Leclercq, Charles H. Talbot, and Henri M. Rochais (Rome: Editiones Cistercienses, 1957–58), 1:3–4.

Selected Bibliography

Adgar. *Le Gracial.* Edited by Pierre Kunstmann. Ottawa: Éditions de l'Université d'Ottawa, 1982.

Batt, Catherine. "Clemence of Barking's Transformations of *Courtoisie* in *La Vie de sainte Catherine d'Alexandrie.*" *New Comparisons* 12 (1991): 102–33.

Calin, William. *The French Tradition and the Literature of Medieval England.* Toronto: University of Toronto Press, 1994.

Dembowski, Peter F., ed. *La Vie de sainte Marie l'Egyptienne: Versions en ancien et en moyen français.* Publications Romanes et Françaises 144. Geneva: Droz, 1977.

Elkins, Sharon. *Holy Women of Twelfth-Century England.* Chapel Hill and London: University of North Carolina Press, 1988.

Gaunt, Simon. *Gender and Genre in Medieval French Literature.* Cambridge: Cambridge University Press, 1995.

MacBain, William. "The Literary Apprenticeship of Clemence of Barking." *Journal of the Australasian Universities Language and Literature Association* 9 (1958): 3–22.

———. "Five Old French Renderings of the *Passio Sancte Katerine Virginis*." In *Medieval Translators and Their Craft*, edited by Jeanette Beer, 41–65. Studies in Medieval Culture, 25. Kalamazoo, Mich.: Medieval Institute Publications, 1989.

MacBain, William, ed. *The Life of St. Catherine of Alexandria by Clemence of Barking*. Anglo-Norman Text Society, 18. Oxford: Blackwell, 1964.

Robertson, Duncan. *The Medieval Saints' Lives: Spiritual Renewal and Old French Literature*. Edward C. Armstrong Monographs on Medieval Literature, 8. Lexington, Ky.: French Forum, 1995.

———. "Writing in the Textual Community: Clemence of Barking's Life of St. Catherine." *French Forum* 21 (1996): 5–28.

———. "The Anglo-Norman Verse Life of St. Mary the Egyptian." *Romance Philology* 52 (1998): 13–44.

Södergård, Östen, ed. *La Vie d'Édouard le Confesseur: Poème anglo-normand du XIIe siècle*. Uppsala: Almqvist & Wiksells, 1948.

Wogan-Browne, Jocelyn. "'Clerc u lai, muïne u dame': Women and Anglo-Norman Hagiography in the Twelfth and Thirteenth Centuries." In *Women and Literature in Britain, 1150–1500*, edited by Carol M. Meale, 61–85. Cambridge Studies in Medieval Literature. Cambridge: Cambridge University Press, 1993.

Wogan-Browne, Jocelyn, and Glyn S. Burgess, eds. and trans. *Virgin Lives and Holy Deaths: Two Exemplary Biographies for Anglo-Norman Women. The Life of St. Catherine. The Life of St. Lawrence*. London and Rutland, Vt.: Everyman, 1996.

2

Virgin, Saint, and Sinners

Women in Gautier de Coinci's *Miracles de Nostre Dame*

Kathy M. Krause

G autier de Coinci's *Miracles de Nostre Dame*[1]—one of the earliest vernacular collections of Marian miracles, and certainly one of the most popular, as judged by the number of extant manuscripts and its influence on later works[2]—devotes a large portion of its narrative to female characters. The Virgin Mary is of course omnipresent; in many of the miracles recounted the protagonist rescued by the Virgin is a woman, and Gautier grants significant textual space to one specific saintly woman, the empress of Rome. Despite the importance of their roles in his text, Gautier's female figures have received little critical attention.[3] While my discussion here cannot hope to compensate for this lack, or to cover the entire gamut of Gautier's female characters, I will attempt a fairly broad analysis of Gautier's depiction of women by examining each of the three categories of women in his work—the Virgin Mary herself, the empress of Rome, and the female protagonists rescued by the Virgin.[4] In particular I want to call attention to the ambiguity that permeates Gautier's representations of women by concentrating on three areas, one for each category: the presentation of the Virgin as a woman; the contrast between the fates of male and female sinners in the *Miracles*; and the ambiguous gender of the empress in the *Miracle de l'Impératrice de Rome*.[5]

The Virgin as Woman

That the Virgin Mary is the true protagonist of Gautier de Coinci's *Miracles de Nostre Dame* seems basically self-evident. She is the major actor in the text taken as a whole, and its dedicatee and "inspiration";[6] she is Gautier's patron, the person who has both "commissioned" the work and provided its subject matter.[7] In the large majority of the miracles, the Virgin commands center stage or at least shares it with the mortal protagonist whom she rescues. The protagonists of the miracles often seem mere pretexts to allow Gautier to write about his beloved Lady. Gautier describes, and delights in describing, a Virgin who intervenes actively, even proactively, in the lives of her faithful. He uses all his poetic and rhetorical powers to portray the Virgin behaving as she is described in Marian theology and popular piety. In the *Miracles* the Virgin takes on flesh—often very clearly gendered female flesh, as I will explore below—through Gautier's elaboration, his concretization, of her epithets and attributes.

All the standard epithets and topoi associated with Marian theology provide fodder for Gautier's poetic invention and his "fleshing out" of his portrait of the Virgin. The topoi are ideal for his purposes, inviting him to literalize, and dramatize, these metaphors as he elaborates his tales. Two topoi in particular stand out, those of Mary as the soul's advocate[8] and as the soul's doctor; they are the most frequent in the *Miracles* and receive the most elaborate development by Gautier.[9] More generally, the development and utilization of such metaphors has been seen as indicative of a real "feminization" of the presentation of the Virgin in medieval discourse and theology. For example, the topos of Mary as the soul's advocate stresses her tender care for her faithful and establishes her rescue of souls after death, in Guy Phillipart's words, as a type of "protection maternante, à l'abri des exigences et des rigueurs de la loi."[10]

Indeed Gautier's (re)presentation of the Virgin, as he concretizes these topoi, does stress her compassion and her *douceur*, emotional qualities associated with her womanhood and motherhood. Thus in one miracle (I Mir 19) the Virgin comforts a poor, dying old woman by sitting at her bedside tenderly wiping her face:

La mere Dieu d'une toaille,
qui blance est plus que flors de lis,
La grant sueur d'entor son vis
A ses blanches mains li essuie. (I Mir 19:228–31)

[The mother of God, using a cloth that is whiter than a lily, with her white hands wipes the great sweat from around her face.]

Calling attention to the maternal aspect of Mary's actions, Gautier here refers to her as "la mere Dieu," a relatively infrequent sobriquet on his part—he much prefers "ma dame" or "nostre dame." Similarly in the miracles where she acts as advocate, it is most often the Virgin's "pitié" or compassion, again associated with motherhood, that motivates her intervention. In several cases, pleading for a soul before the heavenly court, she stresses her status as Christ's mother. Here she urges Him to grant her boon in the *Miracle dou moigne que Nostre Dame resuscita:*

—Fius, fait ele, por pecheeurs
Retraire d'enfer et de painne
Char en mes flans presis humainne.
Por ce, biaus fius, de toi me fi
Tant que toz jors por aus te pri. (I Mir 24:114–18)

[Son, she said, you took on human flesh in my womb in order to save sinners from hell and suffering. Because of this, lovely son, I put my trust in you such that I pray to you always for others.]

Often Gautier presents her preventive intervention in the lives of her faithful—those times she intervenes before the protagonist of the miracle actively sins—as the result of her "womanly" compassion. To cite just one example, in the miracle of the nun who leaves the cloister to marry despite the Virgin's attempts to restrain her (I Mir 43), the Virgin appears to her in a dream thirty years and several children later, chastising her and warning her that if she doesn't take back the veil the doors of heaven will be closed to her. Mary visits the woman not because of anything the woman has done but rather because she "has such a soft heart":

Au siecle fu plus de trente ans
Qu'ainc ne rentra en s'abbeÿe,
Mais ma dame sainte Marie
Ne la volt mie jeter puer.
La douce dame a si doz cuer
Et si gentil, ce dist la letre,
Qu'en oubliance ne puet metre
Nul service que nus li face. (I Mir 43:248–55, my emphasis)

[She was in the world for more than thirty years before she re-
turned to her abbey, but my lady Saint Mary didn't want to throw

her out. The sweet lady has such a soft heart and such a gentle one, as the word says, that she cannot forget any service anyone does for her.]

Each of these cases highlights Mary's compassion, her emotional concern for those of her faithful who are suffering, a trait that can be, and was, seen as "feminine."

The feminization of the medieval presentation of the Virgin visible in Gautier's literalized metaphors and descriptions of his Lady's *douceur* is even more evident when we look at his descriptions of the Virgin's appearance. The *Miracles* contain a large number of images of the Virgin as physically female. Perhaps most obvious are the tales of the Virgin healing sick clerics with milk from her breast (I Mir 17, I Mir 40). In these miracles the Virgin's actions, her exposure of her breast and lactation, are described in terms that conflate the maternal, the sexual, and the spiritual:

Mout sadement par grant delit
De son doz saim trait sa mamele,
Qui tant est douce, sade et bele;
Se li bouta dedenz la bouche,
Mout doucement partot li touche
Et arouse de son doz lait. (I Mir 17:140–45)

[Very graciously, with great pleasure, from her sweet chest she takes out her breast, which is so soft, sweet and lovely; she puts it in his mouth, very softly touches his mouth everywhere and waters it with her sweet milk.]

Gautier, following the Latin miracle tradition which he "translates," again concretizes a spiritual metaphor. Theologians, St. Bernard in the forefront, had used the image of lactation and suckling to describe the process of gaining spiritual, and intellectual, nourishment,[11] but here it is the Virgin's literal breast and literal milk that provide bodily healing. While the metaphoric level remains present, Gautier's extremely literal use of the topos and his very physical, even sensual description of the Virgin's breast and lactation emphasize the Virgin's female form.

Perhaps the strongest feminizing descriptions of the Virgin are those that present her not as a maternal figure but as a young, beautiful woman. In the *Miracle du moine délivré du diable* (I Mir 16), the Virgin rescues a drunken monk from the (literal) attacks of the Devil, who appears successively in the form of a bull, a dog, and a lion. When the Devil first attacks as a raging bull, the Virgin runs to the monk's aid in the guise of a beautiful *demoiselle*. The conflation of drunken fantasy woman, her hair unbound and wearing only an underdress (ll. 35–36), and ardent defender is striking:

> En un chainse mout acesmee
> Acorut toute eschevelee,
> Une toaille en sa main destre.
> «Fui toi! fui toi! Ce ne puet estre,
> Fait la pucele a l'anemi,
> Que riens mesfaces mon ami.»
> La grans biautez de la pucele,
> Qui tant estoit plaisans et bele,
> Le dyable tout esbloï. (I Mir 16:35–43)

[She ran up wearing a shift, she was very graceful, with her hair completely undone, and a cloth in her right hand. "Begone! Begone! This cannot be," said the maiden to the enemy, "nothing shall harm my friend." The great beauty of the maiden, who was so pleasant and lovely, completely dazzled the devil.]

This is the most explicitly feminine description of the Virgin, but she appears as a lovely "pucele" in several other tales, among them the *Miracle du moine de Chartreuse* (II Mir 31). When the Virgin appears to comfort the monk of the title, one of his fellow monks sees her, and the terms used to describe what he sees strongly recall lyric poetry,[12] in particular the comparison with freshly fallen snow ("nois negie"):

> Lors voit devers le ciel descendre,
> Ce li est vis, une pucele
> Si tres florie, si tres bele
> Que rienz n'i fesist nois negie. (II Mir 31: 34–37)

[Then he saw descend from the sky, it seemed to him, a maiden so very flowerlike, so very beautiful that new snow was nothing in comparison.]

These descriptions of Mary as a lovely maiden parallel Gautier's depiction of Mary as the ultimate courtly *amie*. This common topos, developed by many singers of the Virgin's praises in Latin and the vernacular, is literalized and narrativized in the well-known tales of the "fiancé of the Virgin" in which a young man puts a ring on the finger of a statue of the Virgin as a sign of his devotion. When he later plans to marry despite his vow, the Virgin herself appears to remind him of his engagement to her.

In his versions of these tales, Gautier pushes the image so far as to have Mary upbraid several men who decide to forsake the religious life in order to love a mortal woman. Speaking as if she were a jilted, even jealous girlfriend, she complains of their defection to a lesser woman and stresses the quality of her love for them:

> Di moy! di moy! tu qui jadis
> M'amoyes tant de tout ton cuer,
> Pour quoy m'as tu jetee puer?
> Di moy! di moy! ou est dont cele
> Qui plus de moy est bonne et bele?
> . . .
> Enne fais tu trop malvais change
> Quant tu pour une fame estrange
> Me laiz, qui par amorz t'amoye
> Et ja ou ciel t'aparilloye
> En mes chambres un riche lit
> Pour couchier t'ame a grant delit? (II Mir 29:286–308)

[Tell me! tell me! you who once loved me so with all your heart, why have you thrown me out? Tell me! tell me! where then is she who is better and more beautiful than I? . . . Are you not making a terrible exchange when you leave me for a strange woman, I who loved you with love and was already preparing in heaven a rich bed in my rooms in which to lay your soul with great pleasure?]

The vocabulary again recalls troubadour or trouvère love poetry, and the reference to the "rich bed" prepared for the cleric's soul in Mary's chamber conflates once more the spiritual and the sexual. While strongly reminiscent of the Song of Songs and the exegetical tradition that read the beloved of the Song as the human soul,[13] this passage reverses the roles of the Song of Songs and of the normal "courtly" love situation, for here the woman sings of her love and encourages her beloved to come away with her.

This reversal of roles is possible because of Mary's purity, her essential "sinlessness." Dyan Elliott notes how the development of the motif of Mary as a substitute for the male cleric's wife corresponds to an increased emphasis on her purity:

The motif of Mary as substitute wife and antidote to clerical in-
continence would increase as the Middle Ages progressed, as em-
phasized by the steady stream of miracles in which Mary inter-
vened to save the priesthood from sexual errance. . . . The purified
alternative Mary presented to real wives, epitomized in her freedom from pollution in giving birth to Christ and consolidated in
Christendom's cumulative impulse to free her entirely from the
sexually transmitted taint of original sin, exacerbated the dichotomy between Mary and mundane women (epitomized in Eve).[14]

In other words, Mary's ever-greater purity allowed her to be an accept-
able and effective substitute object for the sexual desire of the male
clergy, while increasingly distancing Mary from "real" women. Elliott's
conclusions seem particularly germane to the *Miracles* when one considers that the Virgin's appearances as a lovely maiden occur only to
male protagonists, and in particular to religious men—monks, clerics,
or the young men mentioned above who will take holy orders as a result
of the miracle. Not only does the Virgin appear as a sexually attractive
woman only to male religious characters, she gives milk from her breast
only to religious men. The Virgin in Gautier's *Miracles* comforts her
faithful, celibate male devotees with physical and spiritual health, but
also with a pure object for their sexual fantasy. While the feminine emotional aspects of the Virgin, her tenderness and compassion, are available to all, her physical female appearance, with lactating breasts or
beautiful appearance, is reserved for male religious figures.

Male and Female Sinners

The difference in the physical appearance of the Virgin accorded to male
and female protagonists marks a distinction between them that initially
seems contrary both to Gautier's stated aims for his collection and to his
overall distribution of male and female protagonists. Gautier states in
the prologue to Book One that his aim is to "translate" miracles so that
men and women who cannot read (Latin) will be able to understand
them and realize that it is good to serve the Virgin:

Miracles que truis en latin
Translater voel en rime et metre
Que *cil et celes* qui la letre
N'entendent pas puissent entendre
Qu'a son servise fait boen tendre. (I Prol 1:6–10, my emphasis)

[Miracles that I find in Latin I want to translate into rhyme and meter so that those men and women who don't understand the letter can understand that it is good to give themselves to her service.]

Desirous of demonstrating the virtues of serving the Virgin to both men and women, to all men and women, Gautier includes tales involving characters from all walks of life, utilizing figures with whom his varied audience can identify. For each type of male protagonist there is a corresponding female figure: for every cleric tempted to marry, there is a nun tempted to leave the cloister; for each poor man healed of an infirmity, there is a poor woman cured. The female subjects of the miracles, like the men, represent the range of social classes and positions: noblewomen and *bourgeoises* as well as abbesses and nuns. They run the gamut of moral "character" and situation, from almost unredeemable to saintly, as again do the male characters. Indeed the only story or situation, at least on initial reading, particular to women is that of the pregnant abbess whose child is delivered by the Virgin. However, even this situation can be seen as a female variant of the very common paradigm of a sinful religious whose devotion to the Virgin "saves" him (or her) from his (or her) own folly.

Gautier would seem thus to be a very even-handed polemicist: men and women are similarly sinful, women and men are both rescued by the Virgin. Nevertheless, in the *Miracles* there is one real and striking difference between the situations of the male and female protagonists, or more specifically between male and female protagonists who are saved from the consequences of their sins. Female protagonists who sin are, in almost all cases, saved by the Virgin from public punishment in this life, whereas the men who sin are not subject to public punishment.[15] Rather the Virgin saves sinful men either in private with no human witnesses, as in the case of the drunken monk in I Mir 16, or after they die. If after death, either the men's bodies are recovered from burial in unconsecrated ground, as in the several tales of monks or clerics whose corpses are discovered with roses in their mouths,[16] or the Virgin rescues their souls from devils.[17]

There are no examples like these with a female protagonist; we *never* see a woman's soul rescued after death. Rather, as I stated, women who sin are saved from public punishment in this life. For example, jealous nuns in I Mir 20 accuse their abbess of betraying her vows by becoming pregnant. The Virgin's act of midwifery, delivering the child and sending it via angel nurses to a hermit, saves the abbess from being exposed as a sinner to, and by, the bishop who has her examined, and then examines her himself, the next day. Similarly, in the *Miracle de vne femme de Rome* (I Mir 18) the noblewoman commits incest with her son and then kills the child born of their union. The Devil, disguised as a *maistre*, a lawyer, accuses this female sinner in the emperor's court; accused publicly, she is also publicly succored by the Virgin, here acting as her defense counsel. The difference between this situation and the cases where Mary serves as advocate for sinful men's souls is particularly notable: the Virgin defends the men's souls in heavenly "court"; she defends the noblewoman in the emperor's court.

In both tales Gautier stresses the public nature of the trial. In the abbess's case she is called before her nuns and the bishop, who is seated "en plain chapitre" (l. 242). Murmurs and accusations fill the whole convent:

> Des nonains fu grans plais tenus,
> et grant murmure eut en covent.
> L'une a l'autre eut bien en covent
> Que l'abbeesse honiroit
> Et del noalz toz jors diroit. (I Mir 20:212–16)

[Much conversation was held by the nuns, and there was much murmuring in the convent. They promised one to another to shame the abbess and to speak badly about her always.]

Similarly, the Devil first accuses the noblewoman of Rome of what are in fact her crimes, adultery and infanticide, before the emperor on a day when many are present, deliberately choosing to speak before a full court so as, we assume, to maximize the effect of his words:

> Un jor quant vit q'eut ou palais
> Assez haus homes, clers et lais,
> Lors s'apensa que son affaire
> D'or en avant porroit bien faire. (I Mir 18:195–98)

[One day when he saw that there were many great men, clerics and laymen, at the palace, he thought that he could then carry out his affair well.]

Perhaps the most flagrant example is that of the woman of Laon (II Mir 26) whose crime, indictment, and confession are all caused by public rumor and whose punishment and rescue are equally public. First, rumor accuses her of sharing the favors of her son-in-law with her daughter: "Quar chascuns dit que de sa dame / Tout autel fait com de sa fame"

(II Mir 26:75–76) [For all said that with the lady he did just the same as with his wife]. In despair for her good name, she has her son-in-law murdered, but once again, rumor makes the rounds almost immediately:

> La nouvele, qui tost ala,
> Ala et vint tant ça et la
> Qu'a Loon vint sanz nul delai. (II Mir 26:177–79)

[The news, which quickly spread, went and came here and there so that it arrived at Laon without delay.]

When the family is brought in for questioning, the whole city runs to watch:

> Ainz qu'il viegnent emmi la vile,
> Aqueurent genz plus de dis mile;
> De toutes pars genz i aqueurent. (II Mir 26:225–27)

[As soon as they came into the city more than ten thousand people came looking; they came from everywhere.]

Throughout the rest of the miracle, Gautier continues to stress the crowds that surround and observe the woman. Her confession, her prayers in church before being executed, her march to the place of execution, and finally her appearance unharmed among the ashes and the subsequent account of the Virgin's rescue, all are conducted in the sight of a multitude of townspeople. This is crime, justice, and miraculous clemency as public story and public spectacle.[18]

Such public accusation of female sinners, as opposed to the private chastisement of the men, does not turn upon a question of guilt. While all of these women are in fact guilty of the crimes of which they are accused, so are the male sinners: the monk attacked by the Devil is a drunkard, the pilgrim going to St. James has committed suicide, and so on. The issue is rather the timing of the Virgin's rescue and, more important, the type of "punishment" from which she rescues these sinners. In Gautier de Coinci's *Miracles*, only men are saved after death—although others are, of course, saved while still alive—and only women are saved from, or subject to, public judgment of their sins and/or crimes.[19]

This distinction between the treatment of sinful men and women is a significant one. Men's sins, whether public or private, are often known by the community, as in the case of the lecherous *clerc* whose fellow clerics comment after his death, "C'est a bon droit qu'il est ocis, / Ce dist chascuns. Toute sa vie / A il usee em puterie" (I Mir 15:32–34) [It is right that he is killed, they all said, he spent his whole life in lechery], but they do not seem to demand public censure. Conversely women's sins, as presented in the *Miracles*, are private, hidden sins and they "require" exposure, which then calls forth public condemnation.

There are two exceptions to this overall pattern of public male sin versus private female sin (though none to the concomitant distinction between private and public judgment). Théophile's sin (I Mir 10), his pact with the Devil, is a private affair revealed only when he, in his relief and delight at the Virgin's rescue, confesses publicly. The second case is that of the monk who drowns while crossing a river to visit his leman (I Mir 42). He would seem to be conducting his affair in private, for there is no mention of his fellow monks, in contradistinction to the other cases of sinful religious where the attitude of the community is usually commented upon by Gautier. His rescue is, of course, equally private. In neither case does anyone accuse the man of his sins—Théophile comes to repentance on his own, whereas the drowning monk dies and the Virgin first rescues his soul and then resuscitates him. These exceptions to the "public" nature of men's sins only serve to emphasize the dichotomy between the very different judgments accorded to men and women.[20] The fact that the Virgin saves no women's souls after death may be considered a part of this same public/private dichotomy. The element of public shame added to women's sins subverts Gautier's apparent evenhandedness, his "equality of sin" for men and women. Women are subjected to public shaming and judgment and men are not.

This distinction cannot, however, be read simplistically. It is tempting to see it as yet another example of sexism, in particular of the tendencies in much of Western society throughout the ages to display women to and/or for the public gaze and to punish women more harshly than men for the same crimes—as well as to take (perverse) pleasure in exposing women's sins. Moreover, Gautier would certainly have been imbued with the Church Fathers', and medieval theology's, distrust of women. The equation of woman with deception and trickery—stemming from exegesis of the account of the Fall in Genesis, as well as the larger rejection of the flesh and its desires (again equated with woman) as deceptively enticing the Christian away from God and Spirit—influences all medieval religious writing on, or presentation of, women.[21] In addition, the Church professed and taught that woman was essentially promiscuous, a belief likewise arising, at least in part, from the association of woman and the flesh. In Gautier's text we can see such assumptions operative in characters like the townspeople of Laon, who simply assume the mother is sleeping with her son-in-law, or the empress of

Rome's husband, who immediately accepts his brother's slander of his wife without any evidence:

> Comme son frere bien l'en croit,
> De nule rien ne l'en mescroit.
> Bien seit que fame est tost müee
> Et tost glacie et eslüee. (II Mir 9:835–38)

[As his brother he believed it, he disbelieved nothing of it. He knew well that woman is changeable and slips easily.]

If we move, however, from Gautier's characters to his own discourse, we must admit a caveat or two. First, in the matter of sexual promiscuity, there are in fact more promiscuous men than women in the *Miracles*.[22] Second, as for deceitful language and behavior, while these women have concealed their sins from the communities in which they live, Gautier does not call attention to their deceit; he does not show the women actively lying, and he downplays their attempts to cover up their sin. The issue would then seem rather to be society's unequal perception and treatment of male and female sexual sin, which Gautier "merely" reflects in his text.

Indeed, Gautier addresses this very question in a fairly lengthy passage (II Chast 10:788–823) in his didactic text *La Chasteté aux nonains*, which immediately follows the *Miracle de l'Impératrice* and which is addressed to the nuns of the convent of Notre-Dame de Soissons. He begins:

> N'avez c'un colp, c'en est la somme,
> Ne plus que li hanas de voirre:
> Douter devez comme tonoirre
> Et mal renon et male fame.
> Vos savez bien que toz tanz fame
> Est de si tenre renommee,
> Luez c'un petit est denommee
> D'assez petite vilonnie,
> Mout a envis s'en cure et nie. (II Chast 10:788–96)

[You have only one fault, this is the sum of it, like a glass goblet you must fear like thunder both bad reputation and infamy. You know well that woman always has such a fragile reputation that as soon as she is named just a bit as being a little base she has great difficulty in defending herself or denying it.]

Gautier recognizes that, in his society, women in particular are the objects of rumor and (false) accusations of misconduct; his repeated presentation of women as subject to public punishment, in addition to his direct words in the *Chasteté*, can be read as a warning to the nuns of Notre-Dame de Soissons, and to women in general, that they must be like Caesar's wife, for the world, the *siècle*, will be quick to condemn them.

In the *Miracles*, however, the women subject to public rumor and accusation are, with one exception, not innocent but guilty—and all but one of the sinful women portrayed are guilty of sexual sins:[23] incest (whether real, as with the noblewoman of Rome, or presumed, as with the woman of Laon), forsaking religious vows of chastity (the pregnant abbess and the two nuns who want to leave the convent with their lovers), or stealing another woman's husband (I Mir 33, "De deuz fammes que Nostre Dame converti"). Gautier's text thus not only reflects, and warns against, the *siècle* and its perceptions of women but also reproduces the very stereotypes against which Gautier supposedly warns the nuns of Soissons. This ambiguity, even contradiction, is complicated by another facet of the question of public suffering: in a religious context, suffering—and more specifically public suffering inflicted by "evil" men and borne with or through faith and fortitude—is a strong marker of "holiness," whether male or female. In other words, the fact that the female protagonists are subject to such public suffering and in several cases publicly reveal their devotion to the Virgin Mary places them in the lineage of the martyrs. It is this aspect of the question that I want to explore in more detail in the next section, by examining closely the *Miracle de l'Impératrice de Rome*, a particularly notable case of female suffering and victimization and the one tale of an innocent, thus falsely accused, woman in the *Miracles*.

THE WOMAN IN BETWEEN: THE EMPRESS OF ROME

Gautier begins the two books of the *Miracles* in the same fashion: after the prologue there is a series of songs to and about the Virgin, followed by a "long" miracle. In Book One this is the tale of Théophile. In Book Two this first long miracle is that of the empress of Rome, which runs to nearly four thousand lines—nearly twice as long as that of Théophile, the second longest in the collection. The parallel structure of the two books suggests that the tale of the empress is as important as that of Théophile, and indeed the two are among the best known of the *Miracles*.

The empress's story is a variation on what folklorists have called the

Crescentia saga, from the heroine of the German version of the *Gesta Romanorum*. The tale tells of a woman who is forced into exile by her husband's brother, a jealous rejected suitor; she suffers a number of attacks and accusations by men, then is eventually gifted with miraculous healing ability which she uses at the end of the tale to cure the men who have abused her, by having them first confess their sins publicly. This is a well-known plot in the Middle Ages, found in popular religious literature and theater, in miracle compilations, and in several secular vernacular versions as well.[24] While Gautier's version contains a number of interesting particularities, I want to focus on two aspects of the tale that, while not exclusive to his text, are given special prominence by Gautier, in order to explore more fully the public nature of women's punishment and from there the ambiguous status accorded to women in the *Miracles*.

First, the empress represents a kind of epitome of female victimization; even a brief summary of her tribulations will show how excessive they are. Her travails begin when her husband leaves, not long after their marriage, on a pilgrimage to Jerusalem. Her brother-in-law courts her[25] and his attentions become so persistent and public that she resorts to locking him in a tower. Upon the emperor's return, the brother-in-law retaliates by accusing her of lechery and riotous living. Her husband never gives the empress a chance to defend herself, but immediately accepts his brother's account and hands her over to two serfs who attempt several times to rape her. Rescued from the serfs, she is then "courted" by the brother of her rescuer who, when she refuses him, frames her for the murder of her rescuer's child. In punishment for the murder, rather than being burnt at the stake as suggested initially, she is sent into "exile" on a boat whose captain and sailors again try to rape her when she won't voluntarily have sex with them. Finally they throw her into the sea during a storm and she washes up on a rocky shore. Here the Virgin appears to her in a dream, comforts her, and tells her that the plant she will find under her head when she wakes will cure leprosy and other diseases. The empress then wanders from town to town as a mendicant, healing those in need while losing all her physical beauty because of the harshness of her life. Reunited with her husband— the brother has confessed his sins in order to be healed of leprosy, contracted since his slander and her "exile"—she refuses to rejoin him but instead enters a convent.

The empress's tribulations follow a clear pattern: first a wealthy young man falls in love and desires her, then he slanders/frames her when she won't give in to his advances, and finally in punishment she is given over to low-class men to be raped and/or abused sexually. The *dédouble-ment*, the repetition of the pattern, serves to emphasize both the empress's saintliness and her suffering. She is not just a good and chaste woman, she is an exceptional example of chastity and goodness and clearly worthy to join the company of "virgin" martyr saints, given her suffering, her resistance, and her eventual ability to heal.

Where the majority of the other protagonists of the *Miracles* represent everywoman and everyman—weak and sinful folk from various walks of life who serve as examples, if potentially contradictory ones, to the audience because of their very normality—the empress clearly is in a different category. She is like other women in being publicly judged but unlike them both in the degree of her suffering and in the fact that she is indeed condemned. In all the other cases the women are rescued by the Virgin before judgment is passed and are thus held "not guilty," but the empress, alone among these women, truly is not guilty of the crime of which she is accused. These differences, in particular her innocence, radically modify the position of the empress: whereas the other women, and men, are rescued by the Virgin despite their sins, the empress suffers despite her innocence. The empress becomes a limit-case model of Christian fortitude and virtue, a saint in the making.[26]

Yet despite her perfection there exists a strong tension between the narrator's commentary and his actual presentation of the empress's actions. For example, when she is courted by her brother-in-law we never see her behave anything but chastely and resolutely in her rejection of his advances, but during his narration of the episode Gautier comments at length upon the weakness of women:

> N'est nule fame, tant soit sage,
> S'ele reçoit souvent message
> N'ele oit souvent paroles vainnes,
> Ne li remüent tost les vainnes
> Et ne deviengne a la fin fole.
> N'en doit oïr nes la parole
> Qui talent n'a de faire l'uevre.
> Qui pres de lui lait la culuevre,
> Aucune fois mort ele ou point.
> Aucune fois trueve on en point,
> Se myracle n'est ou merveille,
> Fame qui volentiers oreille. (II Mir 9:373–84)

[There is no woman, no matter how wise, if she often receives messages, or often hears frivolous words, whose weaknesses won't excite her and who will not in the end become foolish. One shouldn't listen to the words who doesn't desire to do the action. Whoever leaves a viper near himself will be bitten or struck sometime. One sometimes finds in the end, if there is no miracle or marvel, a woman who listens willingly.]

Only then does he state that the empress does not behave in this manner:

L'empeeris, la Dieu amie:
Le rosel ne resamble mie
Qui a tous vens vaintre se laisse
Et pour chascun se ploie et plaisse. (II Mir 9:387–90)

[The empress, God's friend, doesn't resemble at all the reed which lets itself be defeated in every wind and bends and submits to everyone.]

Gautier then finishes his argument by contrasting the empress with Potiphar's wife, as if the only behavior for a woman, other than the empress's resolute virtue, were the lechery and evil of that Old Testament symbol of female concupiscence:

Ici me samble que je voie[27]
Que ne vont pas tout d'un acort
L'empeeris dont je recort
Et la fame Phutyfaron,
Qui Joseph au tans Pharaon
Pour sa biauté esforcier volt.
Cele a Joseph sont mantel tolt
Et mout le prie et mout l'asproye.
Ceste est priee, cele proy;
Cele requiert, ceste est requise. (II Mir 9:391–401)

[Here it seems to me that the empress of whom I am speaking and Potiphar's wife, who in Pharaoh's time wanted to rape Joseph because of his beauty, do not behave in the same manner. That one took Joseph's cloak and greatly beseeched and pursued him. This one is beseeched, that one did beseech: that one sought, this one is sought.]

Gautier's moralizing, seemingly in order to exalt his heroine, serves to emphasize every other woman's weakness, all women's sinfulness.

Throughout the next episode—the empress's stay with her rescuer's family which ends with the brother's murder of the rescuer's child and the empress's second "trial" and "exile"—Gautier continues to compare the empress to everywoman in order to demonstrate her remarkable, holy behavior. In particular he comments upon her attitude toward physical beauty and dress—she prefers dirty dresses to festive ones, she washes her face with tears more than rose water (ll. 1197–209)—her preference for spending time in church and chapel rather than dancing and playing (ll. 1189–98), and her wise behavior in fleeing, rather than courting, men who speak "lecherie" (ll. 1216–24). Despite such unworldly behavior she is yet again courted by the brother of her rescuer, and once again Gautier expounds at length on a misogynist commonplace, this time Ovid's maxim that a chaste woman is one whom no man has pursued:

Ovides dist que cele est chaste
Que nus ne prie ne ne haste,
Et il dist voir, par Nostre Dame! (II Mir 9:1335–37)[28]

[Ovid says that she is chaste whom no one beseeches nor pursues, and he speaks truly, by Our Lady!]

After the empress successfully resists this second sexual "temptation," the narrator utters no more of these misogynist commonplaces, nor does he again compare the empress to women in general. Instead his digressions praising the empress, while still concerned with her rejection of worldly values, speak only of her behavior, her attitudes.[29] This development in the presentation of the empress can be seen, at least in part, as purely a result of the narrative line: after this point the empress will be overtly assaulted by the sailors and not "tempted." However, if we read in the other direction, we can also say that Gautier takes every opportunity, every narratively motivated chance, to stress woman's weakness, her tendency toward sin, particularly sexual sin, while highlighting the empress's remarkable virtue and moral strength.[30] This contrastive rhetorical figure distances the empress even further from everywoman, making her virtue indeed "saintly," that is to say, essentially inimitable.[31]

Of the *Miracles'* protagonists tempted to sin, all but the empress "fall"—with the single exception of the nun who doesn't leave the convent to join her beloved (I Mir 26). But this example indeed proves the rule, since the nun renounces her plans only after a dream-vision of the torments of hell completed by a cautionary sermon by the Virgin. If all others fall, the empress's difference stands out ever more clearly, and the conclusion that she is "other" becomes inescapable.

Gautier presents the empress, however, as someone more than, someone other than, simply an exemplar of Christian female constancy, fortitude, and virtue. She not only resists temptation and prefers death to dishonor, she also heals, with the Virgin's gift of the miraculous plant, and she speaks—at some length. Other women in the *Miracles* sermonize in small doses, as when the nun who does not leave the convent preaches chastity to her ex-*ami*, but only the empress and the Virgin have significant speeches. Once again, the empress's singularity stands out.

The empress's long speeches are of two types, prayers and sermons, of which the more significant and more developed are the latter. She preaches on several occasions to the people around her—in particular to the men who "court" her—using the same rhetorical devices as does Gautier when he preaches in his asides, and in his prologues and epilogues. For example, she finishes an argument with her brother-in-law with an *annominatio* on the word *dure:*

Bien me disïez, biaus doz frere,
Que vos m'amïez *dure*ment:
Frere, sachiez seürement
Que l'amors est voyrement *dure*
Qui l'ame *ardoir* fait en l'*ardure*
Qui *dure* autant com Diex *durra*.
Ja mes cuers certes n'*endurra*,
Ne li doz Diex ja ne l'*endurt*,
Si *dure* amors entre nous *durt*." (II Mir 9:324–32, my emphasis)

[Well have you said to me, beloved sweet brother, that you loved me very much: Brother, know surely that love is truly hard which causes the soul to burn in the fire, which endures as long as God will endure. My heart will never endure it, nor sweet God allow if that hard love endures between us.]

She also uses typical sermon topoi, such as the concept that God is no respecter of rank but treats all, rich and poor, equally:

Les pauvres gens ne heit pas Diex.
Ausi grant droit ont es sainz cielz
Li orphenin, li orphenines
Com ont li roy et les roÿnes. (II Mir 9:1433–36)

[Poor people are not despised by God. Orphan boys and orphan girls have as much right in holy heaven as kings and queens.]

Another is the concept that God sees the heart while people see only the exterior:

—Sire, fait ele, mes pensez
Seit Diex mout mielz que nus ne face:
Diex voit ou cuer, hons en la face;
Diex voit le cuer, le vis li hom. (II Mir 9:1478–81)

["Lord," she said, "God knows my thoughts much better than any-one does: God sees into the heart, man on the surface; God sees the heart, man the face."]

The empress speaks her longest sermon (ll. 3381–580) at the end of the miracle, as she informs her husband she wants to become a nun rather than rejoin him: two hundred lines of rhetorical and homiletic expertise. Again we see *annominatio* (here on the well-known homo-phony between *amor* and *amer*)[32] as well as the use of standard topoi of antimarriage and proconvent literature such as an encouragement to prefer God's faithfulness and perfection over human inconstancy and imperfection (ll. 3413–58) or to choose heavenly riches over earthly wealth and an immortal beloved over mortal man (ll. 3568–80). Several passages strongly recall *La chasteté aux nonains*, Gautier's extended exhortation to chastity and sexual purity addressed to the nuns of the convent of Soissons, which directly follows the miracle.

One must say the empress speaks like a cleric, like Gautier himself; he puts into her mouth a discourse normally reserved for religious men. Yet the empress's life, her story, is what gives her the authority to speak. Her prayers, like those of all the protagonists, are always efficacious—God or the Virgin intervenes to rescue her in each of her perilous situa-tions before she is raped or killed. Her sermons, however, have no effect on either her brother-in-law or her rescuer's brother; despite their rhe-torical and theological polish, they do not restrain the men's desire or behavior in any way. Only after her tribulations, and the demonstration of her sanctity through her ability to heal, does her speech succeed in affecting the man to whom she preaches, specifically convincing her husband that she should be released from her marriage vows and be al-lowed to become a nun.

The empress gains the power to speak with authority by her victory over the three forces that assail the Christian soul: the world, the flesh, and the Devil.[33] She demonstrates her victory over the flesh and the

Devil when she rejects both brothers who desire her,[34] and when she prefers death to rape by the sailors. Her victory over the world comes with her rejection of her status and riches as empress, demonstrated by her lifestyle after the Virgin appears to her on the rock, and her sermon to her husband. The vision of the Virgin and the gift of the miraculous healing plant confirm her victory, her status as an *amie Dieu*, as Gautier repeatedly calls her.

Her life after this point—wandering as a mendicant, healing all who ask for her help—demonstrates what a victorious, saintly life should be:

> A Dieu conquerre, a Dieu avoir
> Met si son cuer et son corage
> Que tout le monde comme sage
> Heit et despit pour sauer l'ame.
>
> . . .
>
> Povrement va, povrement vient
> Com povre fame, com estrange.
> Ne vielt loier, los ne losenge
> De nule chose qu'ele face. (II Mir 9:2404–15)

[In order to win God, to have God, she sets her heart and her will such that she, being wise, hated and despised all the world in order to save her soul. . . . She goes and comes in poverty, as a poor woman, as a stranger. She doesn't want wages, approbation nor praise for anything she does.]

This portrait of empress as mendicant exemplifies the patristic teaching that for a woman to become saintly she must become like a man.[35] As we have seen, after just her first "trial" she rejects feminine vanity, wearing dirty dresses and washing her face with tears rather than rose water. Now at the end of her peregrinations her asceticism becomes so intense that it causes her to lose all her physical beauty:

> Tant pleure adez la sainte fame
> Et tant jeüne et eure et veille
> Que sa face clere et vermeille
> Oscure et pale li devient.
>
> . . .
>
> Si esfacie est ja sa face
> Et ses clers vis si deperis
> Ne samble mais l'empeeris
> Qui tant ert bele et tant ert blonde
> C'on en parloit par tot le monde. (II Mir 9:2408–20)

[The saintly woman cried and fasted and stayed awake so much that her clear and rosy face became darkened and pale.... Her face was already so faded and her clear visage so damaged that she didn't look at all like the empress, who was so beautiful and so blond that she was talked about everywhere.]

In short, she loses what caused all her tribulations because it caused men to desire her. It is this aspect of Gautier's presentation of the empress that best illustrates, for me, its deep ambivalence. The empress's sanctity is simultaneously defined by sexual abjection and victimization and by her powerful verbal articulation of her decision to renounce the world. She becomes saintly by rejecting her female humanity, by losing even the physical characteristics that marked her as a woman. Yet such physical denial—which stands in a long tradition of saintly asceticism, St. Alexis and Ste Marie l'Égyptienne being perhaps the most immediate Old French literary examples—leads to her personal choice to become a nun, and to significant power in healing and in speaking.

The empress becomes in a sense the complement, the reverse image, of the Virgin. Both heal, both rescue sinners from the consequences of their sins, but the Virgin can do so while being beautiful, feminine, and in several instances even inviting because she is not of this world, because she is by definition pure and sexless. The empress, owing to her human and thus sinful nature, must reject her femininity to the point of losing the physical marks of her gender in order to accede to such power. In Gautier's textual universe, female beauty in this world is incompatible with female holiness.

Such a conclusion might seem excessively categorical were it not that of the six "good" women in Gautier's *Miracles*, all but one are either already in heaven (the Virgin and Ste Léocade) or physically unattractive (disfigured or dying). The one exception is a virgin of Arras (II Mir 27) who is forced into marriage by her family despite her desire to become a nun. When her husband attempts to force her to have sex, he discovers that she is physically incapable of being penetrated and he stabs her in the vagina. The Virgin intervenes and heals the woman, who is then allowed to enter a convent. Again the exception proves the rule, for if the virgin of Arras is attractive or at least young (we do not get a significant description), she is literally incapable of falling into sexual sin, of losing her virginity even by force. Returning to Dyan Elliott's psychologically influenced analysis, we could say that Gautier's inherent distrust of women, whether due to a Freudian fear of castration or to the ambient homosocial monastic culture, expresses itself in an inability to portray a real woman who remains both desirable and saintly.

With the Virgin and the empress as parallel limit-cases of the "good woman," the female protagonists examined in the middle section, whose female flesh leads them into sexual sin, can be seen to occupy the opposite, negative pole in the analysis. It would seem then that Gautier's text validates the well-worn dichotomy of Eve versus Mary, the evil sexual woman versus the good sexless one.[36] Yet I would argue that some ambiguity does remain, not only in the person of the empress but also in the more general presentation of Gautier's female protagonists. If nearly all the sinful women are guilty of sexual misconduct, their number is dwarfed by that of the men who commit sexual sins. The woman are also, particularly in the most spectacular cases, the object of the narrator's obvious sympathy, while the authorities (bishop, emperor) charged with investigating their crimes are presented as being manipulated by the Devil and/or jealous or venal fellow humans. In the *Miracles*, then, women both are and are not equal in sin and punishment to men. No more sinful than men, they do not receive equal treatment in this world—nor in Gautier's text.

Notes

1. All quotes of Gautier de Coinci's *Miracles* are taken from the Koenig edition. All references are given following Koenig's numbering system: Book (I or II), type of text (miracle, prologue, etc.), text number, and then line numbers within that text. All translations are mine.

2. In the introduction to his edition Koenig states that there are nearly eighty manuscripts, dating from the thirteenth to the fifteenth century. The definitive study of the manuscripts remains Ducrot-Granderye, *Études*. Gautier's influence can be seen in later compilations of miracles, such as the *Vie des Pères*, in Rutebuef (in particular, but not exclusively, in the *Miracle de Théophile*), and in the fifteenth-century *Miracles de Nostre Dame par personnages* where several of the plays derive directly from Gautier's tales, to name just a few examples.

3. One recent exception is Black, "Woman as Savior." Garnier, *Mutations temporelles*, also discusses the miracle of the empress of Rome but is not really concerned with the gender of the protagonist, seeing her travels and trials more as an allegory of the Christian's spiritual progress toward perfection. It is a position often debated among Chaucer scholars in regard to *The Man of Law's Tale*, whose heroine, Custance, is clearly an avatar of the empress of Rome, although not directly derived from Gautier de Coinci. For an overview of the debate, see Edwards, "Critical Approaches."

4. Sainte Léocade, the only true saint (that is to say, dead and canonized) to

appear in the text, also plays an interesting role in the *Miracles*. She has the signal honor of appearing in two separate miracles (the second and last of Book I), and her relics were housed at the monastery at Vic, where Gautier was prior. It is clear from the place and the prominence accorded Sainte Léocade that she holds a special place in Gautier's devotion. However, she is not the protagonist of the miracles in which she appears: in the first the protagonist is the bishop of Toledo, and in the second, which recounts the recovery of her stolen relics, it is Gautier himself who occupies center stage. Thus, although she is a relatively significant female figure in the *Miracles*, she is not a real "actor" in the text. Her presence in the *Miracles* and Gautier de Coinci's "relationship" with her—for example, his fairly obvious identification with the bishop of Toledo or the very personal nature of his remarks in the miracle of her relics—deserve more discussion. But it will have to wait, for reasons of space and cohesion, for another opportunity.

5. The titles of the miracles are as given in the table in the introduction to Koenig's edition (ix–xiii). Although not always as descriptive as one might like, they have the double advantage of being concise and consistent, particularly as the rubrics in the manuscripts can be extremely varied. Note, however, that these titles are not the same as the ones used by Koenig in his indexes or in the edition proper, where he uses the titles in the rubrics of his base manuscript, BN fr. 22928. For ease of reference I also give the Koenig number of the miracle in parentheses after the first mention of the title.

6. She is Gautier's inspiration and *dame* like the lyric *domna* of the *grand chant courtois:*

A la loenge et a la gloire,
En ramembrance et en memoire
De la roïne et de la dame
Cui je commant mon cors et m'ame
A jointes mains soir et matin. (I Prol 1:1–5)
[To the praise and the glory, in thought and in memory, of the queen and the lady to whom I commend my body and my soul, with joined hands evening and morning.]

7. As patron she both causes the work to be written and gives instructions on how to proceed:

La douce dame bien aprise,
Por qu'ai ceste matere enprise,
A traitier si bien la m'apregne
Que boen essample aucuns i pregne
Et qu'ele gre m'en daint savoir. (I Prol 1:15–19)
[May the sweet well-learned lady, for whom I have begun this work, teach me so well to conduct it, that anyone may find a good example in it, and may she judge me worthy of thanks.]

8. For a discussion of the development of the doctrine of Mary as intercessor and rescuer of those devoted to her, see Warner, *Alone of All Her Sex*, 315–31,

and, more specifically concerned with the medieval period and the genre of the miracle, Phillipart, "Le récit miraculaire."

9. The two topoi occur in 35 percent of the miracles. The Virgin acts as advocate in nine of the fifty-eight miracles and as doctor in eleven of them.

10. "Ce que Marie invente en contrepartie, par ses «scandaleuses miracles», c'est l'ordre d'une protection maternante, à l'abri des exigences et des rigueurs de la loi." [What Mary invents in compensation, by her "scandalous miracles," is on the order of a maternal protection, sheltered from the demands and rigors of the law.] Phillipart, "Le récit miraculaire," 576.

11. Bynum, *Jesus as Mother,* 110–69.

12. In a different, rather more expected context, there are also the descriptions and lyric effusions of Gautier's songs in praise of the Virgin at the beginning of both books of the *Miracles.*

13. Matter, *The Voice of My Beloved,* particularly chap. 5.

14. Elliott, *Fallen Bodies,* 114.

15. The one exception to this pattern is the *Miracle du larron pendu* (I Mir 30), where the Virgin rescues a robber from death by hanging and then from the swords of his jailers when they realize he is not dead after three days on the gibbet. But even here the parallel with the women accused of sins and/or crimes is not very strong because there is no scene of judgment: the tale begins with the robber being hanged. Since the Virgin does not save the robber from judgment, as she does the women, but rather from death, I would argue that this miracle falls more into the category of sinful men who are saved after death—several of whom are, in fact, resuscitated by the Virgin.

16. Examples include I Mir 15, "dou clerc mort en cui boche on trova la flor," and I Mir 23, "D'un moigne en cui bouche on trouva cinc roses nouveles."

17. For example, I Mir 25, "de celui qui se tua par l'amonestement dou dyable," or I Mir 28: "dou chevalier a cui la volenté fu contee por fait."

18. The contrast between this miracle and the *Larron pendu* is striking. Both protagonists are guilty of serious crimes, both miracles involve the Virgin rescuing sinners from execution, but in the *larron*'s case there is no trial shown, nor is there any audience mentioned for his execution, nor finally does anyone but the executioners see him alive on the gibbet.

19. Other women subject to public accusations or shame include the empress of Rome (II Mir 1), who will be discussed in detail in the third section, and Gondree (II Mir 24) who, horribly disfigured by illness, is mistreated and abused by all the townspeople and even her own husband because, we assume, they equate physical disfigurement with inner sin, although Gautier mentions no sin on her part.

20. There are a few cases where there is no real sin on the protagonist's part but where he/she suffers anyway. Examples are Gondree, hounded and abused by the townspeople because of her illness and disfigurement, and the priest who knows only one mass, that of Notre Dame, and is kicked out of his parish by the bishop. In these cases the men and women seem to receive essentially equal treatment.

21. The best syntheses, despite their well-debated weaknesses, remain Bloch, *Medieval Misogyny*, chaps. 1–4 in particular, and Pagels, *Adam, Eve, and the Serpent*, as well as the well-known Duby, *Chevalier*. See also Christopher Lucken's discussion of woman and "noise" in this volume.

22. Not counting those cases where there is no consummation of the "illicit" desire (i.e., the cases of the fiancé of the Virgin and the female equivalents), there are six men and three women who are directly presented as being guilty of sexual sins.

23. The one exception is the nun whom the Virgin admonishes for saying too many *saluts* too quickly (I Mir 29).

24. For a discussion of the entire family of texts that recount the tale of the empress, see Wallensköld, *Conte de la femme chaste*.

25. The account of the brother-in-law's falling in love and his sufferings as he initially tries to be honorable afford Gautier a perfect opportunity to demonstrate his mastery of the vocabulary and conventions of *fin'amor* while simultaneously presenting it as deadly, destructive, and inspired by the Devil. Throughout this section (II Mir 9:149–332) the narrator's asides present the empress as the real target of the Devil's attacks and the brother-in-law as "merely" Satan's tool:

La dame ensi teint em prison
Le charbon vif et le tison
Dont li dyables par sousprendre
S'ame et son cors cuida espendre. (II Mir 9:599–602)
[The lady thus keeps in prison the burning coal and the torch by which the devil, by fooling her soul and her body, thinks to own her.]

26. "A woman accedes to sanctity [in Virgin martyr accounts] by prizing her chastity so highly that she dies for it" (Gravdal, *Ravishing Maidens*, 22).

27. Note as well that Gautier doesn't even state that the empress is not like Potiphar's wife, just that it seems to him that he sees that she doesn't behave similarly! Women, even in the person of the saintly empress, are damned with faint praise.

28. One has here at least to wonder if Gautier is not being ironic—to call upon Notre Dame as his guarantor that all women are unchaste! Yet the exposition that follows is utterly serious. In any case, the mere discussion of such a maxim contributes to the misogynist tenor of Gautier's text.

29. For example, the digression in lines 2400–2444.

30. Such a reading is supported by the presence in other miracles of more sermons on the narrator's part decrying the dangers and the sinfulness of women.

31. For a discussion of the question of whether saints were to be seen as "models to be imitated" or rather as "figures to be admired," see Cazelles, *The Lady as Saint*, 21–38.

32. The *annominatio* is quite typical:

Toute autre *amor* m'iert bien *amere*

Por bien *amer* lui et *sa mere.*
Pour Dieu *amer* m'iert tout *amer,*
Car nus sanz Dieu ne sait *amer.* (II Mir 9:3481–84)
[All other love becomes quite bitter to me, from loving Him and His mother
well. To love God all becomes bitter to me, for no one without God knows
how to love.]

33. Gautier explicitly states that she fights against the three enemies of the
faithful:

La lettre dit, si com moy samble,
Qu'a trois champions tout ensamble
Chascun de nos convient combatre,
Et cilz qui il porront abatre,
Saichiez por voir qu'il iert peris.
Souvent tentent l'empeeris
Li mondes, la chars, li dyables. (II Mir 9:2977–83)
[The word says, it seems to me, that each of us must fight against three
adversaries, and those whom they can defeat, know for truth, that they
will perish. The world, the flesh, and the devil often tempt the empress.]

34. The presentation of the empress as so beautiful that men cannot help but
fall in love with her conforms to what Gravdal describes as the "oppressive
contradiction in patristic theology." She argues that many a female saint is
presented as "still so 'sexy' that she leads man to sin, in thought if not in deed,"
and that such a presentation allows "hagiographers [to] maintain the oppressive
contradiction in patristic theology: as long as a woman has a woman's body she
cannot escape her sinful state" (*Ravishing Maidens,* 35).

35. See Bloch, *Medieval Misogyny,* chap. 4.

36. See, for example, Gold, *The Lady and the Virgin.*

Selected Bibliography

Black, Nancy. "Woman as Savior: The Virgin Mary and the Empress of Rome in
Gautier de Coinci's *Miracles.*" *Romanic Review* 88.4 (1998): 503–17.

Bloch, R. Howard. *Medieval Misogyny and the Invention of Western Romantic
Love.* Chicago: University of Chicago Press, 1991.

Bynum, Caroline Walker. *Jesus as Mother: Studies in the Spirituality of the High
Middle Ages.* Berkeley and Los Angeles: University of California Press, 1982.

Cazelles, Brigitte. *The Lady as Saint: A Collection of French Hagiographic Romances of the Thirteenth Century.* Philadelphia: University of Pennsylvania
Press, 1991.

Duby, Georges. *Le Chevalier, la Femme et le Prêtre.* Paris: Librairie Hachette,
1981.

Ducrot-Granderye, Arlette P. *Études sur les miracles Nostre Dame de Gautier
de Coinci.* Annales Academiae Scientiarum Fennicae B-35. Helsinki: Academia
Scientiarum Fennica, 1932.

Edwards, A.S.G. "Critical Approaches to the *Man of Law's Tale*." In *Chaucer's Religious Tales*, edited by C. David Benson and Elizabeth Robertson, 85–94. Cambridge: D. S. Brewer, 1990.

Elliott, Dyan. *Fallen Bodies: Pollution, Sexuality, and Demonology in the Middle Ages*. Philadelphia: University of Pennsylvania Press, 1999.

Garnier, Annette. *Mutations temporelles et cheminement spirituel: Analyse et commentaire du "Miracle de l'Empeeris" de Gautier de Coinci*. Paris: H. Champion, 1988.

Gautier de Coinci. *Les Miracles de Nostre Dame par Gautier de Coinci*. Edited by Frédéric Koenig. 4 vols. Geneva: Droz, 1966–78.

Gold, Penny Shine. *The Lady and the Virgin: Image, Attitude, and Experience in Twelfth-Century France*. Chicago: University of Chicago Press, 1985.

Gravdal, Kathryn. *Ravishing Maidens: Writing Rape in Medieval French Literature and Law*. Philadelphia: University of Pennsylvania Press, 1991.

Matter, E. Ann. *The Voice of My Beloved: The Song of Songs in Western Medieval Christianity*. Philadelphia: University of Pennsylvania Press, 1990.

Pagels, Elaine. *Adam, Eve, and the Serpent*. New York: Random House, 1988.

Phillipart, Guy. "Le récit miraculaire marial dans l'Occident médiéval." In *Marie: Le Culte de la Vièrge dans la société médiévale*, ed. Dominique Iogna-Prat, Eric Palazzo, and Daniel Russo, 563–90. Paris: Beauchesne, 1996.

Wallensköld, A. *Le Conte de la femme chaste convoitée par son beau-frère: Étude de littérature comparée*. Acta Societatis Scientiarum Fennicae 34, no. 1. Helsingfors: Société de littérature finnoise, 1907.

Warner, Marina. *Alone of All Her Sex: The Myth and the Cult of the Virgin Mary*. New York: Knopf, 1976.

3

Women's Voices Raised in Prayer

On the "Epic Credo" in Adenet le Roi's *Berte as grans piés*

David J. Wrisley

Adenet le Roi, in the spirit of medieval continuation, composed a verse narrative entitled *Berte as grans piés* (circa 1273–74) which elaborates on the life of the mother of Charlemagne, Berte, forming what would become the prehistory of the *geste du roi*.[1] In a double gesture of renovation and restoration, Adenet participates in the poetic fiction of *translatio*. He tells us how he takes a material corrupted by its transmission through the jongleurs and recasts the *vraie estoire* of the events of Berte's life, her ancestry, marriage, calumny, and sufferings, into a romance-epic framework (vv. 8–19). The redemptive, reparative paradigms of romance (in turn inspired by hagiographic texts) and the crucial role played by the female protagonists in Adenet's work buttress the world of the chanson de geste. Vernacular speech by women, particularly women's voices raised in prayer which come out in the face of suffering and treachery, forges a *chambre des dames* at the heart of Adenet's story. The performative quality of these prayers, and their ability to revisit narratives of the past, provides the underpinnings for the construction of the exemplary female protagonist—her constancy, her spiritual wisdom, her faith. The "voiced" portraits of both Berte and her mother, Blancheflour, in turn provide a venue in which Adenet's poetic voice forges its own vernacular identity.

* * *

The moment of the Credo prayer said in true faith is a fundamental one in Western Christianity. The manuscripts of the Abelard and Héloïse correspondence end with Abelard's statement of belief. Such a prayer also forms a pivotal moment in liturgical commemoration. Penitential literature likewise structures itself around the moment of confession and the profession of faith. Joinville, the biographer-hagiographer of Louis IX, inserted a Credo into the *Vie de saint Louis*, and composed a much longer prose text entitled *Credo* or *Li romans as ymages des poinz de nostre foi* (1250–51) which glosses the prayer of belief with a colorful mosaic of biblical examples.[2] Medieval literary historians identify a particular kind of Credo, known as the "epic Credo" or the *prière du plus grand péril*, which appears on the brink of despair in both chansons de geste and romances.[3] An analogous and no less important prayer, the Ave Maria, plays a crucial role in romance and lyric contexts alike.[4] Both prayers have a multiple function: they invoke faith and often the intercession of the Virgin or the Holy Spirit; they illustrate the Christian praying, sometimes even in a physical posture of faith, on his knees, hands clasped together; they also review key points of Christian narrative—"des poinz de nostre foi" the clerkly Joinville would say. For the faithful, they are moments in which to express belief through a recollection of a common story, but also they offer the opportunity for petition.

Such an epic Credo prayer, I would suggest, is a "literary speech act" and contains a strong *performative* impulse. In a distinction set forth by J. L. Austin, "performative" utterances are not merely "declarative"— meaning that they communicate statements of fact, inform and describe—but they also "carry out a 'performance' to accomplish an *act* through the very process of their enunciation."[5] By importing powerful narratives from outside the material of the life of Charlemagne's mother, Adenet not only is able to make characters perform their faith, he is also able to "perform" himself; he can back declarative statements of truth value in his own poetic text and the fiction of his tale's genesis with the faithful utterances of royal women. In short, clerkly narrative practice is met by exemplary feminine faith and eloquence in *Berte as grans piés*, and his verse is the canvas on which Adenet sketches such a mutual performance.

Of course, Austin himself and critics following him have recognized the ultimate failure of a clear distinction between a declarative and a performative act of language. In the case of these Credo poems, this is no less true. The recitation of the story (a declarative function) invokes the miracle of divine intercession; in other words, the words of that prayer accomplish an act (a performative function). At the same time, prayer creates a mirroring effect; that is to say, the events of the vernacular romance-epic narrative recounted by the poetic voice fuse with biblical and medieval spiritual intertext. In a ritual moment like prayer, where the time of the event and the time of the evoked narrative seem to collapse, honor is bestowed on the woman uttering these words, and her effort brings value and efficacy to the whole story. The proclamation of such utterances also accomplishes an act in that it has what I call a "thaumaturgic effect," healing sad lovers and disbelievers alike. Adenet's narrative voice promises as much:

L'estoire iert si rimee, *par foi le vous plevi*,
Que li mesentendant en seront abaubi
Et li bien entendant en seront esjoy. (vv. 20–22)

[The story will be set in verse—*I swear to you on my faith*—so that those who do not understand will be amazed and those who do understand will be rejoiced by it.]

In this poem, with its imbricated series of separations and deferrals, the performative act of prayer, by securing an action, also serves as a collateral against the courtly disorder at the beginning of the tale. It assures the ultimate resolution of the story in closure, with recognition and reunion. It is also one of the ways that Adenet creates his world of female exemplarity: Berte and Blancheflour—through prayer to God—bring a perspicacity and spiritual wisdom to the epic material in which he frames their story.

Berte as grans piés is often treated as a chanson de geste because of its formal structure, and yet it owes a great deal to romance narrative also. There are no lengthy accounts of battles or political campaigns; instead scenes of royal marriage, substitution of the bride, separation, wandering in the forest, reunion, and celebration take the center stage as in any of Chrétien de Troyes's romances. When the component of treachery and consequent female suffering is added, romance or romance-inflected hagiographic narratives again come to mind. It is a powerful and rich *conjointure* of diverse material and it serves as an ornate template for the poetic elaboration of the life of Berte, mother of Charlemagne, a life that, as most critics note, is wanting in historical detail.[6] We might see Adenet's *Berte* as similar to his own *Enfances Ogier* and linked to the contemporary vogue for narratives on the childhood of heroes, including Christ—poems that explored, and expanded, the marginal areas of the *geste du roi.* Adenet is sketching a poetic picture of Charlemagne's maternal lineage, and at the same time giving it a characteristic spirituality.[7]

Before I turn to four examples of prayers, some thoughts from Richard Schechner's *Between Theater and Anthropology* can enrich our notion of the performative. His notion of performance as "restored behavior" is particularly illuminating: "Restored behavior is symbolic and reflexive: not empty, but loaded behavior multivocally broadcasting significances. These difficult terms express a single principle: The self can act in/as another; the social or transindividual self is a role or set of roles. . . . Performance means: never for the first time. It means: for the second to the *n*th time. Performance is 'twice-behaved behavior.'"[8] This notion of performance reflects what we find in the female voice and female heroism that one encounters repeatedly in the period of Adenet's writing.[9] What is more, such behavior behaved for "the *n*th time" sets these prayers into the work of clerkly remembrance and thence into a tradition of poetic writing conjoining Christian memory and community.[10] That Berte's life was barely recorded and therefore offered few constraints is precisely what makes it a fruitful terrain for poetic elaboration. Seen from this perspective, Adenet's tale offers a "civilizing" effect on the corrupt legend that he discovered. By inserting Berte and her mother into the roles of penitent Christians, he makes these women act in and as another. Not only are the performances replayed across the text, but the experiences of these women are rendered universal and valid because, in the form of prayer, they appeal to a factor of penitential repeatability; that is to say, the prayers can be uttered by a knight, a clerk, a layman, or a peasant with equally felicitious effect. The power of the "epic Credo" rests in its ability both to evoke and to invoke a memory for "the second to the *n*th time." A tradition is called forth with each of these prayers, and a community assumed in every speech act.[11]

I will examine four central female "prayers" in Adenet's *Berte,* utterances that demonstrate the performative principles outlined above. Jacques de Caluwé's seminal essay on these prayers brings our attention to their variety, in both length and importance.[12] Among the fifteen or so prayers he outlines, many are "embryonic": they consist of a mention of a saint or an address to God that resembles a lead-in to a longer prayer but falls short of being one.[13] Drawing upon the monographic study of Renée Colliot, de Caluwé concentrates essentially on the poetic "originalité" of Berte's prayers, which he says, citing Colliot, paradoxically could apply to numerous circumstances.[14] It is precisely to the tension between the individual "original" utterance and its repeatability or its applicability that I turn; that they can shuttle between the particular and the universal is what makes them exemplary.

In the first *laisse* (vv. 723–33), we find Berte alone—wandering as a hermit would—in the forest of Le Mans. She recalls the Nativity and the story of the Three Magi led by the star announcing Christ's birth. Believing in the truth of that story and underscoring her own wandering, she calls herself a "lasse," a wretch (v. 720). The narrative convergence between the biblical story and Adenet's story reinforces her need for guidance, so that as she heads into the forest "Damedieu reclama, le pere esperital / Lui et sa douce mere, qu'il la gardent de mal" (vv. 724–25) [She invoked Damedieu the spiritual father, and His sweet mother, that They should save her from evil]. Following her petition and invocation, Berte utters a lament to her own mother and the saints. She is described in a sympathetic tone in the next *laisse* as scared—"Ce n'est pas grant merveille se li cuers li doloit" (v. 746) [It is hardly surprising that her heart was suffering]—and as "gente et adroite" (v. 766) [noble and upright]. In *laisse* 30, in contrast, the narrator gives Berte's long genealogy, starting with her mother, Blancheflour, and then her sister Aelis:

La fille Blancheflour, la roÿne au cler vis,
Fu dedens la forest, molt fu ses cuers pensis.
Fille fu au roi Floire, qui fu preus et gentis;
S'il savoit ce meschief, molt seroit abaubis.
Une seror avoit qui ot non Aelis,
Fenme au duc de Sassoigne, et si ert quens marchis,
De Brandebourc tenoit la terre et le paÿs.
Molt fu de haut lignage Berte, ce vous plevis,
De rois, d'empereours et de princes eslis.
Souz un arbre est assise, molt ot poi de delis;
Vermeille ert conme rose, blanche com flours de lis. (vv. 780–90)

[The daughter of Blancheflour, the bright-faced queen, was in the forest and her heart was quite pensive. She was the daughter of Floire, the noble and handsome king; if he knew of this misfortune, he would be much shocked. She had a sister who had the name Aelis, wife of the duke of Saxony, who also was the count-marquis governing the land of Brandenburg. Berte was of very high lineage—this I swear to you—one distinguished by kings, emperors, and princes. She was seated under a tree, hardly delighted at all, scarlet as a rose and white as a lily.]

Not only is the female branch of Berte's family successful in its connections to empire, but these royal women possess beauty and spiritual wisdom. The line (v. 790) contrasting the rose and the fleur-de-lis makes this clear. Her characterization therefore owes both to her suffering, her intelligent response to such pain, and to her royal origins.

The second Credo prayer (*laisses* 42 and 43, vv. 1025–72) comes when Berte is cold, hungry, and on the verge of despair. She invokes both God and her family, kneeling down and lamenting on the image of Calvary, Christ's sufferings on the cross for mankind, and reflecting on his crowning of the faithful in Heaven. From this narrative of redemption whose benefit can be reaped by any Christian praying in good faith, Berte's prayer takes a very personal turn. Compared with the first prayer, this one contains many more verbs in the first person (see italics in the passage below) as well as Berte's acceptance of suffering for the will of God and her double promise never to reveal her marriage with Pepin to anyone and never to lose her virginity:

> . . . ce *sai je* sans douter
> K'en vo saint paradis les faites coronner.
> Puisqu'il vous plaist, biau sire, que *j'aie* a endurer,
> *Je vueil* pour vous mon cors traveillier et pener;
> Or me vueilliez, biau sire, de ce perill geter.
> *Je veuil* pour vostre amour ici endroit vouer
> Un veu que *je tenrai* a tous jours sans fausser,
> Que ja mais ne *dirai*, tant come *porrai* durer,
> Que soie fille a roi ne k'a Pepin le ber
> Soie fenme espousee, ja mais n'en quier parler,
> —*G'iroie* ains d'uis en huis mes aumosnes rouver—
> . . .
> Ma virginité *vueil*, se Dieu plaist, bien garder,
> Car qui pert pucelage, ce est sans recouvrer. (vv. 1044–59)

[*I know* without doubt that you crown them in Heaven. Since it pleases you that *I should* suffer, Lord, *I will* torture and tire my body for You. Please now, Lord, deliver me from this peril. *I will* out of love for You here and now pronounce a vow that *I will* hold true forever: *I will* never *reveal*—as long as *I can* endure—that I am the daughter of a king, nor that I am married to Lord Pepin. Never will I speak about it; *I would* rather *go* from door to door seeking alms. . . . *I will* keep, God willing, my virginity, since she who loses maidenhead, cannot recover it.]

The coronation imagery and the deemphasizing of worldly marriage has the effect of emphasizing Berte's offering of her virginity to God and lends to this scene the character of a female saintly performance; through Berte's repetition of "je vueil" [I will] and its juxtaposition with God's will ("Puisqu'il vous plaist" [Since it pleases you]), she imitates and conforms to the will of God and simultaneously acts out the nuptial union, the performative "I do," that all women saints achieve with Christ. Berte's higher, quasi-saintly aspirations here, in which she espouses faith and the *droite voie*, sketch performative models for the rest of the poetic narrative. The vow to keep her virginity and hide her identity also narratively prefigures—in the fashion of romance narratives—the final test that Berte's faith will undergo; in this way, Berte's prayers make up part of Adenet's own performance of skill at structuring his work and bringing it to closure.

It is with these prayers pronounced by Berte that de Caluwé's and Colliot's lists end. To understand better Berte's textual exemplarity and the structuring role of prayer in Adenet's romance-epic, we must further look at the two complementary prayers of Berte's mother, Blancheflour, which occur halfway through the 3486-line poem. Blancheflour has a terrifying dream in which she is being torn apart by beasts, a dream not unlike the one her grandson Charlemagne will have—or rather, has already had—in the *Chanson de Roland*. Worried, Blancheflour departs for France, and her husband, Floire, sees to it that she leaves in courtly company. Neither Floire nor Blancheflour knows of Margiste's treachery or of the topsy-turvy situation of the court, where Aliste, whom everyone believes to be Berte, has made herself hated. Blancheflour is shocked to find people cursing Berte and her family. She naturally turns to God in complaint. She mentions *melancolie*, the retreat from God in a Saturnian moment, and a distrust of providence; she is also puzzled how such a well-bred girl of old ancestry can attract such harm:

"Dieus," fait ele, "dont vient si faite dyablie?
Ja fu Berte ma fille en si bon lieu norrie
Et s'est nee et estraite de si bonne lignie
Et de pere et de mere de viel ancisserie,
Dont il est or venue ceste melancolie[?]" (vv. 1740–44)

["God," she said, "from where do such diabolical things come? Indeed, my daughter Berte was brought up in such a good place, and was born of such a good lineage and of a father and a mother of old ancestry. From where then did this melancholy come?"]

Then, defending both her honor and that of her husband, she follows Berte's examples and makes a vow: "que tout li ferai rendre ce dont ele est saisie" (v. 1751) [that I shall recover for her everything that has been taken from her]. This invocation, which aims at reversing the perceived injustice—an illusion created by the muddling, obscuring quality of the treacherous substitution—is finally resolved in the next *laisse*, number 72. Preceding her second prayer comes an episode in which Blancheflour, along the way, meets a "paysant vilain" [churlish peasant]. The fellow recognizes her and begins to curse Berte, who, he claims, took away his horse worth sixty sous. He quickly changes his mind when Blancheflour charitably offers him a hundred sous for his trouble. This short scene, mixing courtly generosity with a touch of romance humor, marks the beginning of the "buying back" of Blancheflour's daughter's reputation. The encounter leads Blancheflour to strengthen her vow.

In *laisse* 73, Blancheflour not only speaks to God again, she invokes his name as "qui sesis a la Çaine" (v. 1781) [who sat at the Last Supper]. She goes on to invoke the mother of God, "Mere Dieu debonaire, roÿne souveraine" (v. 1782) [noble mother of God, sovereign queen]. These two gestures show her turning not only to a vow of revenge, as she did above, but also to spiritual narratives and to devotion to Mary; in short, she imitates the example of Berte in order to perform her faith and to accomplish her goal. What is more, the parallel mother-daughter vows, backed up by faith, have a structural function—they mark the midpoint of the poem—while the female collaboration also works to undo the treachery of an evil mother-daughter pair, Margiste-Aliste. This example of the mother-daughter bond anchors a very important lesson at the center of Adenet's romance-epic: remembrance of Christ's life and sufferings is to be equated with continuity, with the avoidance of melancholy and despair, and with protection against peril.

Berte's constancy, displayed in her intelligent decision to turn to prayer, is put to the test not only in the first half of the poem, as we have seen, but also at a crucial moment, a last hurdle for the heroine, recalling scenes from romance (as in Chrétien's *Lancelot*) or a martyr saint's life (as in the *Chanson de sainte Foi*). Pepin, on his way to Anjou, stumbles upon a young woman in a chapel in the woods near the home of Symon and Constance where Berte had taken refuge. Unbeknownst to him, it is his wife. In this instance, the narrator's portrait of Berte offers his own kind of "prayer," in imitation of both his protagonists, for the safety of Berte:

En la chapele ert Berte qui bien fu ensaignie,
Par derriere l'autel s'ert la bele mucie
Ou de cuer prioit molt Dieu et sainte Marie
Que son pere et sa mere doinst Jhesus bonne vie;
Pour le roi Pepin prie, celui n'oublie mie,
Que Damedieus le gart de mal et de folie. (vv. 2636–41)

[Wise Berte was in the chapel and had hidden behind the altar and was praying to God and Mary from her heart that Jesus grant her mother and father safety. She prays for King Pepin—whom she never forgets—that God save him from evil and folly.]

His exemplary portrait of the heroine has internalized—in his own indirect discourse—the kind of spiritual utterances that I have discussed above. He too has learned, at a very important moment, the importance of women's voices raised in prayer. At this juncture Berte is alone, far from the female company of Constance and her daughters, when Pepin solicits sexual involvement from her. The tension can be felt in the verse itself. Anaphora, word repetition, and the alternation of subjects frame the delicate, difficult scene of sexual advances:

Quant Pepins voit son vis vermeil et rouvelent,
Qu'ele ert blanche et vermeille et de joene jouvent,
D'amour et de desir tous li cuers li esprent.
De son cheval a terre tout maintenant descent
Et Berte remest coie, qui nul mal n'i entent,
Et li rois l'araisonne molt debonnairement
Et Berte li respont molt apenseement;
Et li rois assez tost entre ses bras la prent,
Et quant Berte voit ce, *molt ot grant marement,*
Damedieu reclama, qui maint ou firmament. (vv. 2669–78)

[When Pepin sees her scarlet and blushing face, her white and scarlet and youthful appearance sets his heart afire with love and desire. At once he gets down from his horse, and Berte, who perceives no harm in it, keeps still and the king addresses her very nobly and Berte responds cautiously; then the king takes her in his arms, *and Berte felt great distress, and she invoked God who dwells in Heaven.*]

Again Berte turns to prayer. The day, unlike the occasion of her very first prayer, is beautiful, with no rain or wind (v. 2679); such a change in weather would indicate Berte's strength and her stability. She bravely refuses his advances, again evoking a suffering Christ, then she exposes her identity in self-protection (vv. 2729–36). Learning her identity pleases the king very much, even if he does not reveal his own identity in turn: "De la joie qu'il ot ne pot un mot sonner" (v. 2736) [He could not voice a single word of the joy he experienced].

In the complicated reunion sequence that ensues, the first real recognition occurs when Blancheflour and Berte see each other, a scene that sparks many others similar to it. Significantly, it is the female couple of mother and daughter around which recognition turns. In a last biblical invocation, Berte then recognizes her husband Pepin, saying:

Sire, se c'estes vous, Damedieu en graci,
Qui de la Sainte Virge en Bethleem nasqui. (vv. 3128–29)

[Lord, if it is you, thanks to God who of the Blessed Virgin in Bethlehem was born.]

This is more than just a simple description of Christ; Berte has come full circle to the theme of the Nativity evoked in her very first prayer in the forest. Collective joy accompanies the reunion of Berte's parents, Floire and Blancheflour, and her "foster" parents, Symon and Constance, along with her husband, Pepin. The description here is again evocative of royal *geste:* "Symon le voier a la barbe flourie" (v. 3161) [Symon the provost-marshal with the flowery beard] and "ensamble sont assis en la chambre voutie" (v. 3163) [they were seated together in the vaulted room], both turns of phrase used to describe Charlemagne and his court. The last invocation takes on further importance as we learn of two of Berte's children. Adenet mentions Gille, future mother of Roland, who is conceived just after this moment of recognition, and Charlemagne; both are crucial for the French tradition of the *geste du roi.* The futurity that marks this moment of reunion leaves the horizon open for later elaboration. This is what Karl Uitti has called the "ongoingness" of the *geste:* a poetic openness reflected in the chanson de geste's use of temporality as well as a thematic and historical openness to which each poem treating the general material contributes.[15]

Prayers, in Adenet's work, exhibit the exemplarity of our central heroines, Berte and Blancheflour, and form the mortar of this mosaic, this *conjointure* of familiar plot lines—the romance substitution of the bride, the treachery of the evil servant, the sexual confrontation in the forest. The woman's voice raised in prayer is the vehicle through which each of these familiar transgressions is redeemed. These prayers activate the performative element of the written poem at the same time as they form and structure Adenet's continuation of the *geste*. The ritual dimension of the prayers only reinforces them as speech acts. Just as this poem celebrates in its spirit what has already been told (take the case of Blancheflour's terrifying dream) as well as what was, and is, on the horizon of this lineage, it repeats and revisits these same past moments, reinventing them and offering the promise of mythic reenactment. Prayer, as we have seen, is echoed across the poem, starting with Berte and continuing with her mother and finally with the narrator himself, providing the hope for, and the example of, repeatability.[16] As a script for faithful behavior, prayer allows the self "to act in/as another," to borrow the words of Schechner again, that is, in/as an abstract Christian actor; it also provides for the possibility of a future, of this happening for "the *n*th time." A tension, of course, exists at the core of this generic fusion enacted by Adenet between the repeatability of prayer and its single instances manifested here; it is analogous to the tension that exists between the finality and closure of the romance-inspired recognition plots and the open-endedness of the *geste*. Critics have typically received *Berte as grans piés* as a thirteenth-century chanson de geste, even though it is structured on the very romanesque plot of the bridal substitution. Perhaps the alexandrine verse line, the poem's organization in *laisses*, and the focus on Charlemagne's lineage have influenced that classification. For me, the crucial question is not so much where different generic traits manifest themselves as how these two generic modes work together in Adenet's poem. To conclude, I would like to turn to this question.

The very first *laisse*, which functions as a prologue would in romance, gives the origin of the story and describes the context of its composition. The poem does not then begin *in medias res* but rather, in the second and third *laisses*, recounts the story of Charles Martel and his court— also taking place "en sa sale voutie" (v. 38) [in his vaulted hall]—and his struggle with the Vandals. This part brings us close to the legend related in the *Girart de Roussillon* or the *Garin Le Louvain* poems. So violent were those battles that:

Mainte ame en fu de cors sevree et departie,
Et maint hauberc rompu, mainte targe percie,
Mainte tour abatue, mainte vile essillie;
Puis en fu la pais si et faite et establie. (vv. 28–31)

[Many souls were parted from the bodies and many hauberks broken, many shields shattered, many towers struck down, many cit-
ies assailed, and then peace was made.]

From Charles Martel's lineage come Carloman and Pepin; here Adenet
relates briefly the story of Pepin's vanquishing the lion that breaks free
from its cage. These genealogies, not unlike the feminine one given to
Berte in *laisse* 30, are twice repeated at the end of Adenet's poem, in
laisse 129, the one where we first hear of Charlemagne's birth, and then
again in the final *laisse*, number 144. Pepin and Berte have a girl child,
Gille, who will marry Milon and give birth to Roland, and then Berte
brings Charlemagne into the world:

Aprés ot Charlemaine a la chiere hardie,
Qui puis fist seur paiens mainte grant envaie.
Par lui fu la loys Dieu levee et essaucie,
Par lui fu mainte terre de paiens essillie,
Mainte hiaume decoupé, mainte targe percie;
Maint hauberc derrompu, mainte teste trenchie
Molt guerroia de cuer sor la gent paiennie,
Si k'encore s'en duelent cil de cele lignie. (vv. 3479–86)

[Then she had Charlemagne the bold, who later made many attacks on the pagans. Through him was God's law exalted and many
a pagan land besieged, *many helmets cut off, many shields shattered, many hauberks broken, many heads chopped off.* So intently
did he fight the pagan people that that lineage is still suffering.]

The symmetry created by the italicized verses 3483–84 in this passage, found at the end of the poem, and the strikingly similar 28–31 cited
just above, from the beginning, shore up the "ongoing" quality of the
geste, while their formulaic wording creates a *geste*-like refrain within
Adenet's story of treachery and calumny. And the last line quoted, "Si
k'encore s'en duelent cil de cele lignie," memorializes the conquests of
Charlemagne and Roland in Spain, but ultimately reverses the tone of
the emperor's send-off at the end of the Oxford *Roland*: "'Deus,' dist li
reis, 'si penuse est ma vie'" ["God," said the king, "how grievous is my
life"].[17] The sufferings of Charlemagne, and of Berte, have led them to
exalt God's law. This simple trope manages to insert the life of Berte
inside the *geste* of Charlemagne. This reversal—not unlike other textual
symmetries, such as the framing effect of formulaic couplets, and figural
echoes such as the "chambre voutie" and Symon's "barbe fleurie"—but-

tresses the clear intertextual reference to the *Chanson de Roland*. In this light, Berte's suffering and her prayers complement Charlemagne's moments of sad reflection, the moments in which he would tug on his beard. They also gloss the story of Aude and her suffering found in the *Chanson de Roland*. Adenet's poem expands and elaborates on the feminine suffering that precedes the discovery of Ganelon's treachery.

The scribe of the version called Manuscript B elaborates further on what he considers that lineage to be, adding five lines in the last *laisse* to describe the "thaumaturgic effect" that took place during the life of Charlemagne.[18] The colophon of that same manuscript copy goes on to state, "Si fin de berte aus grans piez et comence de son fil challemaine qui fu emperrerers de rome" [Here ends the story of Berte of the Long Feet and begins that of her son Charlemagne who was emperor of Rome], a coda that accomplishes two tasks: first, it logically extends *Berte as grans piés* with the story of Charlemagne; second, it provides a perfect lead-in to the next work in the codex, Gerard d'Amiens's *Charlemagne*, the continuation of Adenet le Roi's Berte poem. All these echoes, both back to the beginning of the poem and forward to the future lineage, characterize convincingly the spirit of the *geste* and Berte's role within it. Adenet's poetic elaboration of the life and the sufferings of Berte, Charlemagne's mother, forms a curious gloss on the *lignie* since it retroactively prefigures and celebrates the losses experienced at Roncevaux in a clerkly gesture not unlike Einhard's account of the battle, which Karl Uitti has qualified as "an important constitutive part of a lengthy series of stories designed to relate Charles' success as Christian emperor-king."[19] In the "great century" marked by continuations—Jean de Meun's *Roman de la Rose* and the prose *Lancelot*, to name just two— Adenet le Roi aims to recover, but also to restore in writing, the legend that *continues the life of Charlemagne into the past*. In turn, his poem is also the object of continuation into the future, in the work of Gerard d'Amiens. To that end, Adenet brings both the eloquence afforded by romance vernacular narrative and the values of constancy and spiritual knowledge in the courtly, exemplary models of the persecuted noble heroine. Again, Manuscript B insists on this point, inserting a couplet after v. 3748 about another daughter of Floire and Blancheflour, also named Constance: "Apres orent constance en cui fu courtoisie / Et noblesce et valeur sanz nule vilonie" [Then they had Constance who embodied courtliness, nobility and noble worth, without any baseness.]

Harmonious with the gesture of continuation, Adenet's text revisits and translates a variety of Old French poetic narratives: the bad dream of the dangerous lion, the vow of virginity, the sexual advances made in the forest, and so on. The plot of the calumny and the restitution of the bride which both opens the intrigue and brings closure and reconciliation is the script from which Adenet sketches his courtly portion of the *geste*. Adenet's art in which he projects forwards and backwards creates the tension, mentioned above, between the closure of the plot line and the openness of his work. The theatricality that has been the subject of inquiry here supports this project. The women's voices raised in prayer, as exemplary, exist both in this particular story and outside of time, both before Berte and Pepin and Charles Martel's time and long after them as well. It is to Adenet's authorial performance that we owe the elegant fusion of past, present, and future. The complex poetic processes of continuation, compilation, and adaptation are composed of a variety of such performances, and the medievalist must look to them in order to witness the collective work of poets, scribes, and continuators.

NOTES

1. Albert Henry has two editions of *Berte as grans piés*. The standard is found in his five-volume *Œuvres d'Adenet le Roi*; the other is *Berte as grans piés*, Textes Littéraires Français 305 (Geneva: Droz, 1982). All quotations here are from the former. All italics and translations are mine.

2. M. Natalis de Wailly, ed., "Credo de Joinville," in *Histoire de saint Louis*, 271–88 (Paris: Renouard, 1868).

3. The "epic Credo" prayers have been the subject of numerous scholarly inquiries which typologically class them according to their form, length, subject, and function. See Labande, "Le 'Credo' épique"; for the use of the term *prière du plus grand péril*, see Frappier, *Les Chansons de gestes*, 2:130; Roy J. Pearcy, "'La Prière du plus grand péril' in Medieval English Literature," *Studies in Honour of H. L. Rogers*, Leeds Studies in English, n.s. 20 (1989): 119–41; Sister Marie Pierre Koch, "An Analysis of the Long Prayers in Old French Literature with Special Reference to the 'Biblical-Creed-Narrative' Prayers," Ph.D. diss., Catholic University of America, 1940.

4. Interesting manifestations and adaptations of this prayer are offered by Rutebeuf in his *Ave Maria*, Gautier de Coincy in his *Salut Nostre Dame*, and Philippe de Remi in his *La Manekine*.

5. Felman, *The Literary Speech Act*, 15; Austin, *How to Do Things with Words*.

6. Paris, *Histoire poétique de Charlemagne*, 223–26; see Henry, *Œuvres*, 4:24–41, for "Le Travail du remanieur."

7. The various *Enfances* poems date from more or less the same period: *Enfances Gauvain*, early thirteenth century; *Enfances Guillaume*, thirteenth cen-

tury; *Enfances Renier*, second half of thirteenth; *Enfances Vivien*, early thirteenth; *Mainet* (a kind of *Enfances Charlemagne*), second half of twelfth.

8. Schechner, *Between Theater and Anthropology*, 36.

9. I address these issues of behavior scripts and the "template" for feminine heroism in chapters 1 and 4 of my Ph.D. dissertation, "Hagiographic Devotion and Christian Historical Verse Narrative in Thirteenth-Century Romance: Philippe de Remi's *Roman de la Manekine*," Princeton University, 1997, 25–96, 264–70, 280–91.

10. On the performative and community, see Paul Zumthor, *La Lettre et la voix: De la 'littérature' médiévale* (Paris: Éditions du Seuil, 1987), 155–77.

11. See "On Linguistic Vulnerability" in Butler, *Excitable Speech*, 1–41.

12. de Caluwé, "Les Prières de *Berte*," 151–60.

13. It is worth commenting that these "embryonic" prayers often are six syllables and complete an alexandrine line. This finishing quality of the invocation of God and the saints inside Adenet's poetics is itself significant and symbolic.

14. Colliot, *Adenet le Roi*, 1:131.

15. Uitti, "'Ço dit la geste,'" 1–27.

16. On the repetition or repeatability of example, see Karlheinz Stierle, "L'Histoire comme Exemple, L'Exemple comme Histoire: Contribution à la pragmatique et à la poétique des textes narratifs," *Poétique* 10 (1972): 176–98.

17. Cesare Segre, ed., *La Chanson de Roland* (Milan and Naples: Ricciardi, 1971), v. 4000.

18. Henry (198 n.) gives the lines that Manuscript B inserts: "Puis vint .I. autres Challes le maisne quen hongrie / Ainssi come dieu vout soufri tele maladie / Que a grant poine en fu sanez jour de sa vie." A description of Manuscript B (Paris: Bibliothèque Nationale, f. fr. 778) is given by Gérard Brault in "Les manuscrits de Girart d'Amiens," *Romania* 80 (1959): 439–41, along with the description of an additional manuscript that pairs incomplete copies of both Adenet's *Berte* and Girart's *Charlemagne* (Bibliothèque Nationale, nouv. acq. fr. 6234).

19. Uitti, "'Ço dit la geste,'" 5.

Selected Bibliography

Austin, J. L. *How to Do Things with Words*. Cambridge: Harvard University Press, 1962.

Butler, Judith. *Excitable Speech: The Politics of the Performative*. New York and London: Routledge, 1997.

Colliot, Renée. *Adenet le Roi*—Berte aus grans piés—*étude littéraire générale*. 2 vols. Paris: Picard, 1970.

de Caluwé, Jacques. "Les Prières de *Berte aus grans piés* dans l'œuvre d'Adenet le Roi." In *Mélanges de langue et de littérature médiévales offerts à Pierre Le Gentil*, 151–60. Paris: Société d'édition d'enseignement supérieur, 1973.

Felman, Shoshana. *The Literary Speech Act: Don Juan with J. L. Austin, or Seduction in Two Languages.* Translated by Catherine Porter. Ithaca: Cornell University Press, 1983.

Frappier, Jean. *Les Chansons de gestes du cycle de Guillaume d'Orange.* 2 vols. Paris: Société d'édition d'enseignement supérieur, 1963–65.

Henry, Albert. *Les Œuvres d'Adenet le Roi.* vol. 4. Université Libre de Bruxelles—Travaux de la faculté de philosophie et lettres 23. Paris: Presses Universitaires de France, 1963.

———. *Berte as grans piés.* Textes Littéraires Français 305. Geneva: Droz, 1982.

Labande, Edmond-René. "Le 'Credo' épique: A propos des prières dans les chansons de geste." In *Recueil de travaux offert à M. Clovis Brunel par ses amis, collègues et élèves,* 2:62–80. Paris: Société de l'École des chartes, 1955.

Morgan, Leslie Z. "*Berta ai piedi grandi:* Historical Figure and Literary Symbol." *Olifant* 19.1–2 (1994–95): 37–56.

Paris, Gaston. *Histoire poétique de Charlemagne.* 1865. Reprint, Paris: E. Bouillon, 1905.

Schechner, Richard. *Between Theater and Anthropology.* Philadelphia: University of Pennsylvania Press, 1995.

Uitti, Karl D. "'Ço dit la geste': Reflections on the Poetic Restoration of History in *The Song of Roland.*" In *Studies in Honor of Hans-Erich Keller: Medieval French and Occitan Literature and Romance Linguistics,* edited by Rupert T. Pickens, 1–27. Kalamazoo, Mich.: Medieval Institute Publications, 1993.

Part II

Amorous Women

Romance and Lyric

4

Melusine's Double Binds

Foundation, Transgression, and the Genealogical Romance

Ana Pairet

I n this essay I would like to analyze the representation of the founding
mother in Jean d'Arras's *Roman de Mélusine* (1393), a prose romance
whose genealogical narrative reflects the political instability of the Hundred Years' War. The romance recounts how the Lusignan fortress in
Poitou was founded by a fairy who bestowed her name upon a powerful
lineage. Jean d'Arras's work constantly associates the marvelous foundation of the fortress with motifs of transgression, which coalesce in the
fiction of the fairy's metamorphic body. The narrative opens as Melusine's mother casts a spell on her daughter, announcing her weekly
metamorphosis, and closes with Melusine's final transformation into a
monstrous creature. Structurally, the romance mirrors the ambivalence
of Melusine herself, who appears as both an eroticized figure of transgression and a founding mother.

To the historian's eye, Melusine appears as an emblem of political
instability. The *Roman de Mélusine* was written under commission as a
eulogy upon the decline and extinction of the elder branch of the Lusignan
family.[1] In an epilogue, Jean d'Arras alludes to a legend that seems to
account for the genesis of the romance he has just brought to completion:

> Et sachiez, quant de moy, que je croy que l'ystoire soit veritable. Et
> dit on pour certain que, depuis qu'elle fu fondée, pour change, pour

acquest ou pour conquest, que la dicte forteresse de Lusignen ne demoura XXX. ans acomplis en main d'ome qui ne feust extraiz de la dessus dicte lignie de par pere ou de mere. (308)[2] [Let it be known, for my part, that I believe the story to be true. And it is held for certain since it was founded that this fortress, whether through exchange, acquisition, or conquest, will not remain for more than thirty years in the hands of a man who, either by his mother or father, does not belong to the Lusignan line.]

As the evocation of the stuff of legend suggests, the construction of the heroine in the *Roman de Mélusine* plays on fears linked to genealogical continuity and its disruption.[3] The "monstrous" character of Melusine's hybrid body has received much critical attention. Yet the exact function of representations of hybridity and monstrosity in the romance, particularly with respect to genealogy and political context, has gone largely unexamined. In fact, as René Girard suggests, if monstrosity can be treated as an excess, it is precisely because it takes part in the phenomenon of the double: "There is no monster who does not tend to duplicate himself or to 'marry' another monster, no double who does not yield a monstrous aspect upon close scrutiny."[4] I would like to pursue Girard's hypothesis by reading Melusine's metamorphic body as an image in which the desire for a stable political identity is inverted. The idea of the monstrous double gives us clues as to how bodily metaphors can signify a more general instability, through an antithesis that sets off the fantastical maternal body against the collective masculine body of her heirs.

In what ways does the genealogical romance stage transgression? While most studies of the genesis of Melusine have adduced a natural evolution of a folkloric motif, the novel clearly, and patiently, reconstructs its own origins. In the so-called Melusinian tales, where a supernatural character follows his or her spouse into the world of mortals, the pact-union-transgression narrative cluster at the center can lead to different outcomes. Inasmuch as Jean d'Arras's work spells out three principal types of resolution, one might argue that the *Roman de Mélusine* itself retraces the evolution of the "Melusinian theme."[5] Indeed, Jean d'Arras's narrative puts forth three distinct versions of the encounter with a fairy.

In the first, the fairy who attempts to enter the world of men disappears forever: no passage exists between the supernatural and the mortal worlds. Jean d'Arras's novel stages the disappearance of the fairy through the story of Remondin's father:

La vraye histoire nous raconte qu'il ot jadiz en la Brute Bretaigne un noble homme, lequel ot riote au nepveu du roy des Bretons, et l'occist. . . . Et, si comme l'ystoire dit, il y trouva un jour, sur une fontaine, une belle dame qui lui dist aucques toute s'aventure. . . . Et bastirent ou lieu et pays desert pluseurs fors, villes et habit-acions firent, et fu le pays en assez brief temps assez peuplez. . . . Mais elle se party de lui soubdainement, de quoy le chevalier fu moult doulens. (15) [True history tells us that there was once in Lower Brittany a gentleman who had an argument with the nephew of the King of Brittany, and killed him. . . . As the story tells it, he discovered one day, seated next to a fountain, a beautiful lady who told him that she knew of everything that had happened to him. . . . And they built in these empty lands several fortresses, made towns and dwellings, and soon thereafter the land was inhabited. . . . But she left him suddenly, and the knight was greatly stricken with sorrow.]

In the second case, the fairy bears offspring with a mortal, but neither she nor her children have a right to stay in the natural world. Elinas, king of Albany in Scotland, encounters a beautiful lady near a fountain. She consents to marriage upon one condition: "Se vous me voulez pren-dre a femme et jurer, se nous avons enfans ensemble, que vous ne mettrez ja peine de moy veoir en ma gesine" (9) [If you wish to take me as your wedded wife and swear that, if we have children together, never shall you try to gaze upon me while I am in labor"]. Melusine's father breaks his promise and loses forever his wife and three daughters.

In the third case, the union of a mortal and a supernatural being re-sults in a new family line. After her double nature is revealed, Melusine too disappears, but leaves her children in the land of mortals.

Transgression appears as a narrative endpoint in folktales alluded to in Jean d'Arras's prologue: "Et si tost qu'ilz defailloient, ilz les perdoient et decheoient de tout leur bon eur petit a petit" (4) [And as soon as they went back on their word, they lost [their spouses] and all their good for-tune disappeared bit by bit]. Turning the tables on exemplary tales, the *Roman de Mélusine* takes transgression as its point of departure. Unlike the nameless nymphs that populate folklore, Melusine inherits trans-gression from her father, only to pass it on to her husband. Moreover, her body is stamped with a sign that resulted from her father's overstepping the line but that also marks her own transgressive nature. Daughter of King Elinas and the fairy Presine, Melusine has inherited human quali-ties from her father, whom she buries alive in Brumborenlion Mountain to avenge her mother. But the mother, displeased, then condemns her to periodic metamorphoses:

> Desormais je te donne le don que tu sera tous les samedis serpente du nombril en aval. Mais, se tu treuves homme qui te veuille prendre a espouse, que il te convenance que jamais le samedy ne te verra, non qu'il te descuevre, ne ne le die a personne, tu vivras cours naturel comme femme naturelle, et mourras naturelment. (12–13) [Henceforth, each and every Saturday, I condemn you to be a serpent from the navel down. But should you find a man who wishes to take your for his spouse and who promises you that he shall never gaze upon you on Saturdays, if he neither discovers your secret nor betrays it to anyone, you shall live a course of life like any natural woman, and shall die naturally.]

Melusine's action against family hierarchy has elicited a punishment by which she must relive each week her mother's story. "Serpente du nombril en aval," she suffers a hybrid existence, rich in narrative possibilities but particularly difficult to bear in the home.

Following the narrative model of the marvelous encounters presented in Jean d'Arras's prologue, the meeting of Remondin and Melusine rights a wrong committed by the male protagonist. Indeed the story of Remondin, third son of the count of Forez, begins with a crime. During a wild boar hunt, the count Aymery of Poitiers and his nephew Remondin are separated from the hunting party and are forced to spend the night in the forest. The learned count examines the night sky and announces to Remondin what the heavens foretell:

> Et l'aventure si est telle que, se, a ceste presente heure, uns subgiez occioit son seigneur, qu'il devendroit ly plus riches, ly plus puissans, li plus honnourez qui feust oncques en son lignaige, et de lui ystroit si tres noble lignie qu'il en seroit mencion et remenbrance jusques en la fin du monde. (21) [Here is what should transpire, if at the present hour a subject were to kill his lord: he would become the richest, most powerful, most honored man ever to come from his lineage, and from him would spring forth such a noble line that one would speak of it and remember it until the end of the world.]

Just as predicted, Remondin kills his uncle in a hunting accident. The young man errs in the forest on horseback, so profoundly afflicted that as he passes by the Fountain of Thirst, he remains oblivious to the presence of three maidens. The noblest of the group of maidens taunts him, reminding him of his duties as a gallant knight. She announces that she knows his name and his destiny, and repeats, nearly to the letter, the count's prophecy: "toutes les paroles que tes sires te dist te seront, a l'aide de Dieu, achevees, et plus qu'il ne t'en dist" (26) [all that your lord has foretold, and more, shall be accomplished with God's help].

The fairy grants Remondin the means to regain his rank, which the killing of his lord had cost him. But readmission to the social order is linked to dissimulation and treachery: Melusine lets the knight know how to feign innocence of his crime. This scene weaves a strong thread between secrecy and transgression. Just as Melusine asks Remondin not to speak of the accident, so too does she make him promise never to attempt to look at her on Saturdays: "Vous me jurerez sur tous les seremens que preudoms doit faire, que le samedy vous ne mettrez jamais peine a moy veoir ne enquerre ou je seray" (26) [Swear to me by all the oaths that a true man of honor should make, that never shall you attempt to gaze upon me on Saturdays, nor ask after my whereabouts]. This closet secret establishes an equivalency between Melusine's body and Remondin's crime, the twin foundations of the Lusignan line.

A third scene, the marriage ceremony, will reinforce their equivalency. Having learned the name and home country of their future in-law, Remondin's brother and cousin demand to know from what lineage Melusine comes. After Remondin asks his interlocutors not to press further, a proleptic intervention by the narrator superposes on the wedding episode the scene of a second crime. Remondin's sixth son will cause the death of the same curious brother who has just pried a bit too far into family affairs: "Las! Depuis l'en failli il, dont Remondin perdy sa femme et le conte de Forest en prist puis mort par Gieffroy au Grant Dent, dont on vous parlera ca avant en l'ystoire" (44) [Alas! He kept his promise not: as a result Remondin lost his wife and the count of Forez died by the hand of Geoffrey of the Big Tooth, as the story will recount]. If Melusine's secret serves to cover up Remondin's transgression, the secret of the fairy's origins will later provoke a displaced reenactment of the very crime it was intended to offset.

Two identical crimes bury in a frame of secrecy the foundations of the Lusignan family line. Similar motifs of dissimulation and discretion appear in the episode of the land grab. Under his wife's sway, Remondin employs Dido's ruse to obtain land from his lord: he asks for as much land as a deerskin can hold. He has the deerskin expertly cut into fine strips and manages to demarcate a large estate around the Fountain of Thirst. When it is time to name the family line, Melusine supplants once again her male counterparts. The assembly of lords, called together by Melusine, insists that she do the honors:

> nul de nous ne s'en meslera par dessus vous, car, par raison, puis que vous en avez tant fait que d'avoir assouvy si belle place comme ceste qui est pour le present la plus forte et la plus belle que j'aye veue, vous ly devez donner don a vostre gré. (47) [Not one among us shall interfere in this matter, for it stands to reason that since you have succeeded in securing and building this fortress, the most beautiful and strongest that I have yet seen, you should name it as you please.]

The feudal lords grant Melusine exceptional if somewhat ambiguous authority: "et nous vous disons pour tous, en general, que vous mesmes lui donnez nom, car il n'a pas en tous nous ensemble tant de sens qu'il a en vous seulement" (47) [we ask you, in the name of all gathered here, to give it a name yourself, for you alone have more judgment than all of us combined]. Melusine follows the count's recommendation to the letter: she uses her own name to derive the toponym "Lusignan," henceforth adopted by her husband Remondin and by the couple's descendants:

> Par foy, dist le conte, ce nom lui affiert tres bien pour deux cas, car vous estes nommee Melusigne d'Albanie, et Albanie en gregois vault autant a dire comme chose qui ne fault, et Melusigne vault autant a dire comme merveilles ou merveilleuse. (47) [By my faith, said the count, this name is fitting for two reasons, for your name is Melusine of Albany, and Albany in Greek means "the thing that errs not," and Melusigne means marvel or marvelous.]

The Lusignan line would seem to be founded on dubious etymologies. While Melusine's patronym suggests stability, her first name joins together in ambiguous fashion two lexemes with opposite meaning: *melas* (black) and *leukos* (white). Black Fairy and White Fairy, "Melusigne" is defined as *merveille* by the very indecipherability of the name she bears.

At the head of a line of warriors, the *Roman de Mélusine* places the enigma of woman defined as excess (through the motif of transgression) and as an unstable identity (through the motif of metamorphosis). The *merveille* resists exploration: as the authorities cited in Jean d'Arras's prologue maintain, it is improper to examine from too close up the mysteries of creation. In the *Roman de Mélusine*, the fairy lives under an ambiguous sign. The following section will show that the representation of Melusine as an ambivalent figure is central to the project of genealogical legitimization.

As the fairy's body forms the object of a prohibition, it condenses elements of transgression dispersed throughout the stories of Remondin and Melusine. According to Mary Douglas, the metaphor of the body "can represent any boundaries which are threatened or precarious."[6] In Jean d'Arras's romance, images of liminality are employed to represent the ambiguity of the fairy's legacy. Ultimately, Melusine's undecidable past serves to justify territorial expansion. Her bodily representation as an ambivalent being stands in contradiction to her role as a founding ancestor, provider, and source of authority. In examining the three roles of fairy, founding mother, and "serpente" that Melusine takes up in succession, I would like to highlight the ways in which each of her bodies is marked by the sign of ambivalence.

FAIRY

Melusine belongs to the imaginary world of the romance and of the *lai merveilleux*, where the fairy invariably inspires ambivalent desires. In her study *Les Fées au Moyen Âge*, Laurence Harf-Lancner has shown how the fairy figure is split into two distinct characters. The first type inherits traits from the ancient *fata* whose prophetic powers were legion, from the erotically charged sylvan nymphs (*fatuae*), and from Gallic goddesses of fertility; she can be characterized as a protective "fairy godmother" figure. Beginning in the twelfth century, with the penetration of Celtic motifs into lay culture, these fairies take on a new visage, that of the supernatural lover. In romance, Morgue will embody a second fairy type. The "Morganian fairy" lures the hero off into the other world, never to return, whereas the "Melusinian fairy" willfully follows her husband into the world of mortals. Morgue, then, belongs to otherness, while Melusine, for her part, is posited as a double. Indeed, in every one of her roles, Melusine is marked by a fundamental duality: she follows Remondin into the world of men, but must hide the secret of her origins. Expelled from her sojourn in the world as a result of her husband's transgression, she continues to return nightly to nurse her children, and later to announce the imminent death of one of her descendants.

Like the fairy in Marie de France's "Lanval," Melusine bestows unlimited power and wealth upon a chosen one. In sociological terms, the fairy lends her body to the fleeting desire of the *juvenis*, a term that in genealogical texts designated either the eldest son of a family whose father was still living or a younger son deprived of inheritance.[7] In search of a temporary solution, the younger sons often had no choice but to leave their native region in the hope that good fortune would bring them what birth had refused them. The male protagonist of the *Roman de Mélusine* finds himself in this very situation: "Et en ot pluseurs enfants masles. Entre les autre[s] il y en ot un, le tiers, que l'en appella Remondin" (15) [And she had of him several male children. Among them there was one, the third-born, that was called Remondin].[8] The Oedipal scenario that frames the departure of the younger sons from the family home is spectacularly dramatized in the romance by the parricide preceding the encounter with the fairy. Approaching Remondin after his crime, Melusine offers a marriage that will bring him great wealth, even greater fertility, and the possibility of establishing a new homeland: "car je te feray le plus seignoury et le plus grant qui oncques feust en ton lignaige, et le plus puissant terrien" (26) [for I will make you into the finest lord ever to come to your lineage and the greatest on Earth].

FOUNDING MOTHER

Melusine is at one and the same time mother and founder: she stakes out the limits of her domain, builds the family fortress, passes on the name to her husband and to their descendants. This image alone is transgressive: medieval society reduces mothers to the role of passive vessel without privilege, through whom land, name, and lineage are transmitted. Melusine's role as both mother and protagonist in the Lusignan family genealogy also breaks with the conventions of courtly discourse, which systematically dissociate female sexuality from reproductive potential. The most representative example of this dissociation is the barren queen, a key figure in the erotics of the French romance. Peggy McCracken appositely contrasts the queen's function in feudal society and the role she plays in the erotic economy of romance: "[T]he queen consort's political role in the medieval court is entirely located in her physical body: the major duty of her office is to produce heirs in order to guarantee succcession and political and social stability. . . . In the major literary traditions surrounding Guenevere and Iseut, and in other less celebrated stories, the queen is barren. Moreover, she is adulterous, and her lack of progeny is most certainly linked to a sexuality that both transgresses moral and civic law and, perhaps more importantly, potentially interrupts proper dynastic succession."[9] Metaphors of lack, doubling, and dismemberment systematically alter the economic and political reality of the female gendered body in order to create a marginalized, transgressive one. The eroticization of the queen's sterile body, McCracken suggests, is akin to rituals of taboo and transgression that aim to diminish the importance of women's bodies in the dynastic economy.

One of the most troubling sources of disjunction in the *Roman de Mélusine* is the constant juxtaposition of narrative conventions associated with courtly eroticism on the one hand and, on the other, images that lend to the lady tangible power, including but not limited to reproduction. This portrayal of female power is quite different from that codified in courtly discourse. Lancelot's example comes to mind here.[10] Reproaching Guenievre for having lowered her eyes and for having refused to speak to him, Lancelot turns silence into the main attribute of the courtly female protagonist: "N'oncques un mot ne me sonastes / A po la mort ne m'an donastes" (vv. 4475–76) [Not a single word did you say to me. / From this you nearly made me die]. Silence and recognition characterize the queen at the window:

Quant Lanceloz voit la reïne
Qui a la fenestre s'acline,
Qui de gros fers estoit ferree,
Ḍ'un dolz salu l'a saluee
Et ele un autre tost li rant,
Que molt estoient desirrant
Il de li et ele de lui. (4583–89)

[When Lancelot sees the queen who leans against the window fitted with large iron bars, he gives her a gentle salute, and she sends it back in kind, for they were greatly desiring, he of her and she of him.]

But Melusine, inverting the conventional flow of erotic exchange, is always the first to speak. During her first encounter with Remondin, who has just passed by on horseback without seeing her, it is she who calls out and gets his attention: "Et quant Remondin l'ouy, si la regarde, et percoit la grant beauté qui estoit en la dame" (24) [When Remondin heard her, he looked at her and realized her great beauty].

At each of the three meetings before the couple's marriage, as well as in the scene immediately following their wedding night, Melusine takes charge of Remondin's destiny. Once she has made her conditions clear, she shows him how to dissimulate his crime and how to obtain an estate from the count of Poitiers. Only after their marriage does she consent to divulge the story of Remondin's father. She then explains to him by what means he can rehabilitate his father's name and reclaim his property. The early encounters of Melusine and Remondin are accompanied by gestures and words that underscore the lady's active role:

> Lors se part des autres et vint a Remondin et print le frain du cheval, et l'arreste tout quoy. . . . Par foy, dist-elle, je croy que cilz jeunes homs dort sur son cheval, ou il est sours et muet. Mais je croy que je le feray ja parler, se il oncques parla nul jour. Lors le prent par la main et le tyre fort et ferme en disant: Sire vassaulx, dormez vous? (24) [She broke away from the others and came toward Remondin, took the horse's bridle and stopped it in its tracks. . . . By my faith, she said, I believe that this young man is asleep on his horse, or else he is deaf and dumb. But I will get him to talk, if ever he spoke. Then she takes him by the hand and gives it a firm tug, saying: Good knight, are you sleeping?]

From the outset, Melusine makes it clear that her favors and good counsel depend entirely on the strict observance of the conditions she has laid out. In compensation for his obedience, Remondin receives Melusine's protection. Her orders are expressed in a formula that serves at once as guarantee, condition, and injunction: "Et alez hardiement, mon amy et ne vous doubtez de rien" (31) [Go forth boldly, my dear, and fear not].

Few examples of founding female figures can be uncovered in medieval literature. The *Roman de Mélusine* explicitly evokes one precursor: Dido, founder of Carthage. Melusine adapts the story of Dido's ruse, recounted in the *Aeneid*, to her own ends. In Vergil's text,[11] the story is told by Venus to Aeneas when he arrives with his men in the outskirts of Carthage. Pygmalion, king of Tyr and brother of Dido, kills his sister's husband and attempts to hide the murder. But the ghost of the slain husband returns to betray the secret to Dido, who is ordered to leave her homeland. The queen of Carthage is portrayed in succession as an unfaithful widow, as the seducer of Aeneas, and, finally, as abandoned lover. Her role as a founder, however, is mentioned only in passing:

> . . . dux femina facti.
> Devenere locos ubi nunc ingentia cernes
> moenia surgentemque novae Karthaginis arcem,
> mercatique solum, facti de nomine Byrsam,
> taurino quantum possent circumdare tergo. (I, 364–68)

[The woman led the whole undertaking. When they arrived at the place where you will now see the great walls and rising citadel of the new city of Carthage, they bought a piece of land called the "Byrsa," the animal's hide, as large an area as they could include within the hide of a bull.]

Jean d'Arras is most likely to have borrowed the Dido material from the twelfth-century *Roman d'Énéas*, a medieval adaptation of the Latin epic which met with great success and influenced the *Parthenopeus de Blois*, one of the models for the *Roman de Mélusine*. In the *Énéas*,[12] Dido is presented as a powerful monarch: "Dame Dido tint le païs; miaus nel tenist quens ne marchis" (vv. 377–78) [Lady Dido held the country; she ruled it better than any count or marquis]. Unlike the Latin text, the medieval rendering underlines Dido's cunning, a character trait that comes to the fore in the ruse by which she founded the city of Carthage:

> par grant angin li alla querre
> qu'il li vandist tant de sa terre
> com porprendroit un cuir de tor,
> doné l'an a argent et or;
> et li princes li otroia,
> qui de l'angin ne se garda.
> Dido trancha par correetes
> lo cuir, qui molt furent grelletes;
> de celes a tant terre prise
> c'une cité i a asise;
> puis conquist tant par sa richece,
> par son angin, par sa proëce,
> que ele avoit tot le païs
> et les barons a soi sozmis. (393–406)

[Through great ruse she went to ask him to sell her as much of his land as the skin of a bull could hold: she gave him silver and gold, and the prince granted her wish, for he was oblivious to the ruse. Dido cut the leather into very thin strips, and with them took so much land that she was able to found a city; she then used her wealth, her wit, and her valor to conquer the whole land and to subjugate the barons.]

The medieval adaptation sings the praises of the valiant warrior-widow, who possesses sovereign power and the virtues of a military leader. She remains, however, a negative influence for the Trojan hero. The relationship between the lovers is depicted as an act of *recréantise:*

An luxure andui se demeinent
lo tens d'iver, d'el ne se poinent;
la dame an laisse son afaire,
nule autre rien ne panse gaire,
et cil en a guerpi sa voie,
et l'un et l'autre s'i foloie. (1573–78)

[In the winter season, they gave themselves over to luxury, not worrying about anything else; the lady left her duties, and thought scarcely of any other matter; and he renounced his journey, and both of them lost their reason.]

Subsequent verses suggest that Dido is principally to blame in the affair: she has held back the warrior and has him at her mercy: "Or a Dido ce qu'el voloit / Del Troïen fait son esploit / Et son talant tot en apert" (vv. 1605–7) [Now Dido has what she wanted. She openly does what she wants and what she pleases with the Trojan]. Énéas, for his part, gives in to illusion: he believes that, as the master of Dido, he also becomes the master of her empire: "toz est livrez a male voe, / et terre et fame tient por soe" (vv. 1613–14) [he lets himself go down a slippery path, and holds for his very own both woman and land].

Expanding on a hypothesis first put forth by Daniel Poirion, Christiane Marchello-Nizia has analyzed the figure of Dido as countermodel for the male hero. In Poirion's reading, the opposition of Dido and Lavinie as Enéas's erotic partners constitutes "one of the first examples of the binary structure error/rectification which would characterize many works of the 12th and 13th centuries."[13] Marchello-Nizia's analysis of the founder's traits in medieval romance sheds new light on the precise function that the Dido model fulfilled in the construction of Melusine. Indeed, the heroine of the *Roman de Mélusine* possesses some of the key featiures that Marchello-Nizia attributes to the founder. For one, the founder, who has often just committed some type of transgression, must arrive "from the exterior" and stake a claim to lost ancestral lands. After the birth of her first son, Melusine tells Remondin the story of his own father and orders her husband off to Brittany to demand restitution of his inheritance. A second trait identified by Marchello-Nizia deals with the territory itself: the founder must break ground in a land as yet untouched. Melusine orders that trees be felled, makes a natural spring flow forth from arid soil, and builds numerous strongholds. As Jacques Le Goff and Emmanuel Le Roy Ladurie once noted, Melusine is the *fée défricheuse* par excellence, the godmother of feudal economy.

In the *Énéas*, Dido functions in the framework of an erotic antithesis: Enéas abandons the queen of Carthage to wed Lavinie and to found the city of Albe. While following Dido's lead as founder, Melusine partici- pates in the hero's quest through the deeds of her ten sons. The Dido/ Lavinie antithesis superposes on Dido the romance model of the ster- ile queen. In contrast, in her role as a progenitor Melusine takes on yet another function of the founder, who must win a princess. Melusine's sons, who leave their homeland to conquer foreign lands, remember the lesson spelled out in the *Énéas:* it is not by marrying a queen that one becomes a founder, but rather by stealing away an heiress from a rival.

"Serpent from the Navel Down"

What renders Melusine strange and menacing is perhaps less her hybrid- ity as half-woman/half-snake than the fundamental instability of her weekly transformation. Jean d'Arras's depiction of metamorphosis un- derscores this instability. The fairy takes on three distinct forms: courtly lady, woman with a snake's tail, and winged dragon.[14] The narrator has systematic recourse to two types of highly codified discourse: courtly discourse and the discourse of the marvelous. It is important to note that those elements in Melusine's story that deal with fairies are rel- egated to the periphery of the novel where they serve to frame the his- tory of the Lusignan line. Melusine's transformation, in Jean d'Arras's story, occurs only after the fairy's exit into the world of legend.

In almost nine-tenths of the text, Melusine's odd inheritance is for- gotten. Presine's curse is pronounced in a mythical time, before the story of the "noble Lusignan castle" begins. Driven by his brother, who ac- cuses Melusine of indulging in unspeakable acts on the day that visiting rights are suspended, Remondin bores a hole in the door behind which Melusine, naked, is bathing "et voit Melusigne en la cuve, qui estoit jusques au nombril en figure de femme et pignoit ses cheveulx, et du nombril en aval estoit en forme de la queue d'un serpent" (242) [and in the tub he sees Melusine, who had the looks of a woman down to the navel and was combing her hair, and from the navel down had the form of a snake's tail]. The scene of discovery is followed by a passage where Melusine, who has reassumed her human form, lies naked next to her husband. In her second, courtly incarnation as woman, nothing further is said of her body: this narrative juxtaposition reinforces the division between the two states of the metamorphic body. A moment of narrative suspense prepares Melusine's final metamorphosis: seated on the windowsill, in full view of the crowd several stories below, Melusine "sault en l'air, et laisse la fenestre et trespasse le vergier. Et lors se mue en une serpente grant et grosse et longue de la longueur de XV. piez" (260) [Melusine jumps into the air, leaves the window behind her and crosses the orchard. Then she changes into a great big snake with the length of fifteen feet]. These three framing scenes are so many individuated moments of one and the same metamorphosis. Indeed, the only passage to evoke a full change, from woman to snake and back again, can be found in the novel's epilogue. There a soldier testifies to having seen the metamorphosis of a "serpente" into a noble lady, shortly before the duc de Berry liberated the Lusignan castle. With this final image, the narrative comes full circle.

How should one read these liminal figures? As the treatment of the founding figure in the medieval rewriting of the *Aeneid* suggests, I would argue that liminality must be understood in reference to the antithesis that opposes the fiction of Melusine's split body and the representation of her sons as conquerors. Stable masculine identity is exposed as a construction antithetical to, but dependent on, the inherent instability of the female protagonist. Here, the uses of liminality as a local figure can be extended to the overarching design of Jean d'Arras's novel: a marvelous character suddenly is taken up in the folds of history. Scenes of deliverance scattered throughout the novel allow us to draw lines of symmetry between the Lusignans' alliances with the houses of Cyprus, Armenia, Bohemia, and Luxemburg and the patronage of Jean de Berry over the Lusignan domain itself. Just as Antoine de Lusignan takes up arms to defend the Kingdom of Luxemburg in the novel, so too do Jean d'Arras and Jean de Berry, a descendent of the Luxemburg line,[15] take up pen and sword to defend the Lusignan domain. Not only do such striking effects of symmetry justify Jean de Berry's sovereignty from a historical point of view, they also help to redefine the symbolic origins of power. In both cases, indeed, military virtue wins out over heredity. The rewriting of the Lusignan history in military terms serves a twofold project: it allows for the matrilineal transmission of rights and privileges and, at the same time, diminishes the symbolic weight of the mother. Such a hypothesis helps to explain just why the figure of the fantastic mother is inscribed at the center of Jean d'Arras's legitimization of legendary genealogies.

NOTES

1. Events contemporary to the completion of the novel echoed the instability of the Lusignan domain, which belonged at the time to the duc de Berry, who had captured it from the English in 1374. Léon de Lusignan, the last Christian king of Little Armenia, died in exile in Paris the year that the romance was composed. See Emmanuèle Baumgartner, "Fiction and History: The Cypriot Episode in Jean d'Arras's *Mélusine*," in Maddox and Sturm-Maddox, *Melusine of Lusignan*, 186–87.

2. All quotes of *Mélusine* are taken from the Stouff edition. Unless otherwise indicated, translations are mine.

3. See Jane H. M. Taylor, "Melusine's Progeny: Patterns and Perplexities," in Maddox and Sturm-Maddox, *Melusine of Lusignan*, 165–84.

4. Girard, *Violence and the Sacred*, 160.

5. Cf. Le Goff and Le Roy Ladurie, "Mélusine maternelle"; Harf-Lancner, *Les Fées*, 119–54; and Lecouteux, *Mélusine*, 15–45.

6. Douglas, *Purity and Danger*, 115.

7. Georges Duby, "Les 'jeunes' dans la société aristocratique dans la France du Nord-Ouest au XIIe siècle," in *Hommes et structures du moyen age* (Paris: Mouton-La Haye, 1973), 213–25.

8. Critics have heretofore neglected an interesting biographical parallel in the life of Jean de Berry, who was also the third son of Jean de France and Bonne de Luxembourg. A present-day biographer evokes the birth of the duc de Berry in the following terms: "Bonne de Luxembourg expected a third child. She had already given [Philip VI] two grandsons, Charles and Louis; the succession to the throne was secure, and this time a girl would be more than welcome. Alas, yet another son was born. Nevertheless, everything leads us to believe that, upon his arrival into the world on the last day of November, the child received a warm welcome" (Lehoux, *Jean de France*, 3–4, translation mine).

9. McCracken, "Body Politic," 38.

10. The two quotes that follow are from Chrétien de Troyes, *Le Chevalier de la charrette*, ed. Mario Roques (Paris: Champion Libraire, 1958).

11. Virgile, *Énéide*, ed. Henri Goelzer (Paris: Société d'Édition Les Belles Lettres, 1964), 19; English translation by David West, *The Aeneid* (New York: Penguin Books, 1991), 14.

12. The five quotes that follow are from the Salverda de Grave edition of the *Énéas*.

13. Marchello-Nizia, "De l'Énéide à l'Énéas," 251.

14. See Kevin Brownlee, "Melusine's Hybrid Body and the Poetics of Metamorphosis," in Maddox and Sturm-Maddox, *Melusine of Lusignan*, 76–99.

15. See Eleanor Roach, ed., *Le Roman de Mélusine, ou Histoire des Lusignan par Coudrette* (Paris: Klincksieck, 1982), 37–43.

SELECTED BIBLIOGRAPHY

Douglas, Mary. *Purity and Danger: An Analysis of the Concepts of Pollution and Taboo*. New York: Routledge, 1966.

Énéas: Roman du XIIe siècle. 2 vols. Edited by Jean-Jacques Salverda de Grave. Paris: Champion, 1925, 1929; reprint, 1985.

Girard, René. *Violence and the Sacred*. Translated by Patrick Gregory. Baltimore: John Hopkins University Press, 1977.

Harf-Lancner, Laurence. *Les Fées au Moyen Âge: Morgane et Mélusine: La naissance des fées*. Geneva: Slatkine, 1984.

Jean d'Arras. *Mélusine. Roman du XIVe siècle*. Edited by Louis Stouff. Dijon: Publications de l'Université, 1932; reprint, Geneva: Slatkine Reprints, 1974.

Le Goff, Jacques, and Emmanuel Le Roy Ladurie. "Mélusine maternelle et défricheuse." *Annales: Économies, Sociétés, Civilisations* 26 (1971): 587–622.

Lecouteux, Claude. *Mélusine et le chevalier au cygne*. Paris: Payot, 1982.

Lehoux, Françoise. *Jean de France, duc de Berri: sa vie, son action politique*. 4 vols. Paris: Picard, 1966–68.

Maddox, Donald, and Sarah Sturm-Maddox, eds. *Melusine of Lusignan: Founding Fiction in Late Medieval France*. Athens: University of Georgia Press, 1996.

Marchello-Nizia, Christiane. "De l'Énéide à l'Énéas: les attributs du fondateur." In *Lectures médiévales de Virgile*, 251–66. Rome: École Française de Rome, 1985.

McCracken, Peggy. "The Body Politic and the Queen's Adulterous Body in French Romance." In *Feminist Approaches to the Body in Medieval Literature*, edited by Linda Lomperis and Sarah Stanbury, 36–84. Philadelphia: University of Pennsylvania Press, 1993.

5

On Fenice's Vain Attempts to Revise a Romantic Archetype and Chrétien's Fabled Hostility to the Cristan Legend

Joan Tasker Grimbert

I n a seminal article published in 1959, Jean Frappier defined what he believed was Chrétien de Troyes's revolutionary stance against the kind of passion depicted in the Tristan legend.[1] He claimed that, whereas the troubadours had used the legend as little more than a rhetorical fig-ure, seeing no conflict between "Tristan-love" and *fin'amors*, Chrétien had recognized the paradox and succeeded in making a lucid distinction between, on the one hand, the fated and fatal passion of Tristan and Iseut and, on the other hand, the essence of courtly love founded on the choice of a beloved that is arrived at through free will and reason. Frappier firmly believed that Chrétien was expressing a marked preference for the latter and that consequently he was hostile toward the kind of pas-sionate love emblematized by the Tristan legend. This view has become so firmly entrenched in the critical canon that most scholars repeat it uncritically, ignoring the evidence brought forth by a few attentive read-ers that would tend to challenge it. In this study, I would like to build on the various observations of these "dissenting" critics and renew the challenge by formulating it more explicitly while reexamining some of the same texts that scholars have cited in support of the canonical view.

Frappier claimed to have found evidence for his belief in two early works by Chrétien. The first is one of the two lyrics attributed unreservedly to Chrétien, *D'amors qui m'a tolu a moi*. In strophe IV of this lyric, according to Frappier, the poet-narrator vaunts the superiority of his own love (inspired by his lady's beauty) to that of Tristan (provoked by a love philtre):

> Onques du buvrage ne bui
> Dont Tristan fu enpoisonnez;
> *Mes plus me fet amer que lui*
> *Fins cuers et bone volentez.*
> Bien en doit estre miens li grez,
> Qu'ainz *de riens efforciez n'en fui,*
> *Fors que tant que mes euz en crui,*
> Par cui sui en la voie entrez
> Donc ja n'istrai n'ainc n'en recrui.[2]

> [Never did I drink of the brew that poisoned Tristan; *rather, a refined heart and goodwill make me love better than he did.* For this I should be most grateful, for *I was not compelled by anything, except insofar as I believed my eyes,* by which I have entered the path that I shall never leave nor renounce.]

However, as Peter Haidu has demonstrated conclusively in a detailed semiotic analysis of this lyric, the comparison is simply a hyperbolic compliment to the poet-narrator's lady, whose beauty is seen as a force as compelling as any love philtre.[3] Indeed, when the poet-narrator claims he was not the least constrained to love except insofar as he believed his eyes, he is saying that in gazing upon his lady's beauty, he became inflamed with love.[4] As we shall see, this is the same process of enamorment that Chrétien describes in *Cligés*.

Indeed, the second work in which Frappier claimed to have found ample evidence that the Champenois poet was hostile to the Tristan legend is *Cligés*,[5] where Chrétien puts Fenice in a situation similar to Iseut's but removes the fatalistic perspective, first by allowing her (according to Frappier) to "choose" freely her beloved, and secondly by having her refuse to conduct herself like Iseut, notably in the matter of sharing her body with two men. Frappier observes:

> L'amour doit-il dépendre d'un breuvage magique, contre la volonté des amants? Fénice, elle, représente au contraire, avec une exigence de pureté, la revendication féminine du libre arbitre en amour. Menacée du même destin, elle refuse de se conduire comme Iseut.

... Le devoir d'Iseut était de rester fidèle à Tristan, de répudier un honteux partage, de ne pas se résigner au divorce de son corps et de son cœur.[6] [Must love depend on a magic potion, against the lovers' wills? Fenice represents on the contrary, with an insistence on purity, the feminine demand for free choice in love. Threatened by the same destiny, she refuses to conduct herself as did Iseut. . . . Iseut's duty was to remain faithful to Tristan and reject a shameful split, to refuse to resign herself to a divorce between her body and her heart.]

Frappier goes on to describe Fenice as "une héroïne de la liberté intérieure. En elle vit la conscience de l'amour, de ses droits, de ses devoirs" [a heroine of inner freedom. In her dwells a consciousness of love, its rights, and its duties] (113). This is an odd kind of overstatement, especially since Frappier is quick to admit that her solution to the problem posed by the Tristan legend is totally unsatisfactory and that Chrétien himself knew that recourse to magical ruses in order to overcome the obstacles of the traditional love triangle was arbitrary and unrealistic (114). Yet by the time Frappier arrives at the conclusion of his chapter on *Cligés*, he seems to have forgotten the irony of which he knew Chrétien to be capable: he accuses him "d'avoir méconnu la vérité humaine et tragique du *Tristan*, de sorte que son adaptation implique un gauchissement du sujet véritable" [of having misunderstood the tragic human truth of the *Tristan*, such that his adaptation implies a perversion of the true/actual subject] (121).

Subsequent studies of this romance have produced much more nuanced readings.[7] Yet Frappier's general interpretation continues to hold sway, leaving us with two outdated assumptions that underlie most interpretations of *Cligés*, including introductions to that romance[8] in recent editions of Chrétien's complete works that will likely have a great deal of influence, since the collections in which they appear are prestigious and confirm the editors' claim that the poet-romancer has been officially admitted into the French literary canon.[9] The first of Frappier's enduring assumptions is that Chrétien was hostile to the Tristan legend and used Fenice to formulate his own criticism of the Cornish lovers. The second assumption is that Chrétien depicted Fenice as a woman who exercises free choice in love and firm and effective control of her destiny. Since the validity of the first assumption depends in large part on that of the second, I shall concentrate most of my attention on the second before returning to the first.

Frappier felt that Chrétien, by eliminating the love philtre and thus removing the fatalistic perspective, had imbued Fenice—and indeed all of the lover-protagonists in *Cligés*—with the power (1) to choose freely their beloved and (2) to conduct themselves in love according to their own will. Although these two issues are related, they need to be examined separately. Regarding the ability to exercise one's own will in the choice of the beloved, I will argue that the process of enamorment described in *Cligés* reveals that free will and reason do not actually preside at the moment at which each protagonist's heart becomes inflamed with love. In *Cligés*, as in Chrétien's lyric, the beloved's beauty is the catalyst—and one that works with as sudden and irreversible a force as any love philtre. It is true that Chrétien's protagonists reflect at length on the effects of love, what Frappier calls the "analyse du tourment amoureux" [analysis of the love torment], but to assert that this reflection leads to its "conciliation avec la volonté et la liberté des amants" [reconciliation with the lovers' will and freedom][10] yields, as we shall see, a curious—indeed paradoxical—notion of the role of free will in this process.

As "proof" that free will is indeed involved in the onset of love in *Cligés*, Frappier observes that both Soredamors and Alixandre declare at one point "Je *veux* aimer" [I *want* to love]. Such an assertion may on the face of it seem quite significant, but when we examine it in the context of the passages in which it occurs, we discover that this expression of the will to love by Alixandre and eventually by Soredamors occurs only *after* each has experienced the onset of love and *after* each has been forced to admit to being wholly under Love's sway. Although it is the result of a considerable amount of reflection, it signifies not free will but rather the willingness to align their own will on that of Love, once they realize that Love demands total obedience and that they are powerless to resist Love's "assault"—which is precisely how the narrator and the two protagonists perceive the onset of love. This may well be what Frappier considers "conciliation avec la volonté et la liberté des amants," but the picture painted by Chrétien is one of lovers who are constrained to make their own will conform to that of the imperious god Love.

Soredamors is a particularly interesting case. The first two things we learn about her are that she is very beautiful and that she is "desdaigneuse . . . d'amors" (v. 446) [scornful of love], a woman who prides herself on never having been moved to love—but on whom Love will soon take its revenge (vv. 456–59). Indeed, as soon as she catches sight of Alixandre, his great beauty inflames her heart, rendering her instantly powerless. In her first monologue she goes through several stages. First, having recognized the role that her eyes have played in what she is experiencing, she accuses them of treason (vv. 475–78). She then realizes that Alixandre's beauty has seduced her eyes but insists that this is not love because one cannot love with one's eyes (vv. 479–500). It would not be fair to blame them in any case, she reasons, because she exercises control over them, and she admits that she would not gaze upon someone if the sight did not please her heart (vv. 501–9). By the end of this first monologue, although she realizes that her heart is somehow engaged, she remains convinced of her ability to control her feelings (vv. 510–23). That she is quite deluded Chrétien underscores by framing this monologue with a commentary in which the narrator assures us that Love has taken its revenge upon this proud beauty. As she is about to begin her monologue he tells us:

> Bien a Amors droit assené,
> Qu'el cuer l'a de son dart ferue.
> Sovant palist, sovant tressue,
> *Et maugré suen amer l'estuet.* (vv. 460–63)

[Love has aimed well: with his arrow he has pierced her to the heart. Often she grows pale and is often bathed in sweat. *Despite herself she is compelled to love.*][11]

After she has finished her lament, he says:

> Vers Amors *se cuide desfandre,*
> *Mes ne li a mestier desfanse.* (vv. 528–29)

[Although *she thinks she can prevail, defense from Love's of no avail.*]

In other words, the reader is assured both at the beginning and at the end of Soredamors's monologue that the heroine is quite mistaken in her confident belief that she can exercise free will and impose that will.

As for Alixandre, he is as seduced by Soredamors's beauty as she is by his. When he gazes upon her, the luminous vision that she represents passes like an arrow through his eyes and lodges in his heart. His long monologue differs considerably from Soredamors's in that he knows his anguish is the result of love, specifically of his reluctance to express it (vv. 626–66). Although he blames Love for hurting its disciples (vv. 667–78), he accepts this ill treatment as a lesson not to be disdained from his master (vv. 679–91). He then speaks more specifically of the wound that

Love has inflicted so deeply that the arrow has gone into his heart, having passed first through his eyes (vv. 692–708). Recognizing that the eyes are the heart's mirror, he proceeds to accuse both his eyes and his heart of treason. They should be his friends, but instead they fulfill entirely their own will, *tote lor volanté* (v. 761), while ignoring his (vv. 709–69). Thus he plainly admits he has no will in this matter, and in order to explain his state he describes the arrow that has subdued his heart (vv. 770–860). Significantly, the description of the arrow becomes interwoven with a portrait of Soredamors, for it is really her great beauty that constitutes Love's arrow:

> Li penon sont les treces sores
> Que je vi l'autre jor an mer.
> C'est li darz qui me fet amer. (vv. 790–92)

> [The feathers are the golden tresses I beheld at sea the other day.
> This is the arrow that makes me love.]

This text is meaningful in that it reminds us that Love made its assault while the two were on the sea, as in the case of Tristan and Iseut, and Chrétien has Alixandre underscore the similarity between the work of Love's arrow and that of the love potion. In both cases, they are symbols for the onset of love in two exemplary individuals who seem destined to love each other and who are powerless to change Love's course, once it has been charted. Thus, here as in strophe IV of *D'Amors, qui m'a tolu a moi*, the allusion to the Tristan legend signifies not *contrast*, as some critics have thought, but rather *similarity*.

Once Alixandre has made the connection between Love's arrow and Soredamors's beauty and recognized the constraint he is under, only then does he commit himself solemnly to do Love's will, whatever the cost:

> Par foi, c'est li max qui me tue,
> Ce est li darz, ce est li rais,
> Don trop vilainnemant m'irais.
> Molt sui vilains qui m'an corroz;
> Ja mes festuz n'an sera roz
> Par desfïance ne par guerre
> Que je doie vers Amors querre.
> Or face de moi tot son buen
> Si com il doit feire del suen,
> Car *je le vuel et si me plest*;
> Ja ne quier que cist max me lest. (vv. 858–68)

·[On my word, this is the sickness that is killing me; this is the arrow, this the ray about which I am so basely enraged. I am churlish to be angered so. Never will an act of defiance or war break any engagement I should seek with Love. Now let him do all his will with me, as he should do with one who is his, for *I desire it, and it pleases me*; never do I wish this sickness to leave me.]

Clearly Alixandre's expression of his willingness to do as Love commands is the result not of free will but of constraint.

This is true for Soredamors as well, but it is not until the middle of her second monologue that she admits the truth: her inability to take her eyes off the man whose sight gives her so much pleasure must mean that she loves him. Love has assailed her and now she will do as it decrees:

Par force a mon orguel *donté,*
Si m'estuet a son pleisir estre.
Or vuel amer, or sui a mestre.
Que m'aprandra Amors? Et quoi!
Confeitemant servir le *doi.* (vv. 944–48)

[*By force he has subdued* my pride, *and I must be at his mercy. Now I wish to love. Now I have a master.* What will Love teach me?—What indeed! How I *must* serve him.

As we can see from the use of vocabulary signifying constraint, Soredamors's admission that she now wants to love is in no way an expression of free will; and the total capitulation of this previously haughty woman is underscored in the passage by the repetition of the word "now" (*or*). We should note that Staines's translation of this passage is based on Manuscript B.N. 794, where the verse numbered 947 in the Luttrell/Gregory edition and 939 in Micha's edition reads: "Or m'aprandra Amors . . . Et quoi?" The iteration of *or* three times makes the change in Soredamors's heart even more striking, and of course her new attitude contrasts dramatically with her earlier one.

In the description of the birth of love in Cligés and Fenice, the determinant role of beauty is even clearer. The narrator provides a hyperbolic description of the couple's beauty, which is so radiant that the two light up the room they enter and attract the awestruck gaze of all who behold them. For Cligés and Fenice it is literally love at first sight, as is symbolized by the exchange of their eyes; almost immediately their hearts are also committed. Although Cligés has many wonderful qualities, it is his beauty that seduces Fenice, for the narrator observes that if she had known more about Cligés than what met her eyes, she would have considered herself even more fortunate:

> Par boene amor, non par losange,
> Ses ialz li baille et prant les suens.
> Molt li sanble cist changes buens,
> Et miaudre assez li sanblast estre
> S'ele auques seüst de son estre.
> *Mes n'an set plus que bel le voit.* (vv. 2788–93)

[In true love, not in deceit, she gives him her eyes and accepts his. This exchange seems very good to her and would have seemed even better if she had known something of his character. *But all she knows is that she finds him handsome.*]

Many scholars who recognize the spontaneous nature of this love persist nevertheless in believing that the lovers exercise free will. For example, Philippe Walter claims that, in criticizing the Tristan legend, Chrétien does not contest "la légitimité de l'amour spontané et fort comme la mort" [the legitimacy of spontaneous love as strong as death], only the idea that love should need a magic potion, which condemns lovers to a disastrous determinism that precludes the exercise of free will; in *Cligés* it is different, for the protagonists dominate their passion. Thus, whereas Walter admits the abrupt onset of Cligés's and Fenice's passion ignited by a gaze—as in the case of Soredamors and Alixandre where the narrator describes at length Love's arrow—he refuses to recognize the constraint involved, preferring to conceive of their passion as "un amour né de la *libre* rencontre de deux corps et de deux cœurs radieux" [a love born of the *free* encounter of two radiant hearts and bodies].[12] Even Michelle Freeman sees Fenice as a free agent in matters of love: "Fenice is in complete and reasoned control of her aims and desires. She has freely accepted to fall in love." She adds that "Thessala is no bungling, ignorant Brangien; she plans and creates the potions administered in *Cligés*. Here free will, implemented by controlled artifice, has replaced tragic passion induced by fate." She concludes that "Fenice's will prevails; she is not a victim of fate as are Dido and Iseut."[13]

Yet in the texts examined above, in no case have we seen a protagonist asserting his or her will to love independently of Love's dictates. In no case have we seen anyone falling in love as a result of having considered any quality of the beloved other than physical beauty. While it is true that in medieval literature physical beauty usually indicates moral goodness, it seems to me highly significant that Chrétien has chosen to describe the onset of love in *Cligés*, a romance replete with echoes of the Tristan legend, as the result of an exterior force to which both sets of lovers must submit. Under these circumstances, it is difficult to agree with Frappier's assertion that "le mérite revient à Chrétien de Troyes d'avoir opposé le plus lucidement à la passion fatale de Tristan et d'Iseut l'essence de l'amour courtois, fondé sur un choix raisonné, une élection motivée qui l'apparente à l'amour cornélien" [Credit goes to Chrétien de Troyes for having established most lucidly the contrast between the fated passion of Tristan and Iseut and the essence of courtly love, founded on a reasoned choice, a motivated selection comparable to the love experienced by Corneille's protagonists].[14]

Freeman's view of Fenice anticipates (and answers according to the canonical view) the next question that we need to consider: If Chrétien's protagonists do not exercise free will at the moment at which they fall in love, do they at least exercise it in conducting affairs of the heart? This is the second issue raised by Frappier's assertions that Chrétien champions the exercise of free will in matters of love. In my examination of this question, I shall concentrate particularly on Fenice, since she is the one who is touted as being the most independent; and of course it is she who uses Iseut as a negative model as she attempts, with the help of Thessala, to gain control of her destiny. Fenice's fate is prefigured in the love story of Cligés's parents, Soredamors and Alixandre, particularly in the way they succumb to love's dictates. By underscoring Soredamors's delusions about her ability to control her destiny, Chrétien has prepared us for Fenice's vain struggle to master *her* own destiny. It will be a more dramatic struggle than Soredamors's, because the love she shares with Cligés will encounter a formidable exterior obstacle, her betrothal to Cligés's uncle, Alis. Like Iseut, she must find a way to indulge her love while fulfilling her role in the traditional social structure.

Most critics express admiration for Fenice's determination to avert the less attractive aspects of the traditional love triangle into which she has unwittingly fallen, especially since Alis is a much less sympathetic figure than King Mark is in the verse *Tristans*: Alis has proved himself unworthy of Fenice by reneging on his promise to his brother never to marry and thus to ensure Cligés's succession to the throne. Fenice has two main reasons for wanting to avoid the situation in which Iseut found herself: she is repulsed by the idea of giving her body to a man who does not have her heart, and she fears that Alis and she might produce a child who would effectively disinherit Cligés. These are admirable motives indeed. What is *not* particularly admirable, on the other hand, is that she is clearly concerned first and foremost with her reputation.[15] Time and again, when asked to choose a solution by which she and her lover can be together, she expresses her refusal—categorical and protracted—to conduct herself in a way that will cause people to speak of Cligés and her as they speak of celebrated lovers who have incurred public reproach, particularly Tristan and Iseut. She can be seen as working consciously to tailor this romantic archetype to her taste. As we shall see, however, her obsession with avoiding public censure paints a devastating portrait of a hollow young woman concerned less with how moral she actually is than with how moral she appears to others.

The Tristan legend is evoked explicitly for the first time when the narrator describes Cligés's qualities. In order to underscore the analogy between the Tristan/Iseut/Mark triangle and the Cligés/Fenice/Alis triangle that he is preparing to describe, the narrator states that Cligés is more skilled in fencing and hunting than Tristan, whom he characterizes as "King Mark's nephew," and then says that Cligés is standing "before his uncle" as the crowd admires his beauty and as he sets eyes for the first time on Fenice:

> Cist sot plus d'escremie et d'arc
> Que *Tristanz li niés le roi Marc*
> Et plus d'oisiax, et plus de chiens:
> En Cligés ne failli nus biens.
> Clygés, si biax com il estoit,
> *Devant son oncle an piez estoit.* (vv. 2769–74)

[He knew more of fencing and archery and hawks and hunting dogs than *King Mark's nephew, Tristan.* In Cligés no good quality was lacking. In all his beauty Cligés *stood before his uncle.*]

Fenice herself makes the analogy explicit when she first tells Thessala that she is in Iseut's situation and begs her nurse to help her find a way to avoid giving her body to a man who does not have her heart. She herself would rather be *dismembered* than be *remembered* for having engaged in the kind of irrational behavior for which Iseut garnered public reproach:

> *Mialz voldroie estre desmanbree*
> *Que de nos .ii. fust remanbree*

> *L'amors d'Ysolt et de Tristan,*
> Don tantes folies dit an
> Que honte m'est a reconter.
> *Ja ne m'i porroie acorder*
> *A la vie qu'Isolz mena.*
> Amors en li trop vilena,
> Que ses cuers fu a un entiers
> Et ses cors fu a .ii. rentiers.
> Ensi tote sa vie usa
> C'onques les .ii. ne refusa. (vv. 3125–36)

> [*I'd rather be torn limb from limb than have the two of us call to
> mind the love of Tristan and Iseult.* So much madness that I am
> ashamed to repeat is uttered about them. *I could never be recon-
> ciled to the life Iseult led.* Love debased itself too much in her, for
> her heart belonged entirely to one man and her body was possessed
> by two. Thus she passed all her life, never refusing the two.]

Although Fenice goes on to express a personal repugnance for the heart/
body split and laudable scruples about the possibility that she might
give birth to an heir who would effectively disinherit Cligés, her reputation nevertheless appears to be foremost in her mind.

Her concern for her reputation is confirmed in a second long speech,
this one addressed to Cligés. Thessala had provided her with the means
to prevent Alis from enjoying her body. She has only to complete her
plan to grant her body to the man who already has her heart. She begins
by informing Cligés that Alis has never enjoyed her body. She is proud to
have avoided the baser aspects of the traditional love triangle, and she
asserts that she will never become an example of villainous conduct:
"Ne ja nus par mon essanplaire / N'aprendra vilenie a faire" (vv. 5231–
32). She and Cligés must never be compared to Tristan and Iseut, because then love would be debased:

> Se je vos aim, et vos m'amez,
> *Ja n'en seroiz Tristanz clamez,*
> *Ne je n'an serai ja Yseuz,*
> Car puis ne seroit l'amors preuz,
> *Qu'il i avroit blasme ne vice.* (vv. 5239–43)

> [If I love you and you love me, *you will never be called Tristan nor
> shall I ever be Iseult,* for then love would not be honorable but
> base and *subject to reproach.*]

This preamble is analogous to the first part of Fenice's speech to Thessala. She then goes on to warn Cligés that he will never have her body unless she can be spirited away from Alis without ever being found and without incurring public reproach:

> Ja de mon cors n'avroiz delice
> Autre que vos or en avez,
> Se apanser ne vos savez
> Comant je puisse estre an anblee
> A vostre oncle et desasanblee
> Si que ja mes ne me retruisse
> *Ne moi ne vos blasmer ne puisse*
> *Ne ja ne s'an sache a cui prandre.* (vv. 5244–51)

> [Never will you have pleasure from my body other than what you have now unless you can figure out how I can be abducted from your uncle in such a way that he can never again find me, *nor be able to blame you or me, nor ever know whom to accuse.*]

Once again, Fenice's concern for her reputation has come to the fore, and it will be reiterated the next day when she responds to Cligés's suggestion that they simply leave Constantinople and take refuge in King Arthur's court. He has had the ill-conceived idea to compare the joy that their arrival in Britain would undoubtedly arouse with that felt in Troy when Paris arrived there after abducting Helen. The remembrance of this other provocative romantic couple arouses Fenice's ire, and in the remarkable speech that follows, she mentions four times her obsession about avoiding blame:

> Cele respont: "Et je dirai
> *Ja avoec vos ensi n'irai,*
> *Car lors seroit par tot le monde*
> *Ausi come d'Ysolt la blonde*
> *Et de Tristant de nos parlé.*
> Quant nos en serïens alé,
> Et ci et la *totes et tuit*
> *Blasmeroient nostre deduit.*
> Nus ne crerroit, ne devroit croirre
> La chose si com ele est voire.
> De vostre oncle qui crerroit dons
> Que je se li fusse an pardons
> Pucele estorse et eschapee?

Por trop baude et trop estapee
Me tendroit l'en et vos por fol.
Mes le comandemant saint Pol
Fet boen garder et retenir:
Qui chaste ne se vialt tenir,
Sainz Pos a feire bien anseingne
Si sagemant que il n'an preingne
Ne cri ne blasme ne reproche.
Bien estoper fet male boche." (vv. 5289–5310)

["And I shall say," she replied, *"never shall I go with you in this*
fashion, for then everyone would talk of us the way they do of
Iseult the Blonde and Tristan. After we have gone, *people all over*
would censure our pleasure. None would believe—nor should they
—that what happened is true. Whoever would believe I evaded
your uncle and remained a virgin? *They'd think me quite shame-*
less and dissolute, and you they'd take for a fool. It is good to
remember and to observe Saint Paul's command. Whoever will
not remain chaste Saint Paul instructs to behave so discreetly as
to *not arouse outcry, censure, or reproach. It's wise to still an evil*
tongue."]

Fenice refuses to run off with Cligés because everyone would speak of
them as they had Tristan and Iseut, never imagining that she had man-
aged to keep herself chaste. (Of course, her scruples appear to have dissi-
pated by the end of the romance when the couple decide to flee to Britain to enlist Arthur's help.) Fenice justifies her desire to avoid censure
by citing a garbled version of Saint Paul's counsel regarding chastity (vv.
5304–9)—"advice" that she punctuates with a proverb. Paul, of course,
wished that all could practice chastity as he himself did, and the only
recommendation he made was to marry if one could not exercise self-
control (I Cor. 7:7–9). Although critics have long noted with amusement
that Fenice misconstrues totally Paul's advice, those who admire her
seem unperturbed by the fact that her interpretation makes of both her
and Paul consummate cynics. And it is a cynical solution indeed that
Fenice finds in her attempt to follow this advice: after outlining her plan
to feign death, she says that it must be done cleverly so that no one can
find fault with it: "Et se la chose est par san feite, / Ja en mal ne sera
retreite, / Ne ja nus n'en porra mesdire" (vv. 5342–43) [And if the plan is
ably executed, it *will never be described as wicked. None will ever be*
able to speak ill of it].

Many years ago Gaston Paris highlighted Fenice's obsession with her reputation, but he did so in order to demonstrate that Chrétien had failed in his attempt to portray a heroine more moral than Iseut.[16] Few critics today would claim that Chrétien did not have complete control over Fenice's characterization. Given the number of verses devoted to this aspect of her character, it is clear that he was trying to show that Fenice's efforts to tailor a romantic archetype fail to yield a conception of love that is more refined than that of Tristan-love. Her determination to avoid the heart/body split lauded by so many critics is motivated in large part by her obsession with avoiding public censure. And the means she employs to this end certainly do not put her on a higher moral plane than Iseut. Her discourse may be noble, but her actions are not.[17] In the end she will be revealed for what she has always been: a woman whose conduct belies her noble appearance and discourse. Fenice views her life in superficial terms. She judges Iseut harshly as a woman who debased love by trying to fulfill her duties to her husband while following her heart, but she never considers the ultimate immorality of her own conduct—her refusal to fulfill her duty vis-à-vis her husband and her subjects.[18] No one is more cognizant than Chrétien of the gap that can exist between words and deeds. The lesson that all of his heroes, particularly his male protagonists, must learn is the necessity of backing up their word (what they say) or reputation (what others say about them) with deeds that support that *parole*.[19]

Fenice is clearly a woman who is determined to control her destiny, and she does succeed in achieving her goal of granting her body only to the man who has her heart. She does it by refashioning to her taste two of the most characteristic motifs of the romantic archetype with which she is obsessed: (1) the legendary love philtre, which provoked Tristan and Iseut to grant each other their hearts and their bodies, becomes the potion by which Alis is deluded into thinking he enjoys Fenice's body; (2) the Cornish lovers' death, which signals their inability to endure any longer the suffering involved in their attempt to reconcile their need to fulfill their roles in society and their need to be together, becomes a feigned death, by which Fenice removes herself from society to live with Cligés like Mabonagrain and his lady in a *locus amoenus*, a lovers' retreat. The Tristan and Iseut of the early verse romances, for whom social alienation represented a living death,[20] would have considered this a steep price indeed to pay for their personal happiness, and Chrétien himself could not possibly have approved of this solution.[21] Indeed, the magical means to which he has his heroine resort to overcome the obstacles to her bliss, and the "happy ending" that has Alis conveniently die off so that the lovers can marry, lend Fenice's enterprise a hollowness that anticipates its ultimate failure.

For fail she does. It is true that she manages to dictate the course of her love life, but only with the extraordinarily efficacious help of Thessala. Her activist attitude, which has seduced so many critics, should not blind us to the fact that, though Fenice may make the decisions, it is Thessala who provides the means to transform her desires into reality.[22] Moreover, Fenice cannot control her fame—or the notoriety attached to her actions. And, given the overriding importance in her mind of the need to preserve her reputation in her life and for all time, this concern would have to be the primary yardstick by which we gauge the success of her attempt to control her fate.[23] Although she achieves all of her earthly goals and ends up living as Cligés's spouse and empress in Constantinople, her ingenious schemes will become common knowledge and earn her the reputation of the faithless empress *par excellence,* as she is transformed for all time into what she had most feared—a negative exemplum:

> Qu'einz puis n'i ot empereor
> N'eüst de sa fame peor
> Qu'ele nel deüst decevoir,
> *Se il oï ramantevoir*
> *Comant Fenice Alis deçut,*
> Primes par la poison qu'il but
> Et puis par l'autre traïson.
> Por ce einsi com an prison
> Est gardee an Costantinoble,
> Ja n'iert tant haute ne tant noble,
> L'empererriz, quex qu'ele soit,
> *Que l'empereres ne la croit*
> *Tant con de cesti li remanbre.*
> Toz jorz la fet garder en chanbre
> Plus por peor que por le hasle,
> Ne ja avoec li n'avra masle
> Qui ne soit chastrez en anfance:
> De ce n'est crienme ne dotance
> *Qu'Amors les lit an son lïen.*
> Ci fenist l'uevre Crestïen. (vv. 6743–62)

[Ever since, there has never been an emperor who did not fear being deceived by his wife *after he had heard the story of how Fenice deceived Alis,* first with the potion he drank, and then with the other treachery. For this reason, every empress, no matter who she may be, no matter how highborn or noble, is guarded in Constantinople as though imprisoned. *For the emperor has no trust in her so long as he remembers Fenice.* He has her always kept under guard in her chamber more out of fear than to protect her from the sun. Never may she have a male in her company unless he has been castrated from childhood, so there is no doubt or fear *that love might bind them in its fetters.* Here ends Christian's work.]

Because of Fenice's notoriety, all future empresses of Constantinople live under virtual house guard, and the only men admitted into their presence are eunuchs, so that there can be no fear that Love will ensnáre them. Here, at the end of the romance, love is seen as being *restrained* from doing its usual work of *constraining* people to love. This, then, is where Fenice's "noble" quest has led; this is the fallout from her dogged pursuit of what so many critics have been pleased to call a love "more refined" than Tristan-love.[24] The final irony is that in the last two lines of this remarkable closing commentary, in a couplet where the verb *fenist* recalls Alis's notorious consort, *lïen* is made to rhyme with *Crestïen.* Our poet could not have provided more conclusive proof that he did not share his earnest heroine's belief in the role of free will in love.

Thus, although Chrétien's depiction of Soredamors and Fenice as women determined to exercise free choice and ultimate control in matters of love may at first blush seem refreshing, it soon becomes apparent that the poet seeks above all to demonstrate the extent of their *delusions* about that choice and that control. Frappier firmly believed—as do the vast majority of romance scholars—that Chrétien disapproved of Tristan and Iseut. Since that conviction is predicated on the mistaken belief that the poet had depicted characters whose conduct in love was founded on free choice and reason, surely we must look elsewhere for evidence that Chrétien actually was hostile to the Cornish lovers.

Matilda Bruckner claims that Chrétien's pervasive irony and the intertextual web he weaves in his romances make it impossible to know how he really felt about the Tristan legend.[25] Perhaps. Certainly, the mere presence in his works of multiple allusions does not prove that he was "haunted" by it or that he sought to exorcise the "demon" of a subversive myth.[26] It proves only that the Tristan legend was a crucial text in the formation and development of the romance genre.[27] Tristan and Iseut, so celebrated for their ardent love, their extraordinary cleverness, and their sublime beauty, provided a yardstick against which lovers in lyric poetry and romance would inevitably be measured.[28] This is how Chrétien used them in all of his works, especially in *Cligés*, but this practice implied no moral judgment, and if he allowed Fenice to judge Tristan and Iseut, he was careful both to distance himself from his heroine and to invalidate her judgment by demonstrating her abject failure to achieve a more "refined" love than theirs.[29]

NOTES

1. Frappier, "Vues." This view is developed more at length in his influential book *Chrétien de Troyes: l'homme et l'œuvre* (1957). All translations from these two studies are my own.

2. Berthelot, *Chansons courtoises*, 1048–49. My translation and emphasis.

3. Haidu, "Text and History," especially 22–25. This important article, published nearly twenty years ago, has unfortunately escaped the notice of most romance scholars—but see Bruckner's incisive review of Peter Noble's *Love and Marriage in Chrétien de Troyes*. Unfortunately, Haidu's article appeared too late to inform either Noble's study or another book that concentrates on Chrétien's ideas on love, Topsfield, *Chrétien de Troyes*.

4. On the determinant role of the eyes in the onset of love see Cline, "Heart and Eyes." I examine this phenomenon as it relates to Chrétien in a forthcoming study, "Chrétien, the Troubadours, and the Tristan Legend."

5. In referring to this romance and its protagonists, I use the forms found most frequently in modern editions of the Old French romance—Alixandre, Cligés, Fenice, and so on—except, of course, in citing critics who use other forms, such as the modern French equivalents Alexandre, Cligès, Fénice.

6. Frappier, *Chrétien*, 112–13.

7. See especially Curtis, "Validity"; Haidu, *Aesthetic Distance*; Freeman, *Poetics of "Translatio studii"*; Lacy, *Craft of Chrétien de Troyes*; Lefay-Toury, "Roman breton et mythes courtois"; and Polak, *Chrétien de Troyes: "Cligés."*

8. See Walter, "Notice," and the general introduction to Chrétien by Jean-Marie Fritz in *Romans*, by Chrétien de Troyes, 9–42. All translations from these works are my own.

9. On Chrétien's "canonization," see Keith Busby's review of these editions in *Speculum*, especially 405–6. Another recent indication of this phenomenon is the publication of Philippe Walter's *Que sais-je?* volume, *Chrétien de Troyes*.

10. Quotations in these two paragraphs are from Frappier, "Vues," 153.

11. Verse numbers for Chrétien's *Cligés* refer to the recent critical edition by Stewart Gregory and Claude Luttrell. Any italics are mine. My translations of these passages owe a great deal to the prose translation of David Staines and the verse translation of Ruth Harwood Cline. If I were not attempting as literal a

translation as possible, I would use Cline's renderings throughout. They are ingenious and amazingly accurate. She translates this passage as follows: "Love
aimed his arrow, straight and true, / and through the heart she was impaled / and
often sweat and often paled. / She loved in spite of her disdain" (p. 14).

12. Walter, "Notice," 1126–27. My emphasis.

13. Freeman, Poetics of "Translatio studii," 48–51.

14. Frappier, "Vues," 153.

15. On this concern, see Lacy, 14.

16. Paris, "Cligès." Commenting on Fenice's distortion of Paul's advice, Paris
concludes: "Ainsi ce qui importe aux yeux de cette personne, qui incarne l'idéal
'rigoureusement moral' de Chrétien, ce n'est pas la chasteté, c'est la bonne
réputation" [Thus what matters to this person, who incarnates Chrétien's "rigor-
ously moral" ideal, is not chastity but a good reputation] (292, n. 1). As Haidu
notes: "Rarely has the encounter of critic and literary work resulted in a greater
mismatch than in Paris' lengthy essay on Cligès" (Aesthetic Distance, 91, n. 137).

17. See Lefay-Toury, "Roman breton et mythes courtois," 286: "Le mensonge
réside pour elle dans l'hiatus qui s'étend entre ses paroles et ses actes, entre la
lettre et l'esprit du roman. Ce ne sont pas les mots qui mentent, ce sont les faits"
[The lie dwells in the gap between her words and her actions, between the letter
and the spirit of the romance. It is not the words that lie but rather the facts].

18. Curtis, "Validity," 299–300.

19. See my discussion of this theme in "Yvain" dans le miroir.

20. Grimbert, "Love, Honor, and Alienation in Thomas's Roman de Tristan."

21. On the tower episode Haidu remarks: "A love lived or endured in isolation
is always false for Chrétien." Indeed, the Joie de la Cort episode in Erec et Enide
demonstrates "that love, for Chrétien, is possible and real only in a socialized
setting. The love of two partners who isolate themselves from the world and
other men is, however pleasurable, a living death for Chrétien" (Aesthetic Distance, 103).

22. Lefay-Toury, "Roman breton et mythes courtois," 195. Lefay-Toury's the-
sis is that Chrétien, in each successive romance, endows his heroine with increasingly less power to control her fate.

23. Haidu, Aesthetic Distance, 105.

24. Walter duly notes the pall that this turn of events casts over Fenice's
"triumph." Nevertheless, he remains unshaken in his conviction that Cligés
was written to exorcise the fascination with the Tristan legend: "Cette conclusion peu engageante vient ternir le dénouement triomphal du roman. Est-ce
bien cependant la conclusion essentielle à retenir de l'œuvre? L'intérêt capital
de Cligès réside dans l'opposition manifeste au roman de Tristan" [This rather
unattractive conclusion tarnishes the romance's triumphal denouement. But is
this really the essential lesson of the work? The main interest of Cligès resides
in its obvious opposition to the Tristan] ("Notice," 1124).

25. Bruckner, review of Love and Marriage, 511.

26. Cf. Pierre Gallais, "La hantise tristanesque de Chrétien de Troyes," chap. 7 of *Genèse du roman occidental*, especially 56–64; and Payen, "Lancelot contre Tristan."

27. Freeman goes even further: in *Poetics of "Translatio studii"* she stresses the nature of Cligés as a self-conscious model of twelfth-century romance composition. On Chrétien's creative intertextual use of the Tristan legend, see also her "Transpositions."

28. Thus, for example, the simple fact that a romance author characterizes his heroine as more beautiful than Iseut does not imply that he disapproves of Iseut, only that she is a paragon of beauty to which he is pleased to compare his heroine.

29. As Curtis observes: "Although Chrétien never openly expresses any disapproval of Fénice, she is nonetheless, of all the heroines he created, the most unscrupulous, deceitful, and immoral" ("Validity," 299).

SELECTED BIBLIOGRAPHY

Berthelot, Anne, ed. and trans. *Chansons courtoises*. In *Œuvres complètes*, by Chrétien de Troyes, edited and translated by Daniel Poirion et al., 1041–49. Paris: Gallimard, 1994.

Bruckner, Matilda Tomaryn. Review of *Love and Marriage in Chrétien de Troyes*, by Peter S. Noble. *Romance Philology* 39 (1986): 508–13.

Busby, Keith. Review of *Œuvres complètes*, by Chrétien de Troyes, edited and translated by Daniel Poirion et al., and of *Romans*, by Chrétien de Troyes, edited and translated by Michel Zink et al. *Speculum* 71 (1996): 405–9.

Chrétien de Troyes. *Cligés*. Edited by Stewart Gregory and Claude Luttrell. Arthurian Studies 28. Cambridge: Brewer, 1993.

———. *Cligés*. Edited by Alexandre Micha. In Classiques français du moyen âge. Paris: Champion, 1957.

———. *Œuvres complètes*. Edited and translated by Daniel Poirion et al. Bibliothèque de la Pléiade 408. Paris: Gallimard, 1994.

———. *Romans*. Edited and translated by Michel Zink et al. Classiques modernes. Paris: Livre de Poche, 1994.

Cline, Ruth H. "Heart and Eyes." *Romance Philology* 25 (1971): 263–97.

Cline, Ruth Harwood, trans. *Cligès*, by Chrétien de Troyes. Athens and London: University of Georgia Press, 2000.

Curtis, Renée. "The Validity of Fénice's Criticism of Tristan and Iseut in Chrétien's *Cligés*." *Bibliographical Bulletin of the International Arthurian Society* 41 (1989): 293–300.

Frappier, Jean. *Chrétien de Troyes: l'homme et l'œuvre*. 1957; 2d ed. Paris: Hatier, 1968.

———. "Vues sur les conceptions courtoises dans les littératures d'oc et d'oïl au XIIe siècle." *Cahiers de Civilisation médiévale* 2 (1959): 135–56.

Freeman, Michelle A. *The Poetics of "Translatio studii" and "Conjointure":*

Chrétien de Troyes's "Cligés." French Forum Monographs 12. Lexington, Ky.: French Forum, 1979.

———. "Transpositions structurelles et intertextualité: le 'Cligès' de Chrétien." *Littérature* 41 (February 1981): 50–61.

Gallais, Pierre. *Genèse du roman occidental. Essais sur Tristan et Iseut et son modèle persan.* Paris: Têtes de Feuilles et Éditions Sirac, 1974.

Grimbert, Joan Tasker. "Chrétien, the Troubadours, and the Tristan Legend: The Rhetoric of Passionate Love in *D'amors qui m'a tolu a moi* and *Cligés.*" In *Philologies Old and New: Essays in Honor of Peter Florian Dembowski,* edited by Joan Tasker Grimbert and Carol J. Chase. Forthcoming.

———. "Love, Honor, and Alienation in Thomas's *Roman de Tristan.*" In *The Arthurian Yearbook* 4, edited by Keith Busby, 77–98. New York and London: Garland Publishing, 1992.

———. *"Yvain" dans le miroir: Une poétique de la réflexion dans le "Chevalier au lion" de Chrétien de Troyes.* Purdue University Monographs in Romance Languages 25. Amsterdam and Philadelphia: John Benjamins, 1988.

Haidu, Peter. *Aesthetic Distance in Chrétien de Troyes: Irony and Comedy in "Cligès" and "Perceval."* Geneva: Droz, 1968.

———. "Text and History: The Semiosis of Twelfth-Century Lyric as Sociohistorical Phenomenon (Chrétien de Troyes: 'D'Amors qui m'a tolu')." *Semiotica* 33 (1981): 1–62.

Lacy, Norris J. *The Craft of Chrétien de Troyes: An Essay on Narrative Art.* Leiden: Brill, 1980.

Lefay-Toury, Marie-Noëlle. "Roman breton et mythes courtois." *Cahiers de Civilisation médiévale* 15 (1972): 193–204; 283–93.

Noble, Peter S. *Love and Marriage in Chrétien de Troyes.* Cardiff: University of Wales Press, 1982.

Paris, Gaston. *"Cligès."* In *Mélanges de littérature française du moyen âge,* edited by Mario Roques, 229–327. Paris: Champion, 1910.

Payen, Jean-Charles. "Lancelot contre Tristan: la conjuration d'un mythe subversif (Réflexions sur l'idéologie romanesque au moyen âge)." In *Mélanges de langue et de littérature médiévales offerts à Pierre Le Gentil,* 617–32. Paris: Société d'édition d'enseignement supérieur et Centre de documentation universitaire Réunis, 1973.

Polak, Lucie. *Chrétien de Troyes: "Cligés."* Critical Guides to French Texts 23. London: Grant & Cutler, 1983.

Staines, David, trans. *The Complete Romances of Chrétien de Troyes.* Bloomington and Indianapolis: Indiana University Press, 1993.

Topsfield, L. T. *Chrétien de Troyes: A Study of the Arthurian Romances.* Cambridge: Cambridge University Press, 1981.

Walter, Philippe. *Chrétien de Troyes.* Collection *Que sais-je?* Paris: Presses universitaires de France, 1997.

———. "Notice." In *Œuvres complètes,* by Chrétien de Troyes, edited and translated by Daniel Poirion et al., 1114–30. Paris: Gallimard, 1994.

6

The Lyric Lady in Narrative

William D. Paden

I approach the lyric lady in narrative from the direction of lyric itself, particularly troubadour lyric, and from the problematic of *fin'amor*. The *domna* of troubadour lyric poetry, we are told, was married and superior in rank to the poet. In an article published in 1975 I challenged these assumptions, not on the grounds that we can definitely establish that she was anything else, but rather that we cannot find adequate evidence either way.[1] Assumptions that run counter to demonstrable truth are easier to combat, but these have no demonstrable relation to truth; they are gratuitous, I argued, and should be discarded because they impose baseless notions upon our reading.

Twenty years later my claim was debated by Don Monson. Monson disputed my interpretation of several key terms in the lyric (without persuading me of his views), but then came to this surprising conclusion: "We do catch occasional glimpses of a certain social reality lurking behind the poetry. . . . Such insights into social reality are exceptional, however. In most cases we must resign ourselves to the fact that the public forum of poetry can provide only a fleeting and distorted image of such private and intimate aspects of human behavior."[2] I could not have asked for better. Since Monson acknowledges in these words that the poetry does not provide support for the views he defends, we are obliged to ask why he and others defend them. The literary evidence is weak, and the historical evidence, as has long been recognized, is nil.[3] I have argued more recently that the motivation underlying these assumptions stems from certain nineteenth-century suppositions about realism and sexuality.[4] We tend to suppose, as though we were trained in the reading of Stendhal, Balzac, and Flaubert, that fiction imitates reality and reality explains fiction; therefore we tend to suppose that if the troubadour's lady is inaccessible, it must be because she is married, and if the troubadour says he looks up to her, she must occupy a superior social position. It may make sense to read nineteenth-century novels this way, but not the troubadours. By assuming that the troubadour's desire was adulterous, we satisfy the nineteenth-century imperative to talk about forbidden sex, an imperative that produced critical moments such as the *amour courtois* of Gaston Paris,[5] literary moments such as the novel of adultery, and cultural moments such as Freudian psychoanalysis.

Here I will explore another avenue that might shed further light on the matter, namely the romances with lyric insertions. In these French texts bits of lyric are employed as a locutionary device, as something that a character might say, or rather sing; and since these characters are involved in narrative, they have the qualities of narrative characters—they function in an explicit narrative context, they have explicit relations with one another, and they perform actions that add up to explicit identities. These qualities of characters-in-narrative are lacking in characters-in-lyric such as the lover and his lady in troubadour song. The assumptions I question flesh out lyric characters by enclosing them in presumed minimal narrative contexts, but do so at the risk of arbitrariness since, by definition, the lyric characters lack precisely those narrative features we seek. If we need narrative context in order to understand lyric, however, we have actual medieval narrative contexts for lyric lovers at our disposal in the romances with lyric insertions. Better to approach the lyric through real medieval narratives, I say, than through factitious quasi-narratives that we extrapolate from the lyric ourselves.[6]

I began this investigation with a simple hypothesis that the lyric insertions in romance might confirm these assumptions, if romance characters sang love songs for ladies who were married and superior to their lovers—or might disprove them if the insertions were used in other ways. Of course my intention was not impartial. I reasoned thus: the two earliest romances with lyric insertions, the *Roman de la Rose* by Jean Renart and the *Roman de la Violette* by Gerbert de Montreuil, both focus sharply on the virginity of the heroine, seen as an essential condition for marriage; if the men who love them sing snatches of lyric, then, these lyrics do not concern adulterous desire for women who are already married to someone else. In the *Rose* the lover is Conrad, emperor and king; in the *Violette* it is Gérart, count of Nevers.[7] Conrad is superior in rank to his beloved Lïenor, sister of his vassal Guillaume de Dole. Gérart seems to be superior to his beloved Eurïaut, though her social position is not made clear. In neither case is the lady of superior rank.

These two romances seem to suggest that the lyric, then as now, expresses the desire of a young man for a young woman, desire that in these cases leads to marriage. In such a reading the desire sung by the troubadours is not so different from that sung by the Beatles or more recent popular singers. If we found reason to adopt such a reading, we would lose the quaint medieval quality of the traditional assumptions, so piquant, so feudal, so titillating to antiquarian taste. We might gain a less sentimental, less cumbersome, more simple, direct, and honest view of *fin'amor*.

Turning to the romances themselves, I found that things are somewhat more complicated. In the *Roman de la Rose* Jean Renart includes three songs from Occitan originals, but none of them is actually sung by either of the principals in the love story, Conrad or his beloved Lïenor. One is sung by Guillaume, Lïenor's brother, and two by nameless minor characters with no other function but to sing them. Guillaume and his companions, making their way to visit the king's court, burst out in chorus with the first stanza of Jaufre Rudel's song of *amor de lonh*, not because Guillaume is in love with anyone far or near, but because he has been summoned by the emperor, a summons that offers exciting possibilities of preferment.[8] Furthermore it is summertime, so the days really are long; and finally, when these young men hear birds singing beside the road, they naturally feel an urge to sing too. Their communal performance of the stanza expresses a shared cultural value of courtliness.

The two other Occitan songs, performed by characters with no significance for the plot, are nevertheless associated with Lïenor and Guillaume. As Lïenor prepares to defend herself against the false accusation that she has yielded her maidenhood to the seneschal, she hears someone singing a *chançon auvrignace*, a song from the Auvergne by Daude de Pradas, and she could have sung it very well herself, the narrator assures us, if she had not been so distressed. The song speaks of the nightingale and the coming of spring, but concludes that the speaker needs joy to heal and cure his *cors*—his body, his self, or, just possibly, his heart (vv. 4653–59). Conrad, waiting in the next room for the woman he loves to defend herself against the charge of unchastity, and nearly mad with mixed emotions, takes no comfort in words or song (v. 4663), that is, this song. The *chançon* expresses the need for joy that both Lïenor and Conrad, in their distinct ways, feel acutely at this stressful moment.

The third Occitan insertion is performed by a knight in Guillaume's company as Guillaume returns to court for the triumphal marriage of his sister and the king (vv. 5212–27).[9] In the Occitan original Bernart de Ventadorn sings out of the lover's stinging grief and his envy of the lark, but the inserted version shifts the emphasis to the lark's joy, corresponding to Guillaume's elation at his brilliant prospects.

In sum, then, none of these Occitan insertions in the *Rose* gives direct expression to a lover's desire for his lady, although all of them serve to enrich our sensation of the world that revolves around the love of Conrad and Lïenor. As Maureen Boulton has put it,[10] these insertions describe social occasions rather than the love of the character who sings them.

If we expand our consideration to encompass all the insertions in the *Roman de la Rose*, however, we find that the leading characters in the love story do sing out their hearts. Three-quarters of the insertions (thirty-five of forty-seven) describe social occasions, but the remaining dozen serve to spotlight the love that guides the story. Conrad's nine *chansons courtoises* trace the lover's progress up to his triumph in marriage, which he celebrates festively with a *chanson à danser*.[11] Lïenor has only two opportunities to express her love in song. In two *chansons de femme*, specifically *chansons de toile*, she sings her yearning for "amors d'autre païs"—such as the love of Conrad—and retells the story of Doe and Doon, emblematic of her own faithful love (vv. 1183–92, 1204–16).

The principal genres are the courtly songs in what Bec has called the *registre aristocratisant*, mostly by known authors, and the anonymous dance songs and women's songs in the *registre popularisant*.[12] They are distributed in an articulate pattern. The romance begins with ten dance songs during the long picnic sequence; it ends, after the marriage of Conrad and Lïenor, with a final sequence that begins with two dance songs, develops with two courtly songs sung by minor characters as part of the general festivity, and concludes with two more dance songs. Between these introductory and concluding sequences, the love story develops through Conrad's courtly songs. He launches it with two of them, and then Lïenor and her mother contribute three women's songs. The courtship proper is narrated through an alternation of courtly and dance songs, *chansons de toile*, and a few less conspicuous genres such as the *pastourelle.* The lyric does not disrupt the narrative line but carries it; the octosyllabic couplets that intervene between the lyrics serve to knit them together. The songs tell the story.[13]

Conrad's courtly songs bear out my initial hypothesis about the nature of *fin'amor.* He adapts lyrics by Gace Brulé, the Châtelain de Couci, Renaut de Beaujeu, Renaut de Sabloeil, and several anonymous poets in order to express his situation, which is that of a young but mature man, a young king but still a bachelor, who loves a maiden, the sister of one of his vassals. The Occitan lyric insertions do not express this love so directly, but participate in its celebration. In the dance songs the singer's persona sometimes defies the jealous one or ones (vv. 310–15, 318–22), but it is impossible to tell whether the word *jalous* is singular or plural—possibly referring to a husband, or else to members of the girl's family jealous of her honor—and Jean Renart tells us specifically that the lady who sings the first of these songs is "une dame sans vilonie" (v. 307). In a *chanson de toile* sung by a nameless bachelor, Bele Aiglentine has been made pregnant by Count Henri; when she asks him if he will marry her, he agrees joyfully and makes her his countess (v. 2292). Plainly Aiglentine and Henri, like Lïenor and Conrad, were unmarried at the time of the song.

If we were to take seriously the attitude that *fin'amors,* either Occitan or French, concerns love for a married woman superior in rank to the lover, we would oblige ourselves to feel a powerful intertextual irony in all this—an irony that, I submit, seems quite foreign to the *Roman de la Rose.* Jean Renart does not draw upon lyrics of cynical experience and distort them to fit a world of innocence. I cannot imagine that Conrad launders tunes about social-climbing adultery; the conflict within the *Rose* concerns another kind of problem altogether, the jealous malevolence of the seneschal. Conrad's love begs to be heard as pure, appealing, sympathetic desire, unsullied by any presumed worldly amorality of the thirteenth century, the nineteenth, or the twentieth—just as, in my estimation, do the lyrics of the troubadours and *fin'amor* in general.

In the *Roman de la Violette* Gerbert de Montreuil uses songs more expressively.[14] Of the forty songs in the romance, twenty are sung by the hero, Gérart de Nevers, three by his beloved Eurïaut, and six by other women who love him, for a total of twenty-nine, so just short of three-quarters of the songs in the work have expressive function. There are two insertions from Occitan, one sung by Gérart and the other by Eurïaut. Both are from Bernart de Ventadorn. Gérart hears a lark singing, thinks of *fine amour,* and remembers the maiden Aiglente, a duke's daughter with whom he fell in love when he forgot Eurïaut, his true love, under the influence of a potion.[15] So he sings the beginning of Bernart's song of the lark (vv. 4187–94). Earlier Eurïaut was inspired by *amours* to sing a stanza castigating the envious just when she met the envious villain Lisïart (vv. 324–31); there is no doubt in my mind that Gerbert de Montreuil intended his audience to appreciate the irony, although neither Eurïaut nor Lisïart seems to have noticed it.

Once again the lovers' songs guide us through the story, and once again the songs observe a carefully designed alternation in genres. But Gerbert innovates with the refrain, not a stanza but a snatch of lyric from an existing song, usually two lines long (in the *Violette*), occasionally three lines or only one. The refrains take over the subordinate function that was carried by the dance songs in the *Roman de la Rose,* alternating with the dominant *chansons courtoises.* At the Easter court with which the story begins—corresponding to the picnic sequence in the *Rose*—we hear a series of refrains sung by noblewomen. They all concern love, of course. Some of them concern extramarital love while others do not. A countess sings of grief in love, and then a duchess sings flirtatiously; a maiden, sister of a count, sings that she will never marry, but will fall in love instead ("par amors amerai," v. 120); the sister of another count sings that she is happy in love, and defies the gossips; a *damoisiele* sings that she is afraid because she is going to her lover all alone; a *castelainne* (presumably the wife of a *châtelain*) sings "Aprendés a valoir maris, / Ou vous m'avés perdue" (vv. 141–42) [Learn to be good for something, husband, / Or you have lost me], and a lady from Normandy, who they said was in love with the king himself, sings that she cares for her lover despite her husband.

In contrast with the ten dance songs that open the *Rose,* this sequence of refrains comes closer to the traditional assumptions about *fin'amors.* We should remember, however, that they are subordinate to the central love story, which, in the *Violette* as in the *Rose,* concerns two unmarried and marriageable young people. The introductory sequence peaks when Gérart himself is invited to sing; he performs a courtly stanza castigating the envious (vv. 191–98) which anticipates the envy of Lisïart, and then sings two refrains, first rejoicing in love—which starts him boasting— and then adding that he has the prettiest *amie* of all. As in the *Rose,* the songs tell the story. In the foreground we have Gérart preening himself with reckless self-indulgence, in the background a chorus line, as it were, including the ladies who sing the refrains, both married and unmarried, all swooning with desire. From this point onward the insertions obey a regular alternation of genres, usually one courtly song followed by two refrains, sometimes two courtly songs in a row or three refrains instead of two. After a series of adventures and travails, including Gérart's entanglement with three other women, the lovers are reunited and finally marry.

It all began when Eurïaut sang two songs, the Occitan stanza against envy directed to Lisïart and then a French stanza adapted from a song by Moniot d'Arras, which is of particular interest for my purpose.[16] In this *chanson de femme* the speaker swears that she will cuckold her husband if she gets the chance, and compares her lover and herself to Tristan and Iseut (vv. 51–53). The refrain refers to the husband unambiguously as "li jalous": "Quant plus m'i bat et destraint li jalous, / tant ai [j]e miex en amor ma pensée" [The more the jealous one beats and restrains me, / the more I have my thoughts on love]. When the maiden Eurïaut sings this song, she adapts it to her circumstances, replacing the refrain and producing a song that says she has an *ami*, so this fool who is trying to seduce her is wasting his words (vv. 441–49). That is, Eurïaut rebuffs Lisïart as the *mal mariée* rebuffs her husband, because each prefers her lover—in Eurïaut's case Gérart, whom she will eventually marry.

Does this mean that Lisïart enjoys a situation comparable to that of a husband, or that Eurïaut will prove too amorous to be contained within the restraints of marriage? Surely not. Moniot's *mal mariée* functions in a way analogous to the refrains sung by the restive wives at the Easter court, refrains that provide counterpoint to Gérart's satisfaction with the love of Eurïaut. The love that unites the hero and the heroine forms a contrast with unsatisfactory conjugal love as expressed in some of the introductory refrains (but not in others) and in the song by Moniot embedded intertextually in Eurïaut's.

The protagonists surpass less distinguished lovers, some of whom are married while others are not, as the major key dominates the minor, or, to pursue the musical metaphor, as consonance, characterized by major chords with their pleasing final effect, dominates dissonance with its minor chords and lack of resolution. The dissonance expressed in the *mal mariée* marks it as subordinate to the harmony of the main story line with its culmination in marriage.

And that is what I think I have learned from these romances with lyric insertions. If we drop our concern with finding direct association with the Occitan lyric and look to other romances with lyric insertions, we can extend this conclusion. In Machaut's *Remede de Fortune*, for example, and in Christine de Pizan's *Dit de la Pastoure*, snatches of lyric are set within narratives of desire free of marital constraints.[17] Looking further afield, we see that in the thirteenth-century German *Frauendienst* of Ulrich von Lichtenstein, in Dante's *Vita nuova*, in the fourteenth-century Spanish *Libro de buen amor* and in Chaucer's Knight's Tale, narratives are signed in various ways with the lyric signature.[18] None of these narratives explicitly concerns the love of a poet for a married woman of superior rank.[19] The Knight's Tale culminates in the marriage of Palamon and Emily.

Within the Occitan domain itself, however, a counterexample comes readily to mind. In *Flamenca* the lover Guilhem de Nevers, who is capable of every other courtly accomplishment, is also a poet; he loves Flamenca, the wife of the jealous Archambaut. When Guilhem first manages to speak to Flamenca, he whispers two syllables to her during Mass ("Hai las!"), thus beginning a dialogue of two-syllable utterances that continues over what seems a month of Sundays. These syllables reconstitute a stanza (a lyric insertion of a special kind) from a pre-existing courtly song by Peire Rogier, a troubadour who was active about a century before the composition of the romance.[20] When Flamenca signifies to Guilhem that she reciprocates his desire, their passion soon reaches climax in a celebrated scene at the baths of Aix. This romance seems to confirm everything I have challenged.

That is, it does so if we read it as the fulfillment of an erotic situation that was already immanent in the poetry of the troubadours generally, and not as an exception, innovation, or dissonance within that context. We have another late thirteenth-century narrative to consider as well, the "Perilhos tractatz d'amor de donas" in the *Breviari d'amor* begun by Matfre Ermengaud in 1288.[21] In the manner of the romances with lyric insertions, Matfre introduces into his disquisition stanzas plucked from the troubadours he most admires, including nine selections he wrote himself. And Matfre asserts that the love sung by the troubadours leads not only to marriage but even to love of children.

Scholars persuaded of the traditional view logically must regard *Flamenca* as the very exemplification of troubadour love, and discount Matfre's assertion as a groundless attempt, against all odds, to reconcile the troubadours with the church. But perhaps this is not so. Perhaps the troubadours make a spectacle not of their lady, whatever her civil status, but of their love; perhaps this love is not usually identified in relation to marriage at all, but simply as desire; and perhaps this desire, unencumbered by marital impediments, serves as the dominant element of their erotics, played off on occasion against a subordinate element of illicit desire marked distinctively as extramarital. If such is the case, then Matfre Ermengaud was truer to the troubadours than *Flamenca* was, in that he saw their desire potentially leading to marriage, just as the authors of some romances with lyric insertions and other romancers did. One may also cite the mid-thirteenth-century troubadour Guilhem de Montanhagol, whose celebrated formula "D'amor mou castitatz" is correctly understood to mean that marital fidelity begins in love.[22] Guilhem anticipated Matfre Ermengaud.

And *Flamenca*, boldly reversing the general mode of troubadour lyric, sang an extended narrative on a dissonant melody. *Flamenca* was neither the only romance to do so nor the first. We could trace a dissonant tradition that began with the *Tristan* of Thomas about 1175, continued in Chrétien's *Lancelot* about 1180, and was taken by Gaston Paris as exemplary of medieval love despite the fact that all Chrétien's other romances contradicted him.[23] *Tristan, Lancelot,* and *Flamenca* perform variations, tragic or comic, on the theme of adulterous love, but we have no warrant to extend their assumptions onto the rest of medieval love poetry. Rather we should recognize that we have two complementary traditions, a dominant or consonant one in which the lyric of love could, if embedded within narrative, lead to marriage, and a subordinate or dissonant one in which desire defied marital sanction. *Flamenca* transforms the *mal mariée* into narrative, as Matfre Ermengaud transforms the *canso*.

Traditional scholarship has read the *canso* as though the *mal mariée* —a Northern French genre scarcely attested in Occitan—provided the key to understanding it, and has thus mistaken the dissonant tradition for the dominant one in order, it seems, to satisfy an obscure need to make the world of medieval poetry more wicked, hence more thrilling, than the reader's. But we have plain evidence in these two romances, at least, that the lyric could sing of love leading to marriage with thrills aplenty. If we cast off that obscure need, we are free to recognize that the troubadours were more like us than we have been told.

NOTES

1. Paden et al., "Marital Status and Social Rank."
2. Monson, "The Troubadour's Lady Reconsidered Again," 273.
3. "Nous ne connaissons l'amour courtois que par la littérature": Marc Bloch, *La société féodale* (Paris: Albin Michel, 1939–40), 2:41.

4. Paden, "View through Thick History."

5. Paris, "Lancelot du Lac, II."

6. If by the same logic we look to the Occitan vidas and razos, we find that about a third of them say the troubadour loved another man's wife, and about a tenth of them that he loved a lady of higher rank (Paden et al., "Marital Status and Social Rank," 46–47). But the vidas and razos "reduced all manner of poetic statements to commonplace expressions of unrequited passion" (46); their tendency to take the troubadours' figurative language literally lies at the source of the assumptions I challenge.

7. Gérard is not called quens, but he undoubtedly holds the conté that he loses, provisionally, to Lisïart. See Buffum, Le Roman de la Violette, vv. 994, 1461.

8. Lecoy, Roman de la Rose, vv. 1301–7. In this section, all verse references are to the Lecoy edition of Rose. On the three Occitan insertions, see Paden, "Old Occitan as a Lyric Language," 42–46.

9. Guillaume's delight at the prospect of material advancement might possibly be expressed in his version of the song, if rent in v. 5226 might be taken as "rent, income"—"Yet she does not take from me income"—despite the fact that the sense is first attested in the fourteenth century, according to Adolf Tobler and Erhard Lommatzsch (Tobler-Lommatzsch Altfranzösisches Wörterbuch [Berlin: Weidmann, 1925–], 8:8381). See also Paden, "Old Occitan as a Lyric Language," 46n.38.

10. Boulton, The Song in the Story, 3.

11. First Conrad sings that he has been smitten by Lïenor sight unseen, on the basis of a description by his singer Juglet (vv. 846–52). He thinks this may be just an amorete, but it grows into a loial amor, and he says it gives him good hope (vv. 923–30). Emboldened, he tells Guillaume in a song that "une amor me desvoie" [a love turns me from my road]; when Guillaume becomes Conrad's vassal and agrees to the marriage, Conrad sings that he will be loyal in love forever (vv. 1456–69, 1769–76). Then in a moment of naive trust he sings in the hearing of the seneschal that he has fine amors but must beware of the losengier (vv. 3180–95). The seneschal, an absolute losengier, learns of Lïenor's birthmark; when Conrad presses him to know why he opposes the marriage, he commits his slander, and Conrad sings that he regrets having insisted, out of jealousy, on learning what he did not want to know (vv. 3625–31). Grief-stricken, he sings that love has slain him without reason; feeling worse and worse, he sings that he has deserved to die (vv. 3751–59, 3883–90). But when Lïenor vindicates herself, a dance song flies out of his heart (vv. 5106–11), and everything ends happily.

12. Bec, Lyrique française, 1:33–35.

13. Pace Boulton, who writes: "As an element of narrative technique, the lyric insertion device introduces an element of disruption into the narrative work" (The Song in the Story, 3).

14. On the Occitan insertions, see Paden, "Old Occitan as a Lyric Language," 48–51.

15. She and her servant Flourentine, who loves Gérart too, are both *pucieles* (v. 2752).

16. Moniot d'Arras wrote between 1213 and 1239: see Geneviève Hasenohr and Michel Zink, eds., *Dictionnaire des lettres françaises: Le Moyen Âge*, 2d ed. (Paris: Fayard, 1992), 1024. The *chanson de mal mariée* here cited ("Amors me fait renvoisier et chanter") is in Bec, *Lyrique française*, 2:18–20.

17. Boulton lists seventy romances with lyric insertions written from the early thirteenth century (Jean Renart's *Roman de la Rose*, dated 1215–28) to 1425 (*The Song in the Story*, 295–97). On Christine's *Dit de la Pastoure* as a version of her own marriage and bereavement, see Paden, "Christine de Pizan."

18. In the *Frauendienst* Ulrich von Lichtenstein intersperses fifty-five lyric compositions within narrative verse: see Reinhold Bechstein, ed., *Ulrich von Lichtenstein Frauendienst* (Leipzig: Brockhaus, 1888), and J. W. Thomas, trans., *Ulrich von Liechtenstein's Service of Ladies* (Chapel Hill: University of North Carolina Press, 1969). Juan Ruiz, in the *Libro de buen amor*, alternates between narrative *cuaderna vía* and twenty-one lyrics: see Raymond S. Willis, ed., *Juan Ruiz: Libro de buen amor* (Princeton: Princeton University Press, 1972). In the *Vita nuova* Dante alternates between prose commentary and lyric poetry: see Tommaso Casini and Luigi Pietrobono, eds., *La Vita Nuova di Dante Alighieri*, 3rd ed. (Firenze: Sansoni, 1964). The first part of the Knight's Tale ends with a "questioun" in the manner of the *jeu parti*:

> Yow loveres axe I now this questioun:
> Who hath the worse, Arcite or Palamoun?
> That oon may seen his lady day by day
> But in prison he moot dwelle alway;
> That oother wher hym list may ride or go,
> But seen his lady shal he nevere mo.
> Now demeth as yow liste, ye that kan,
> For I wol telle forth as I bigan.

(Larry D. Benson, ed., *The Riverside Chaucer*, 3rd ed. [Boston: Houghton Mifflin, 1987], vv. 1347–54).

The Middle English *Owl and the Nightingale* is a late twelfth-century debate poem in which the owl represents traditional morality and the nightingale defends courtly values. The nightingale denies that she teaches "wives to break their vows," protesting, "Through me was wedlock never broken"; she goes on, "But if a wife be weak of will . . . And . . . once perform an act of shame, Shall I for that be held to blame?" (Brian Stone, trans., *The Owl and the Nightingale; Cleanness; St Erkenwald* [Harmondsworth: Penguin, 1971], 228–29; Eric Gerald Stanley, ed., *The Owl and the Nightingale* [London: Nelson, 1960], vv. 1331–36, 1349–56).

19. Though we learn very little about the lady whom Ulrich von Lichtenstein serves, at one point during his adventures "he recounts that he took a few days off to have a pleasant visit with his wife"; see Hubert H. Heinen, "Thwarted

Expectations: Medieval and Modern Views of Genre in Germany," in *Medieval Lyric: Genre in Historical Context*, ed. William D. Paden (Urbana: University of Illinois Press, 2000), 342. Dante fell in love with Beatrice when both were nine years old; his love for her continued, growing ever more sublime, although he married another woman nine years later, and she married another man two years after that—assuming she was in real life Beatrice Portinari, as Boccaccio asserts. Nor was Dante's love defeated by the death of Beatrice at age twenty-four.

20. See Gschwind, *Roman de Flamenca*. The Peire Rogier song, "Ges non puesc en bon vers fallir," is in Nicholson, *Poems of the Troubadour Peire Rogier*, no. 6, stanza 6; it is discussed by Limentani, *L'eccezione narrativa*, 275–84, and Kay, *Subjectivity in Troubadour Poetry*, 207–10.

21. See Paden, review, 104–10.

22. "Ar ab lo coinde pascor," in Ricketts, *Poésies de Guilhem de Montan-hagol*, no. 12, v. 18. "What does Montanhagol mean by *castitatz*? Probably not 'chastity' in the modern sense, but the control and ordering of sexual desire" (Topsfield, *Troubadours and Love*, 247). "Chaste marriage was a designation frequently used by medieval authorities, especially in the high and late Middle Ages, to designate a union in which the individuals were true to their marriage vows" (Dyan Elliott, *Spiritual Marriage: Sexual Abstinence in Medieval Wed-lock* [Princeton: Princeton University Press, 1993], 4).

23. "Chrétien prônait la passion amoureuse aboutissant au mariage et ne concevait pas la possibilité d'un amour vrai en dehors du mariage" (Lazar, *Amour courtois et fin'amors*, 233). The dissonant tradition goes back in lyric form to the bawdy songs of Guilhem IX, who also sings of desire uninhibited by marriage, as in "Ab la dolchor del tems novel"; see Bond, *Poetry of William VII*, no. 10. Of course Guilhem was married himself, like Ulrich von Lichtenstein and the mature Dante Alighieri later on.

Selected Bibliography

Bec, Pierre. *La Lyrique française au moyen âge (XIIe–XIIIe siècles): Contribution à une typologie des genres poétiques médiévaux, Études et textes*. 2 vols. Paris: Picard, 1977–78.

Bond, Gerald A., ed. *The Poetry of William VII, Count of Poitiers, IX Duke of Aquitaine*. New York: Garland, 1982.

Boulton, Maureen Barry McCann. *The Song in the Story: Lyric Insertions in French Narrative Fiction, 1200–1400*. Philadelphia: University of Pennsylvania Press, 1993.

Buffum, Douglas Labaree, ed. *Le Roman de la Violette ou de Gerart de Nevers par Gerbert de Montreuil*. Société des Anciens Textes Français. Paris: Champion, 1928.

Gschwind, Ulrich, ed. *Le Roman de Flamenca: Nouvelle occitane du 13e siècle*. 2 vols. Berne: Francke, 1976.

Kay, Sarah. *Subjectivity in Troubadour Poetry.* Cambridge: Cambridge University Press, 1990.

Lazar, Moshé. *Amour courtois et fin'amors dans la littérature du XIIe siècle.* Paris: Klincksieck, 1964.

Lecoy, Félix, ed. *Jean Renart: Le Roman de la Rose ou de Guillaume de Dole.* Classiques Français du Moyen Âge 91. Paris: Champion, 1962.

Limentani, Alberto. *L'eccezione narrativa: la Provenza medievale e l'arte del racconto.* Torino: Einaudi, 1977.

Monson, Don A. "The Troubadour's Lady Reconsidered Again." *Speculum* 70 (1995): 255–74.

Nicholson, Derek E. T., ed. *The Poems of the Troubadour Peire Rogier.* Manchester: Manchester University Press, 1976.

Paden, William D. "Christine de Pizan as a Reader of the Medieval Pastourelle." In *Conjunctures: Medieval Studies in Honor of Douglas Kelly*, edited by Keith Busby and Norris J. Lacy, 387–405. Amsterdam: Rodopi, 1994.

———. "Old Occitan as a Lyric Language: The Insertions from Occitan in Three Thirteenth-Century French Romances." *Speculum* 68 (1993): 36–53.

———. Review of *Die Troubadourzitate im Breviari d'amor*, edited by Reinhilt Richter, and of *Le Breviari d'amor de Matfre Ermengaud*, edited by Peter T. Ricketts. *Romance Philology* 37 (1983): 104–10.

———. "The Troubadour's Lady: A View through Thick History." *Exemplaria* 11 (1999): 221–44.

Paden, William D., with Mireille Bardin, Michèle Hall, Patricia Kelly, F. Gregg Ney, Simone Pavlovich, and Alice South. "The Troubadour's Lady: Her Marital Status and Social Rank." *Studies in Philology* 72 (1975): 28–50.

Paris, Gaston. "Lancelot du Lac, II: Le Conte de la charrette." *Romania* 12 (1883): 459–534.

Richter, Reinhilt, ed. *Die Troubadourzitate im Breviari d'amor: Kritische Ausgabe der provenzalischen Überlieferung.* Modena: S.T.E.M.-Mucchi, 1976.

Ricketts, Peter T., ed. *Les Poésies de Guilhem de Montanhagol, troubadour provençal du XIIIe siècle.* Toronto: Pontifical Institute of Mediaeval Studies, 1964.

———. *Le Breviari d'amor de Matfre Ermengaud.* Vol. 2, London: Westfield College, 1989; Vol. 3, London: Royal Holloway, 1998; vol. 5, Leiden: Brill, 1976;

Topsfield, L. T. *Troubadours and Love.* Cambridge: Cambridge University Press, 1975.

Part III

Dissenting Women

Lyric and Farce

7

"Fine Words on Closed Ears"

Impertinent Women, Discordant Voices, Discourteous Words

Nadine Bordessoule

Feminist critics are today rereading and analyzing medieval texts with a view to bringing out another, or other, voices. Contained in the text but masked by more than a century of medieval studies that have either manipulated or overlooked the feminine presence, these voices express something that is not stated explicitly, and that therefore eludes both philology and taxonomy. By attempting to set aside the prejudices surrounding a given text or author, such as the one concerning Jean de Meun's "misogyny," I hope to pay attention to the discordant, impertinent, or discourteous voices that tell us something different about women in the Middle Ages.

In the literature of the late Middle Ages—i.e., between about 1275 and 1500—we can detect a desire to put a new slant on the established textual ways of representing women. While still allowing the topoi of courtly poetry to resonate, these writings also seek to give voice to a distinctive tone that uses the traditional expectations of the genre the better to bend them to a more impertinent manner, one less respectful of courtly topoi. The dominant traits and characteristics of the female characters authorized by this new form of expression contributed to the rise of a literature in which the courtly heritage was questioned and challenged and, in some cases, quite simply subverted.

This subversion could be defined as putting in place a mechanism that plays with the readers' expectations by letting them think that what they have before them is a classic courtly text, in the sense that the female character serves as a receptacle, a foil for the narcissistic complaint of the knight or troubadour, but then, having done this, undermines those expectations by endowing the female character with a distinctly discordant discourse or mode of behavior.

This questioning of the assumptions of courtly discourse is possible only when the female characters break with the traditional posture that confined them to providing a supportive listener (as for the poems of the troubadours) or a narcissistically enhancing gaze focused on knightly deeds (as in *Lancelot* when the queen, hidden in the tower, watches her beloved in combat) and begin to speak, at the risk of surprising or shocking or disappointing. I will begin by considering how this dual heritage of Provençal poetry and Arthurian romance is called into question in the thirteenth century following the impact of the *Roman de la Rose*.[1]

In a famous passage in *Roman de la Rose*, la Vieille (the Old Woman), with much experience of life and of men, offers advice on matters of the heart to Bel Accueil (Fair Welcome), a personification of the young Rose for whom she is responsible. Her lengthy admonition warns the innocent young woman of the dangers of love and the misery of marriage that would imprison her youth, concluding that it is better to have many lovers than one jealous husband.

The old woman's advocacy of pleasure and wariness of the bonds of marriage is but one instance of an idea that Jean de Meun expresses on a number of occasions in this work. Other characters, too, manifest their dissatisfaction with the way love is treated in society. Le Jaloux (the Jealous Husband) complains of the perverse effects of the marital institution as a result of which a woman's flighty nature is hidden until the marriage has been sealed. As for Genius, he embarks on a cosmic encomium of universal procreation in which he emphasizes the point that, given the need to perpetuate the work of Nature, it is men's duty to plow the fields, to engender and multiply the generations so as to win ultimate victory over the Grim Reaper.

In relation to the central theme of sexuality and its social regulation, which is questioned or criticized by all the characters of *Le Roman de la Rose* in turn, la Vieille's discourse stands out because the position she expounds is exclusively feminine. Most suggestively, this woman's view makes no allowance for the concerns of jealous husbands or young seducers. Marriage and customs notwithstanding, what matters most

to la Vieille is that women should recover their original liberty to act
and love as they see fit:

D'autre part el sut franches nees;
loi les a condicionees
qui les ostes de leur franchises
ou Nature les avoit mises. (ll. 13845–48)[2]

[Women are freeborn; they've restricted been
By law, that takes away the liberty
That Nature gave them.] (p. 289)

The discourse of la Vieille, seen for many years as one of the central
expressions of Jean de Meun's rabid misogyny, was paradoxically also
the source of a new way of speaking about matters feminine (if not feminist), one that writers in the centuries following would continually
develop. This female desire for independence and fear of constrictive
marital bonds cannot be reduced to a vision of female inconstancy and
infidelity. On the contrary, it is above all a celebration of the freedom of
love, one that seems at first glance to link up with the literary topos of
adulterous and secretive courtly love.

But while her mistrust of marriage recalls the courtly ideal, la Vieille's words reflect a more practical set of intentions aimed at attaining
a less fallacious ideal of love than the one sung by the poets of *fin'amor*.
As adviser to the inexperienced young woman, she goes against all the
rules of seduction as expounded since antiquity in, for example, Ovid's
seminal text in the matter, the *Ars Amatoria*. La Vieille proffers a number of tactical recommendations and seductive practices that belong to
a very different code from the one traditionally used by courtly authors.
Not without venality, the old madam insists that the damsel should win
herself a troupe of rich and generous lovers by using all the artifices of
toilette and appearance.

She goes on to advocate being unfaithful and swearing love to any
number of suitors at the same time, arguing that this is exactly what
men do and merely a question of fighting with the same weapons. She
subtly backs up her case with references to mythology showing the suffering of the women betrayed in love by the heroes Jason and Paris, and
the despair of Dido when, having offered to share her life and kingdom
with him, she is abandoned by Aeneas.

Instead of devoting herself to a single lover, the lady must win herself
as many suitors as she can, keeping them captive with her charms and

transforming her natural beauty into weapons of combat. She must learn to feign laughter and tears, to dress, make herself up, eat with delicacy, and generally behave in such a way as to arouse desire. As a catalogue of tips on hygiene, ways of pushing up pendulous breasts, and recipes for paints and unguents, as well as a treatise on comportment for an inexpert virgin, the old woman's discourse acknowledges two aims. The skillful use of her charms, enhanced if necessary, should enable the young woman to win many lovers and thus enjoy the games of love while at the same time giving her enough control to ensure material comfort for her old age, when the time of love is past.

Reversing the image of female passivity in the face of her many suitors, la Vieille suggests that the lady behave as a hunter rather than as a prey, increasing her chances of pleasure in the present and of a comfortable retirement in the future by pursuing the largest possible number of men:

> Ausinc doit fame par tout tendre
> ses raiz por touz homes prendre . . .
> a touz doit son croc estachier. (ll. 13559–64)

> [A woman everywhere should spread her nets
> To capture all the men; . . .
> She'll try to hook them all.] (p. 283)

In order to get beyond the idea that Jean de Meun's description bespeaks a misogynistic, caricatural vision of artifice and deceit, I would point to the insistence with which, through the character of la Vieille, the author insists on claiming a role for women that allows them to be enterprising and free in their amorous choices—in a word, hunters and not hunted.

In this essay, by reconsidering the *Roman de la Rose* in the light of some recent American feminist critical readings, I will reexamine a number of traditional assumptions that exclude the *Rose* from the category of texts that formulate a progressive discourse on the female condition.

One tendency of this new medievalist criticism is concerned with the representations of women and the place of the feminine in French medieval texts. This enterprise is defined by feminist critics as a back-and-forth between two tendencies, that is to say, ideally, as a creative questioning of the way in which "gender" influences not only medieval thought but also the present-day study of medieval thought. By focusing on the complexity of relations between representations of the feminine and feminine identities, the purpose is to determine the position of the female subject in medieval literary studies.

Gaston Paris, who was the first person to hold a chair of medieval literature in France, is now at the center of a critique that sets out to reread medieval texts by problematizing, for example, courtly love from the viewpoint of woman's subjectivity and woman's relation as subject with the social class into which she was born. However, to appreciate the originality of this undertaking we first need to get beyond the old debate over the misogyny of courtly literature by admitting, for example, that the idealization of woman in Arthurian romance has more to do with a nineteenth-century vision of desirable femininity, conceived at a time when women's social and political status was in upheaval, than with the historical reality of the twelfth century. Also destined for the historical dustbin are the bourgeois definitions of "female nature" and "the eternal feminine" from the first half of the twentieth century. Both are serious obstacles to our understanding of the specificity of the feminine in texts, and even of woman herself, during the Middle Ages.

Once we have understood this, the voice of these women critics can be heard clearly and at the same time situated within the overall movement of the new criticism. Among the researchers working to produce a new reading of femininity, we find, for example, Helen Solterer with her study of verbal insults in medieval disputes,[3] which examines the figure of the woman who answers back like an impertinent Minerva, retorting to the masters of discourse from Jean de Meun to Alain Chartier. Another aspect of this attempt to offer a distinctive reading of the feminine in medieval texts is particularly well illustrated by the arguments put forward by E. Jane Burns[4] when she listens for discordant voices proffered in response to the stereotyped *gentes dames* of the romances and shrews of the fabliaux—a response that is always articulated in the body, through "bodytalk," and not in what is said by or about the characters.

Breaking free of the clichés condemning female sexuality to the closed sphere of conjugal obedience, courtly love, or adultery, which are so often deployed to define and demarcate medieval womanhood, this critic tracks down and interprets those moments where the feminine differs and distances itself, articulates itself in opposition to the traditional roles transmitted via fictive anatomies. Burns reveals this classical portrait of the heroine to be the product of a fictive and idealized composition of the female body. By looking at the physical details of the body, free of fantasy projections, whether in the play of orifices in the fabliaux or the severed tongue of Philomena or the thighs of Iseult, Burns's

feminist analysis underscores a bodily presence that is in profound dis-
agreement with the apparent coherence of a masculine discourse on
women whose paradigmatic instance would be Ovid's tale of Pygmalion.
Whether it is Philomena the violated virgin, Enide the wife and lover,
or Iseult the adulterous queen, these courtly women slip free of the
reductive portraits that make of them magnificent bodies constructed
by male desire and the male gaze, and they begin to move, to relate
"a different (hi)story" from the one assigned to the codified beauty
imposed on them.

For Burns, the adulterous queen Iseult offers the most telling illus-
tration of the double nature of femininity, its resistance to reduction
by discourse. More than Melusine, Iseult is par excellence the woman
with two bodies. It is by disarticulating the courtly rhetoric that seeks
to define Iseult by the position of her body in relation to Tristan or King
Mark that Burns's feminist interpretation clarifies the text and offers a
new reading of Iseult's subjectivity. The ideology of marriage, of king-
ship, and of patriarchy in general has different ways of imposing this
disjunctive logic regarding the way Iseult's body belongs to one man or
another, at the same time defining her identity as faithful courtly queen
or discourteous adulteress with all the social consequences that result
from each position. When accused, Iseult refuses to define herself by
choosing one or the other of the two disjunctive terms (wife or adulteress); she rather replaces them with another definition of her subjectivity
through a conjunction (wife *and* adulteress), thus uniting Tristan and
Mark in one male figure.

Taking the lead from these critical interpretations of classical texts,
it is possible to reread the purportedly misogynistic characterization in
the work of Jean de Meun and his successors in terms that offer an alternative representation of femininity by insisting on the positive questioning of the courtly convention that limits female figures to a purely
passive role.

This amorous dialectic, which reverses the passivity of the Lady and
changes her into a huntress, inspired many fourteenth-century poets. In
La Prise amoureuse (1322) Jehan Acart de Hesdin depicts a young poet
who, like Actaeon, is chased through the woods of Jonece by a pack of
dogs who finally corner him and tear him to pieces. Each of these dogs
metaphorically represents one of the Lady's qualities. Thus *Renom* (Re-
nown) and *Réputation* attack the young man's hearing, *Beauté* blinds
him, *Gouster* and *Taster* (Taste and Savor) madden his senses, and so on,

until the poet is stripped bare. Although its form and intention are courtly, this poem is symptomatic of a significant change in the representation of the Lady during the fourteenth century.

The quarrel provoked by Alain Chartier's text *La Belle Dame sans merci* at the beginning of the fifteenth century clearly illustrates the unease created by this irruption of female discourse that disarticulates the courtly dialogue.[5] Rejecting the alienating rhetoric of the idealization of women in courtly discourse,[6] the Lady asks the insistent lover how much longer he is going to harbor this *fol pensement* [foolish/mad thought]. Then, when he claims to have been wounded by her *doubz regart* [sweet regard], she allows herself this impertinent remark:

Il a grant faim de vivre en deuil
Et fait de son cuer lasche garde
Qui contre ung tout seul regart d'ueil
Sa paix et sa joie ne garde. (233–36)[7]

[He hungers to live in grief and guards his heart lightly, who, against a single eye's glimpse, his peace and happiness cannot retain.]

Her disdainful attitude toward the amorous commonplace that sees the gaze as a mirror of the heart signifies a break with the courtly tradition. The distinction becomes even more marked when the woman adds that "les yuelz sont fait pour regarder" [the eyes are made for looking], replacing the poetic ideal of the eyes as mirror of the soul with a prosaic optical function. This refusal to hear and, consequently, to speak/sing her part in the courtly dialogue enables the Lady to assert a position that we may describe as discourtly (discourteous). Echoing the advice of la Vieille in *Le Roman de la Rose*, the Lady now states her desire to retain her freedom and independence:

Je suis franche et franche vueil estre
Sans moy de mon cuer dassaisir
Pour en faire .j. autre le maistre. (285–88)

[I am free and free want to be, without giving up my heart to make another its master.]

The ensuing dialogue between the jilted lover and the Lady further clarifies the latter's *discourtly* position. In addition to her desire to remain free, she has a sharp distrust of courtly discourse, which she describes as "plaisans bourdes, confites en belles parolles" [pleasant gaffes got up in fine words]. This assertion of independence calls into question the economy of courtly relations by redefining the active/passive roles, or by quite simply canceling the hunted/hunter relation that underpins all courtly discourse. In the process we observe a displacement of the amorous dialogue, which moves away from the play of seduction and the panting quest of desire and toward the annihilation of any romantic possibilities in this refusal of courtly dialogue. As Helen Solterer has shown, what is upsetting in these discourtly words is the fact that the Lady's indifference can be seen shifting toward a potential hostility that could, ultimately, kill the lover: "it showcases a woman able to claim her *franchise*, yet it reprimands her for her liberty's cruel ends—the lover's death."[8]

Generally considered emblematic of the denial of courtly rhetoric, *La Belle Dame* and her quest for *franchise* or frankness prompted many a debate in the fifteenth century.[9] By heralding the end of a static idealization of women, *La Belle Dame sans merci* opened the way to other representations of women that were less cramped and rigid than those articulated by *fin'amor*.

The final step in this process, going from the refusal of love to the betrayal thereof, from discourtly words to discourtly actions, was represented by another author of the late Middle Ages, Antoine de la Sale. Inheriting some of the vulgarity of the female characters of the fabliaux, the heroine of his *Jehan de Saintré* betrays the love of her noble knight with an ignoble, corpulent old abbot. The young knight, able to speak to his belle only in courtly terms, is faced with the inanity of their content when the lady refuses to listen: "Scavez vous autre chanssons canter que ceste? se n'en scavez, si vous taisiez" [Know you no other songs to sing than this one? If not, keep your peace].[10] Emptied of its evocative power, dispossessed of its role as a vector of emotion and reduced by these discourtly women to mere prattle, courtly discourse falls silent. By refusing to hear, by distancing themselves from these "fine words," these female characters at the same time carve out their own discursive space.

The appearance of these impertinent ladies in the literature of the late Middle Ages who, either by refusing to listen or by changing the amorous code, call into question the dominant discursive position of the male characters, coincides with the collapse of the courtly ideal. While most of these texts seem a priori to be based on misogynistic prejudices, we may catch other echoes in the discourse of the female characters. These women are not only expressing their distrust, lassitude, or indifference toward amorous discourse, thus echoing the themes of contemporary fictions,[11] they are also articulating their desire for freedom or their determination to love according to their own code and not according to the courtly code of a bygone age.

NOTES

1. See Hicks, *Débat*.
2. Guillaume de Lorris and Jean de Meun, *Roman de la Rose*. The line numbers in this section refer to the Lecoy edition, the page numbers to the Robbins translation.
3. Solterer, *Master and Minerva*.
4. Burns, *Bodytalk*.
5. Solterer, *Master and Minerva*, 177–99.
6. "Courtliness is, at bottom, a competing mode of coercion that will, alongside misogyny, continue to hide its disenfranchising effects behind the seduction of courtesy, and thus dominate the discourse of lovers in the West" (Bloch, *Medieval Misogyny*, 197).
7. All quotations of Chartier's *La Belle Dame sans merci* are from the Champion edition. The translation of this passage is by Kathy M. Krause. Unless otherwise stated, translations from the *Belle Dame* are by Charles Penwarden.
8. Solterer, *Master and Minerva*, 181.
9. Many poems followed Alain Chartier's example and represented the theme of the lover spurned by a damsel who prefers her independence. See Piaget, "*La Belle Dame.*"
10. de la Sale, *Jehan de Saintré*, 273.
11. See, for example, the role played by the French actress Jeanne Balibar in the film *J'ai horreur de l'Amour* (I Loathe Love), 1997.

SELECTED BIBLIOGRAPHY

Bloch, R. Howard. *Medieval Misogyny and the Invention of Western Romantic Love*. Chicago: University of Chicago Press, 1991.
Burns, E. Jane. *Bodytalk: When Women Speak in Old French Literature*. Philadelphia: University of Pennsylvania Press, 1993.
Burns, E. Jane, Sarah Kay, Roberta Krueger, and Helen Solterer. "Feminism and the Discipline of Old French Studies: Une Bele Disjointure." In *Medievalism and the Modernist Temper*, edited by R. Howard Bloch and Stephen G. Nichols, 225–68. Baltimore: Johns Hopkins University Press, 1995.
Chartier, Alain. *La Belle Dame sans merci*. Paris: Champion, 1973.
de la Sale, Antoine. *Le Petit Jehan de Saintré*. Edited by J. Misrahi and C. A. Knudson. Geneva: Droz, 1978.
de Lorris, Guillaume, and Jean de Meun. *Le Roman de la Rose*. Edited by F. Lecoy. 3 vols. Paris: Champion, 1965–70.

————. *The Romance of the Rose*. Translated by Harry W. Robbins. Edited and with an introduction by Charles W. Dunn. New York: E. P. Dutton, 1962.

Hicks, Eric, ed. *Le débat sur le Roman de la Rose*. Paris: Champion, 1977.

Piaget, A. "*La Belle Dame sans merci* et ses imitations," *Romania* 30 (1901): 22–48; 31 (1902): 315–49; 33 (1904): 179–208; 34 (1905): 375–428, 559–97.

Solterer, Helen. *The Master and Minerva: Disputing Women in French Medieval Culture*. Berkeley and Los Angeles: University of California Press, 1995.

8

Poetic Justice

The Revenge of La Guignarde in the *Livre des Cent Ballades*

Sally Tartline Carden

The *Livre des Cent Ballades*, a lyric collection composed in 1389 by multiple authors, recounts the adventures of a young knight about to be initiated into the mysteries and pleasures of love. In its most complete version, this collection actually contains a total of 113 ballads, of which the final 13 are responses to the original hundred.[1] The protagonist and narrator of the story, Jean le Seneschal, also serves as the primary author of the text. The two major narrative episodes of the *Livre* divide the text approximately in half. The first 50 ballads describe the narrator's encounter with an older knight, Hutin de Vermeilles, who offers conventional advice proclaiming Loyalty as the guiding principle in all amorous relations. Ballads LV through XCVIII introduce the only female voice in the text, that of la Guignarde. She too attempts to advise Jean in matters of love, but suggests strategies that contradict the wise counsel of Hutin and offend the young knight's courtly sensibilities. Frequently, critics pass over la Guignarde as a conventional portrait of anticourtly behavior in the tradition of the *entremetteuse*, such as la Vieille in the *Roman de la Rose*. However, her role in this text extends well beyond such conventions, as she participates as an equal in a courtly dialogue modeled on the *jeu-parti*, which echoes and rewrites elements of the *pastourelle*. She challenges and destabilizes the foundations of courtly language, revealing dangerous inconsistencies that threaten to undermine the entire system.

The structure of the *Livre des Cent Ballades* resembles that of the *jeu-parti*, a type of poetic debate inspired by the Provençal *partimens* and practiced by French noblemen primarily during the second half of the thirteenth century.[2] Social constraints regulated access to this dialogue. According to Mirela Saïm, "le droit du sujet à la parole dialogique est fondé sur sa position dans l'ordre social: ce droit constitue *une mise en demeure discursive de l'hégémonie sociale*" [the right of the subject to dialogue is founded on his position in the social order: this right constitutes a *discursive formalization of social hegemony*].[3] In the case of the *Livre des Cent Ballades*, an indirect debate develops between the knight Hutin and la Guignarde, whose arguments the narrator, protagonist, and author, Jean le Seneschal, pits against one another. This mediation is essential, since it would be highly unusual for a woman such as la Guignarde to participate in a poetic debate of this type.[4] Her gender and social status preclude her participation in such a traditionally male domain.

Traditionally, each lyric debate was followed by an appeal to judges who were charged with deciding in favor of one side or the other. In the case of the *jeu-parti*, this decision existed outside the text itself and frequently was never rendered or not recorded.[5] In order to resolve the conflict between her advice and that of her opponent Hutin, la Guignarde suggests an appeal to outside authorities—other courtly lovers—to pronounce judgment. This judgment materializes in the thirteen response poems appended to the *Livre*. Although these poems represent the work of thirteen different men, none of whom participated in the writing of the original text, they play a fundamental role in the development of the *Livre des Cent Ballades*, particularly with regard to the role of la Guignarde. The configuration of the material book itself illustrates the critical importance of these additional ballads: several blank pages (a number of which now contain the responses) follow the *explicit*, ready to receive the responses solicited in the last of the initial 100 ballads.

Because la Guignarde's discourse responds to and opposes that of Hutin, it is essential to examine first the material and presentation of these initial arguments. In the first ballad of the collection, Jean reveals that he relates events that occurred approximately six months prior to the composition of the ballads. The scene he describes resembles a conventional *pastourelle* opening. While riding his horse one day between Angers and Pont-de-Cé, he was approached by an older knight who, recognizing the innocence of youth, immediately engaged him in a conversation about love. Although Jean himself does not identify this man, he is later identified in one of the response ballads as "le bon Hutin," once celebrated by Christine de Pizan as an exemplary knight and lover:

> . . . bon Hutin exemple
> De Vermeilles, ou bonté ot si ample
> Qu'oncques nulz homs n'y sceut que reprochier,
> Ne nul mesdit en diffamant n'ot chier;
> Souvrainement porta honneur aux femmes,
> Ne peust ouïr d'elles blasme ou diffames;
> Chevalier fu preux, sage, et bien amé,
> Pour ce fu il et sera renommé.[6]

> [. . . good, exemplary Hutin de Vermeilles, who possessed such great goodness that never could he reproach any man, nor did he hold dear any negative words in slander. He brought unequaled honor to women. He could never hear them blamed or defamed. He was a brave, well-advised, and well-loved knight. On account of this, he was and will be celebrated.]

Hutin de Vermeilles indeed appears worthy of this reputation, with an illustrious military career and marriage to Marguerite de Bourbon, a member of the royal house of France. Jean himself recognizes Hutin's status and addresses him appropriately as "sire." In addition, he describes his counselor in terms similar to those of Christine de Pizan:

> [Le] chevalier qui sans pareil
> Fu, ce m'est viz; de grace plain,
> Beauz et preuz, devot et mondain
> En fait, en parler gracieux. (51, vv. 3–6)[7]

> [The knight who was without equal, in my opinion, full of benevolence, handsome and brave, pious and worldly in actions, and gracious in speech.]

Hutin exhibits a similar respect and affection for his protégé, referring to him frequently with variations of "frere."[8]

Hutin's female counterpart also remains unidentified in the hundred ballads. She is merely one among others in a "compagnie . . . De gens gracieux et plaisans" (53, v. 3) [assembly of charming and agreeable people]. Regnaut de Trie reveals her "identity" in the first response ballad, calling her la Guignarde or the Flirt. In responses 6 and 12, she is further described as "la Guignarde jolie" [the pretty Flirt] and "la Guignarde au muable talent" [the Flirt with fickle desires]. Although both characters represent hyperbolic stereotypes, the exaggeration clearly privileges the male character. The fact that the (male) readers of the *Livre des Cent Ballades* attribute a precise, historically accurate, exemplary identity to the male character, while identifying his female rival simply by an undetermined, impersonal, and somewhat pejorative epithet, reveals the force of the message being communicated either overtly or covertly in Jean's text. For the authors of this collection, the female figure is associated with anticourtly values, which precludes full participation in this profoundly male domain of courtly behavior. The negative connotations associated with la Guignarde are taken to the extreme in a rubric accompanying one miniature in Manuscript A, which goes so far as to label her Maquerelle, or procuress, a judgment hardly supported by textual evidence.

A certain ambiguity characterizes this negative portrait of la Guignarde, however, because she is described as a member of courtly society entitled to all the rights and privileges thereof. In spite of his opposition to her advice, Jean refers to her respectfully as "dame,"[9] an appropriate form of address for any lady at court. For her part, la Guignarde opens her dialogue with Jean using terms that might indicate a romantic relationship between the two, addressing him as "beau sire" (ballad 55) and "beaux amis doulx" (59). On one occasion she repeats the term used by Hutin, "frere," which seems to indicate that she and the knight enjoy an equal status. As her discourse develops, the term "filz" replaces all other forms of address. This shift establishes a balance of power that favors la Guignarde. She plays on this superiority, at one point calling Jean "couart" because he fears declaring his love openly to the lady he desires. La Guignarde and Jean may be social equals, but in matters of love, she, like Hutin, reigns supreme as the voice of experience.

In spite of her purported authority in such matters, la Guignarde's arguments fall on deaf ears, because Hutin has already persuaded the young knight to follow his example and submit to the God of Love. Hutin's encounter with the narrator develops an ideal model of courtly behavior, describing the advantages to be gained through loyalty, and condemning the evils of unfaithful love. He describes a conventional portrait of a young lover whose pleasant demeanor, judicious use of words, and active participation in courtly activities such as tournaments and dances will endear him to all, and especially to the lady whose favors he desires. A true dialogue between the older and younger knight never actually materializes, because the advice of Hutin takes the form more of a lecture than a conversation. Ceding to a higher authority, Hutin quotes the advice offered to him by the God of Love. Although love initially dominates the discussion, the commandments of Amours soon become reoriented toward issues of military service and *prouesse*. The discussion becomes rather technical, as the God of Love recommends situating oneself in the *avant-garde* and *guet*, positions that tend to provide more adventure and consequently more opportunities to increase one's reputation. He also describes methods of undertaking and defending against a siege and proclaims naval battles the most noteworthy of all types of military engagement. In addition, he recommends to all young lovers

De hanter le mestier de guerre
Soies sages, preux, et preudom
Ainsi pourras honneur conquerre. (12, vv. 18–20)

[Frequent the activities of war, be noble, well-informed, and brave. In this way you will be able to gain honor.]

He then suggests military exploits in the Holy Land—in Syria, Arabia, or Turkey—as appropriate substitutes if war is not being waged closer to home. Successful combat against the Turks in particular, who have become "de guerre plus adurée" (14, v. 21) [more hardened to war] will double one's reputation. This endorsement of military action represents a significant transformation of the traditional discourse of the God of Love, as the pursuit of personal glory replaces a seemingly forgotten object of love. The traditional topos of *prouesse* as a means of winning the lady here is rewritten, as the lady's favor becomes only a secondary consequence of military success.

This intrusion of *chevalerie* into the domain of courtly love emphasizes the male perspective being developed in the collection and further specifies it as that of male noblemen. Only male members of the nobility may participate in these types of armed activity. Having thus established his authority in such matters by combining his personal experience and reputation with the words of the God of Love himself, Hutin promises that his past mirrors Jean's future if Jean promises "tout pour Loiauté maintenir" (21, v. 13) [everything to uphold Loyalty]. He concludes by warning against Fausseté:

Et comme elle est desavenant
En corps de lignage vaillant
Et en cuer qui monter voudroit
A hautesse le chemin droit
Qui affiert a chevalerie. (50, vv. 4–7)

[And how it is unsuitable in a body with noble lineage and in a heart that would like to go up the straight path of glory which belongs to knighthood.]

Once again, Hutin highlights the importance of social status, based on noble lineage passed from father to son. Inspired by these arguments, Jean pledges himself to the service of Amours, indicating his desire to uphold his commandments, and the two part company.

After a brief reflection on the knight's advice and a declaration of his intentions to uphold Loiauté, Jean finds himself amidst a courtly assembly along the banks of the Loire. Uninterested by these men and women, he loses himself in thoughts of his beloved, while gazing into the waters of the river:

En pensant a ma dame belle.
Car plus me plaisoit ce penser
Que tous les biens qu'autres donner
Me pourroient, car tant amoie. (54, vv. 3–6)

[Thinking of my beautiful lady, because this thought pleased me more than all the rewards that any others could give me, for I loved so much.]

Nearby, one of the ladies notices him and, suspecting love as the source of his musings, decides to question him directly. She then offers advice for the same reasons as Hutin, in an attempt to enlighten and form youthful inexperience:

Et pour ce que vous voy ester
En jeunesse, conseil donner
Vous vouldray bien bon. (55, vv. 28–30)

[And because I recognize your youthfulness, I would like to give you very good advice.]

At this point, the protagonist finds himself in a position almost identical to that of the opening ballad which describes his encounter with Hutin. Seeing him lost in thought and suspecting the cause, an older, experienced individual approaches and offers advice about love. Jean has allowed Hutin to speak with no resistance, offering only a minimal reply to his initial inquiry:

«A quoy pensez vous, amis chiers?»
Je lui dis que je ne savoie.
Lors m'aparla trop volentiers. (1, vv. 5–7)

["What are you thinking about, dear friend?" I told him that I did
not know. Then he spoke to me very willingly.]

In the case of la Guignarde, however, he resists such a dialogue, annoyed
by the unsolicited intrusion into his pleasant thoughts. These contradictory reactions may reflect the fact that Hutin appears before Jean falls in
love, with him "en voie Amoureuse" (1, vv. 9–10) [on the loving path]
but not yet having arrived. Jean pledges himself to the God of Love in
ballad 51 and uses for the first time the verb *aimer* in the first person
in ballad 52, where he explicitly mentions "ma dame." So when la Guignarde appears, she finds Jean actually in love, not merely in the state of
indifference that characterized him earlier. She represents a double threat
to his happiness, as a woman who challenges, both with her attention
and with her doctrine, the sovereignty of his lady. In addition, he may be
resisting her unorthodox participation in a courtly activity traditionally
reserved for men—the poetic debate.

Attempting to ignore this affront to his serene contemplations, the
young man remains silent. His resistance does not, however, discourage
la Guignarde, who finally succeeds in eliciting a response, however
minimal:

Et doucement me demanda
Se mon cuer bien et fort amoit:
Lors dit «Oÿ» car vray estoie. (56, vv. 25–27)

[And sweetly she asked me if my heart loved well and deeply: Then
I said "Yes" because it was true.]

She aggressively pursues the conversation, forcing Jean to reveal the
nature of his love and obliging him to hear her opinions.

The ensuing dialogue represents a much more balanced exchange
than the conversation between Jean and Hutin, although la Guignarde
clearly dominates the discussion. She initially poses a series of questions
designed to ascertain the lover's character. Twice Jean attempts to put
an end to the exchange, but each time his female counselor ignores him.
La Guignarde discovers that the young knight has not yet declared his
love to his lady and subsists on Esperance alone. She inquires whether
he would pursue the favors of another lady should she express an interest in him. Jean vehemently declares that he will love none other than
his chosen lady. When asked if he would renounce this love if the lady
refused his advances, he again states that he will remain faithful under
any circumstances, for "autre ne quier, ne veul amer" (60, v. 16) [I do not
desire or want to love another]. La Guignarde then explains to Jean that

he has no idea what suffering will result from this "fol penser" [crazy thinking] and proceeds to elaborate her theory of love that provides the only path to fulfillment.

Reversing the arguments of Amours and Hutin, la Guignarde advises that one must "priez partout" (61, v. 35) [court everywhere] and seek pleasure with many women. Instead of recommending submission to the God of Love, she insists that one must resist this act of weakness and "garde[r] qu'Amours ne vous surmonte" (61, v. 21) [watch that love does not dominate you]. Like her masculine counterpart, she does, however, link the discussion of love to issues of *prouesse*, honor, and reputation. La Guignarde explains that those who are not controlled by love will seek out adventure and chivalric combat for which they will be richly rewarded. Having lovers in many places, they can satisfy themselves anywhere without compromising their duty. The knight who loves too much, on the contrary, will be unable to remain separated from the object of his affection long enough to accomplish anything noteworthy. His heart will lead him to return too early, thus missing out on the military action, and his reputation will suffer in favor of the others who return successful. The ladies, of course, will prefer those with a greater reputation.

However, whereas the advice of Hutin recommended the pursuit of *prouesse* as a sufficiently noble enterprise in and of itself, la Guignarde sees it in the more traditional sense as a means to gaining the lady's favor. Success with one woman not only will allow a lover to become more skillful at seduction but also will cause his reputation *among women* to grow. This ultimately is the opinion that matters, since the ladies hold exclusive control over the rewards the lover seeks. The resulting confidence will inspire the lover to undertake more military actions, which will in turn contribute to his reputation. A self-perpetuating cycle of fulfillment develops, from which the loyal lover must necessarily be excluded. Says la Guignarde, "Qui partout seme, partout queult" (91, v. 12) [He who sows everywhere reaps everywhere]. Jean himself expresses opposition to this idea in the refrain to ballad 68, where he declares: "Tout doit perdre qui tout convoite" [He who desires everything must lose everything].

La Guignarde manipulates several of Hutin's main arguments to suit her rather divergent purpose. Whereas Hutin entreats Jean to flatter his lady and "loe ses faiz, ses riz, ses jeux" (5, v. 26) [praise her actions, her smiles, her loving ways], la Guignarde easily applies this same technique to many women: "Loez *leurs* fais et *leur* beauté" (62, v. 18, emphasis mine) [praise *their* acts and *their* beauty]. She also adopts her predecessor's concern for discretion. Amours and Hutin teach what all courtly lovers know: the love relationship must remain a secret. Among his commandments, the God of Love includes "d'estre secret maintien les voies" (7, v. 15) [maintain the paths of discretion]. If the love relationship is discovered, the *médisants* certainly will attempt to destroy it. La Guignarde recommends that everything be undertaken "secretement," declaring "Moult est avenant faire et taire" (63, v. 24) [It is quite suitable to act and be silent]. Her concern lies not specifically with the *médisants*, but rather with the other women involved who might discover a lover's multiple attachments. Those who love too much in one place cannot adequately control their emotions and end up revealing their feelings to everyone, violating the rule of courtly discretion, inviting the wrath of the *médisants*, and putting the lady's reputation in jeopardy.

The most dangerous and overtly anticourtly aspects of la Guignarde's discourse involve the use of deception, and deceptive language in particular, to accomplish the romantic goals she champions. Appearances play an essential role in a lover's behavior. She recommends maintaining an air of innocence that borders on naïveté in order to avoid suspicion. This outward appearance, however, conceals "secretes sentelles" (66, v. 23) [secret paths] by which the clever lover reaches the hearts of many women. According to la Guignarde, this deception does not constitute disloyalty if, when with each lady, a lover devotes himself completely to her:

Car desloiauté tant ne quant
N'a en plusieurs femmes amer
Et faire a chascune semblant
D'elle seule cherir, doubter
Servir, obeïr, honnorer. (85, vv. 17–21)

[Because there is no disloyalty at all in loving many women and pretending to each one to cherish, respect, serve, obey, and honor only her.]

Ambiguous language supports such false appearances:

Promettre pouez seurement
A chascune qui nom d'ami
Vous dourra, que si loiaument
L'amez, qu'en tout ce monde cy
N'amez rien autant comme li;

Et certes lui direz voir
Tant que serez en ce parti,
D'autre amour ne vous peut chaloir.
S'ainsi le juriëz a cent,
A nulle ariëz menti. (86, vv. 1–10)

[You can certainly promise to each one who will call you friend
that you love her faithfully and that in all of this world you love
nothing as much as her. And surely you will speak the truth to
her. As long as you are in this situation, no other love can interest
you. If you made such a promise to a hundred, you would have
lied to none.]

La Guignarde thus promises success through the use of deceptive
language. This results in the destabilization of courtly discourse and the
destruction of the conventions that guaranteed the truth of the love declaration. Courtly language no longer guarantees courtly behavior. This
type of behavior recalls that of the chevalier in the *pastourelle*. In one of
the most common types of *pastourelle*, a knight happens upon a young
and naive shepherdess whom he attempts to seduce with flattery, gifts,
or promises of marriage, all delivered in attractive and conventional
courtly language. The force of this type of poem lies in the opposition
between the social classes to which the two characters belong as well as
in the contradiction between the knight's status and his patently offen-
sive and boorish behavior.[10] The authors of the *Livre des Cent Ballades*
reverse this situation by regendering the dominant figure. Here it is the
older, experienced woman, la Guignarde, who encounters "le jeune naïf"
and attempts to seduce him, not with her body, but with her rhetoric and
intellect. Her arguments, though, embody exactly the type of behavior
exhibited by the knights of the *pastourelle*. In order to "rescue" Jean
from this apparent threat, like the shepherds who frequently arrive just
in time to preserve the virtue of the shepherdess, his peers are called
in to help him resist la Guignarde. Philippe d'Artois, Bouciquaut, and
Creseques all appear in the final two ballads to assure Jean that the uncourtly advice offered by the brazen woman should be rejected in favor
of Hutin. Reinforcements arrive in the response ballads, with seven out
of thirteen voices declaring themselves also supporters of Loyalty.

When Jean rejects la Guignarde's teachings, he relates the story of his
encounter with Hutin, whose advice, unlike hers, pleased him greatly.
She insists on knowing the identity of this individual and a detailed account of his arguments. Jean obliges, thus initiating an indirect debate

between the two counselors. Jean's recourse to a "real-life" example to support his position inspires la Guignarde to seek similar support for her side, asserting that "Ainçois qu'un y eust bien trouvé, / A un miller en prendroit mal" (96, vv. 9–10) [Before one person found good in such a situation, a thousand would be miserable]. As a way of proving this assertion, she proposes a judgment of the debate, seeking the authority she lacks among Jean's peers. The adversaries agree to solicit opinions "aus bons compagnons esliz, / Qu'amors a en ses las mis" (97, vv. 6–7) [of the worthy chosen companions whom the God of Love has caught in his trap]. This call for judgment initiated by la Guignarde seems to signal the final step in the marginalization of the only female voice (albeit a fictive female voice created by male authors) in the text. Because the opinions to be solicited belong to male lovers only,[11] she appears to argue herself right out of the picture, effectively ending female participation of any kind in this debate to which she seemingly had no claim to begin with. However, the dialogic dynamic and structural principles that define the collection and the response series lead to quite a different conclusion.

Jean agrees to propose a judgment to determine which brings more joy to lovers,

Loiauté ou Faux Semblant
En amant
Fausseté la losengiere. (98, vv. 10–12)

[Loyalty or False Appearance in love, Falseness the slanderer.]

According to la Guignarde, however, he naively misinterprets her arguments. She insists that she never glorified Fausseté at the expense of Loiauté and indeed recognizes the premier role of the latter:

Ains la [Fausseté] dois mettre derriere
Et baniere
De Loiauté mettre avant,
Ou droit est, c'est ma priere. (98, vv. 25–28)

[Rather, you must put Falseness behind and the banner of Loyalty in front where it belongs. This is my desire.]

She refuses to acknowledge that the behavior she encourages, "pourchaçant / En mains lieux joie pleniere" (98, vv. 32–33) [pursuing complete joy in many places], constitutes "Fausseté la losengiere." La Guignarde engages in a battle of semantics that Jean is ill-equipped to join.

The debate continues following the simple opposition developed by Hutin between Loiauté and Fausseté.

The penultimate ballad of the *Livre des Cent Ballades* describes the first judgment rendered in the debate. Predictably, Philippe d'Artois, the comte d'Eu, aligns himself with Jean and Hutin:

> Enquestay de ceste affaire
> Au conte d'Eu, que je truiz
> Pretz et duiz
> A toute loiauté faire. (99, vv. 9–12)

[I interrogated the count of Eu concerning this matter and found him ready and willing to do anything for loyalty.]

Together these allies then secure the support of Jean Bouciquaut and Jean de Creseques, both well-known knights of the royal court. Thus the anonymous fictional protagonist again associates himself with historically real individuals known for their role at court as well as their military exploits. This association further valorizes the male characters as "true" in opposition to the fictive uncertainty embodied by la Guignarde.

Bouciquaut and Creseques not only declare themselves partisans of loyalty, they also signal their role in the composition of the *Livre des Cent Ballades*, stating: "Par nous fu ce livre estruiz" (99, v. 34) [This book was constructed by us]. This verse contains the only reference in the entire collection to the actual composition of the text. The identification of multiple authors creates a certain ambiguity in this text that from the outset defined itself as a narrative in the first person based on the experiences of a particular individual. The exact nature of the collaboration remains unclear, although stylistic features support the hypothesis that the text was written by a single author. This does not, of course, preclude the possibility of contributions by multiple individuals in the conception, composition, or revision of the *Cent Ballades*.

The final ballad foregrounds the collaborative nature of this collection with the appeal by the authors to the public, requesting the continuation of the debate with judgments written in ballad form. The authors (no longer with the participation of la Guignarde) seek a truthful declaration "sans decevoir" (100, v. 23) [without deception]—one that rejects the trickery and deceit endorsed by their female rival. The judgment lacking in the *jeu-parti* here appears within the text itself as well as outside the textual boundaries in the thirteen response ballads.

Of the thirteen respondents to the appeal of Jean and his collabora-
tors, seven declare themselves openly in support of Hutin and loyalty;
three others, including two abandoned by Amours on account of their
vieillesce (response 6, v. 23), take the side of la Guignarde, leaving three
who remain undecided or do not directly support either Hutin or la Guignarde. Traditionally, critics have accepted the quantitative advantage
of Hutin's supporters in the responses as an uncontestable judgment
in favor of loyalty. In the introduction to his edition, Gaston Raynaud
declares: "On sait qu'elle ne réussit pas à convaincre son interlocuteur,
non plus que plupart des autres *amoureux* consultés. La poétique du
temps, plus encore que leur penchant personnel, interdisait de porter
un autre jugement" (p. xl) [We know that she did not succeed in convincing her interlocutor any more than the majority of the other lovers
consulted. The poetics of the time, even more than their personal preference, made it impossible to render any other judgment]. This "rush to
judgment" by Raynaud fails to understand the significance of the message communicated by la Guignarde throughout the text as well as the
subtle reinforcement of this message found in the responses. Although
the proponents of loyalty do enjoy a slight numerical superiority, the
uncertainty and instability of language created by the minority nullify
this apparent advantage.

In one of the undecided votes, found in response ballad 8, Jehan de
Mally asserts the advantages of both sides. For those who choose to love
only one, "De toutes meurs Loiauté va devant" (v. 17) [Before all rules,
Loyalty goes in front]. On the other hand, if a lover can successfully
attend to "cent dames, et bien, et largement" (v. 24) [a hundred ladies
well and generously], he should reap great rewards. If he then decides
he wants to devote himself to only one lady, he should abandon this
practice. The poet concludes by stating that he cannot judge such an
important issue, and everyone must decide for himself:

Ne ne me sçay auquel plus accorder
Et pour ce dy: selon mon sentement,
A chascun d'eulx feroit il bon sembler. (response 8, vv. 8–10)

[I do not know which I should favor more and for this reason I say:
According to my feeling, each one should do what seems best.]

Interestingly, Jehan de Mally's argument in favor of loyalty echoes la
Guignarde's defense of her position when confronted by Jean's accusations of falsity. She also recommends that "Loiauté va devant," but only
to lead the way for Fausseté, which follows closely behind.

Two of the responses that do not subscribe directly to either la Guignarde's or Hutin's view present a much more troubling analysis of the situation. In poem 7, which occupies the exact midpoint of the response series, Monseigneur de Berry (Duke Jean de Berry) enthusiastically proclaims, "On peut l'un dire et l'autre doit on faire" (v. 30) [You can say one thing and should do the other]. He suggests a strategy based on deceptive language that separates the words from the actions they represent:

Dire qu'on veult seulement Louiauté
Et que c'est droiz que tout cuer s'i atire;
Mais du faire n'aiez ja volenté. (response 7, vv. 11–13)

[Say that one wants only Loyalty and that it is right that all hearts aspire to this, but do not ever do it willingly.]

In the final poem of the collection, the Bastard de Coucy presents a similarly polyvalent judgment. His ballad resembles a conventional lover's complaint, describing amorous suffering so painful only death can bring relief. All of these declarations occur in a slightly modified context, however, as he concludes each stanza with the refrain "Ains dit on, mais n'en sera riens" (response 13, vv. 8, 16, 24, 28) [So they say, but nothing will come of it]. His strategy resembles that suggested by la Guignarde in ballad 64 in the case of a lady's refusal:

Donnez en a Amours le blasme
En luy priant que vous pardonne;
Dittes que tant est belle et bonne
Qu'au fort amer la vous convient. (64, vv. 5–8)

[Give Love the blame for it, while begging that she forgive you; Say that she is so beautiful and good that it is appropriate that you love her so passionately.]

The lover must manipulate words to his advantage.

The most serious threat to the destabilization of courtly discourse occurs towards the end of this final response poem. After describing language and behavior designed to deceive the lady whose favors one seeks, the Bastard de Coucy comments directly on the debate between Hutin and la Guignarde, highlighting the risks of deceptive language:

Veïr pouez de ceulx qui ont plaisir
A fort promettre et tenir pou convent,
Et qui semblant font qu'ilz veulent morir

Pour bien amer; et puis font serement
Que la Guignarde n'ensuyront nullement,
Hutin croyront, estre veulent des siens
A tousjours maiz et amer loyaulment:
Ains dist on, mais il n'en sera riens. (response 13, vv. 17–24)

[You can see from those who enjoy promising a lot and keeping their word very little and who pretend that they want to die on account of love; then they swear that they will not follow la Guignarde in any way. They will believe Hutin; they want to be one of his forever and love loyally. So they say, but nothing will come of it.]

This analysis condemns as false not only la Guignarde and her supporters but also the voices that apparently condemn her. Although their language appears to support Hutin, their actions may not follow accordingly. As the final ballad of the collection, the Bastard de Coucy's words recontextualize everything that precedes and force a circumspect rereading of the entire *Livre*.

These proponents of uncourtly behavior and deceptive speech distinguish themselves from traditional anticourtly figures such as la Vieille in the *Roman de la Rose* or the *losengiers* of the lyric tradition because they are historically real male members of the most prestigious courts of France. These noblemen can counter the authority of Hutin on his own terms, as la Guignarde herself was unable to do. She cannot argue as one of Jean's peers; access to the debate depends on gender and social status. One must bear in mind, of course, that this entire exchange constitutes a social game, with fictions responding to other fictions. It would be naive to suggest that the respondents express their true feelings in these ballads. Seven of the thirteen respondents, including the duc de Berry, would later become charter members of the Cour d'Amour, dedicated to loyalty and the service of women. However, the overt support of uncourtliness proffered by a court figure of the stature of Jean de Berry must be recognized as a significant departure from courtly literary conventions. This innovation becomes especially significant with regard to the establishment of la Guignarde's authority.

The spatial distribution of the responses that either reject Hutin's and Jean's discourse on loyalty or threaten the foundations thereof determines the ultimate failure of the authors' quest for truth. The ballads in the critical initial, medial, and final positions (one, seven, and thirteen) destabilize the system and undermine the truth value of the entire collection. The very first response ballad firmly situates the author on the side of la Guignarde, whom the poet identifies for the first time in his refrain: "Je me tendray a la Guignarde" (vv. 12, 24, 36) [I will uphold la Guignarde]. The central and final ballads discussed above suggest a divorce between words and actions. Jehan de Mally, the author immediately following Berry, remains indecisive, perhaps troubled by the latter's assertions. Moreover, when Ivry declares in the next ballad, "car / Je me tieng et me tendray a une" (response 9, v. 10) [I remain and will remain faithful to one], the reader can no longer accept the statement at face value. Perhaps following the advice of the duc de Berry, he says one thing but does another. The arrangement of these responses with opposing voices structuring the series recontextualizes the debate, challenging the judgment offered in the closing ballad of the original hundred.

The conception of the collection as a structured whole rather than as a series of unrelated fragments allows this dynamic to function effectively in the response ballads. It is interesting to speculate on the origin of this strategy, given the multiple authors of the *Livre* itself and the attribution of each response ballad to a different individual. The fact that several respondents refer to earlier responses in their ballads indicates either a collective activity or the circulation of the responses among the members of a group. The arrangement of the responses is neither random (recorded, as it were, in the order that they were received by a scribe) nor the responsibility of the authors of the *Livre des Cent Ballades*. Testifying to this hypothesis is the seemingly impossible chronological ordering of the first three ballads, with the author of the third responding to and naming the two preceding poets. Also, the author of response ballad 6 refers to the opinion offered in response 9, indicating that the poets situated earlier in the series had access to the later poems. Thus the ordering of the responses clearly is designed to be meaningful, situating opposing voices at critical points in the series.

In his introduction to the *Livre des Cent Ballades*, Raynaud suggests that, following the composition of the first hundred ballads during the imprisonment of the authors (Jean le Seneschal, Jean Bouciquaut, Jean de Creseques, and Philippe d'Artois) in Egypt, a poetic debate similar to a *puy* (a poetry festival/competition) took place in Avignon from October 31 through November 6, 1390, during which the response poems were written. Several of the respondents are known to have accompanied Charles VI on this particular visit to the South. Raynaud offers further evidence that the remaining response poets probably also attended in the retinues of various noblemen such as the duc de Bourbon and the sire de Coucy.[12] It is impossible to verify that the authors indicated in the text actually composed the poems attributed to them, although this type of poetic exchange among noblemen was very popular during the period. If one rejects Raynaud's theory, the judgment ballads may be seen either as a group of independent responses gathered and assembled by a scribe at a later date or as the fictional creation of an individual poet who invented the entire series. In any case, the meaningful ordering of the responses in the manuscript remains central to the discussion.

The compiler of the response ballads, whether scribe or poet, clearly counters the intention of the original four authors, to uphold the virtues of loyalty in love. This movement responds to arguments presented by la Guignarde and builds on evidence contained within the judgment ballads themselves. A brief consideration of the references incorporated into the response ballads reveals a significant dichotomy between the two groups. The proponents of loyalty who uphold the ideal embodied by Hutin mention almost exclusively other members of their restricted community and the main characters involved in the debate. For example, in response ballad 3, Monseigneur de Touraine entreats Regnaut de Trie and Chambrillac, both authors of responses, to abandon their position and support loyalty. In his ballad, the sixth, Tignonville mentions eight of the authors participating in the debate of the *Cent Ballades*.[13]

Interestingly, however, the supporters of la Guignarde employ literary references to the exclusion of individual participants in the debate. These poets mention la Guignarde herself and Hutin who, as protagonists in the *Livre des Cent Ballades*, also qualify in this category. In the first response ballad, Regnaut de Trie indicates that Hutin's loyalty ultimately destroyed him. He offers further proof of the dangers inherent in loyal love with the example of Kahedin, a character in the *Tristan en prose* who died as a result of his love for Iseut la blonde. In the following ballad, Chambrillac invokes a series of literary figures in an attempt to discredit loyalty and illustrate the advantages of having many lovers. The devoted Troilus lost Criseyda to Diomedes, and the loyalty of Tristan and Iseut was never fully rewarded. However, Gauvain, the celebrated knight of the Round Table

> . . . qui tant pot valoir
> En proesce et en courtoisie,
> Ot en maint lieu dame choisie. (response 2, vv. 29–31)

[. . . who succeeded so well in showcasing his valor and courtliness, had a chosen lady in many places.]

These literary examples expand the limits of the debate, increasing its relevance as a literary rather than merely a social exercise. Furthermore, this strategy authorizes and valorizes the voice of la Guignarde who, like these exemplary figures, exists only as the fictional creation of male authors.

Thus the compiler of the response ballads subtly exploits the disjunction between words and actions and the ambiguity of courtly language described by la Guignarde. Using the forum set up by the supporters of loyalty, he or she manipulates the exchanges into an example of and testament to the power of language to convey multiple and even contradictory messages. This apparent female threat, however, exists in a text that originates in and is directed toward the restricted society of male noblemen. The authors write for and dialogue with their peers. In this masculine universe, then, la Guignarde signals difference—things are not as they seem. As la Guignarde teaches, one must always look "derriere [la] baniere / De Loiauté" to see what appearances may conceal. Her lesson encourages us to look beyond outward appearance and through conventional language to discover what lurks in the shadows. Hidden beneath the pretty trappings of a courtly lady, one just might find a knight bent on seduction using lies and ungentlemanly force. In spite of attempts to silence her, the dialogic dynamic and the poetics of compilation amplify the voice of dissent embodied by la Guignarde, and it is ultimately she who has the last word—one that speaks directly to Jean le Seneschal and all of his courtly companions.

NOTES

Author's note: An earlier version of this paper was presented at the South Atlantic Modern Language Association Convention in Atlanta in November 1997.

1. My analysis will focus on the edition of Gaston Raynaud, which is based on Manuscript C, corrected against Manuscripts A, B, and G. The complete text of the response ballads is found in Manuscript A. See Raynaud, *Les Cent Ballades*, for a complete discussion of the manuscripts and the edition.

2. For a more detailed discussion of the *jeu-parti*, see Gally, "Disputer d'amour" and "Jeux partis de Thibaut."

3. Saïm, "Altérité et socialité," 83–92; emphasis is Saïm's, translation is mine.

4. This does not mean that no women could participate in a literary debate. Christine de Pizan participated actively in many political and literary debates with her male contemporaries. However, she was a professional poet and not a

courtly lady. The *dame* functions as the object rather than the subject of courtly love poetry.

5. Reed, *Middle English Debate Poetry*, 147.

6. Christine de Pizan, *Oeuvres poétiques de Christine de Pizan*, ed. Maurice Roy (Paris: Firmin Didot, 1891), 2:97. This character is identified as Pierre d'Aumont, known as Hutin in the *Mémoires de la Société de l'histoire de Paris* (Paris, 1890), 2:308–9.

7. All citations of the *Livre des Cent Ballades* are taken from Raynaud's edition and are identified by ballad and verse numbers; all translations are my own.

8. See ballads 20, 22, 38, 49, and 50.

9. See ballads 68 and 94.

10. Faral, "La Pastourelle," 211.

11. Although the terms used to identify the prospective respondents to the debate (*amoureux, compagnons*) could be gender neutral, the words used with them specify masculine virtues specifically associated with *chevalerie*. The context in which these terms are used (Jean refers to "compagnons," which would be his peers, thus male noblemen) also suggests that only male responses are envisioned. This hypothesis is confirmed not only by courtly convention but by the response ballads themselves.

12. Reynaud, preface to *Les Cent Ballades*, xlviii–l.

13. In response ballad 9, Yvry lists a number of women whose favors disloyal lovers may seek. These references are simply common female names and do not refer to specific individuals or literary figures: "Prier Belon et sadaier Mabire, / Guignier d'un oeil a Agnez et sourrire / A Marote" (vv. 4–6) [Court Belon and put on airs with Mabire, wink at Agnez and smile at Marote]. It is interesting to note that he uses the diminutive forms, which occur frequently in the *pastourelle* tradition.

Selected Bibliography

Cottrell, Robert. "Le Conflit des générations dans les *Cent Ballades*." *French Review* 37 (1964): 517–23.

Faral, Edmond. "La pastourelle." *Romania* 99 (1975): 204–59.

Gally, Michèle. "Disputer d'amour: Les Arrageois et le jeu-parti." *Romania* 107 (1986): 55–76.

———. "Jeux partis de Thibaut de Champagne: Poétique d'un genre mineur." In *Thibaut de Champagne, Prince et poète au XIIIe siècle*, edited by Yvonne Bellenger and Danielle Quéruel, 89–97. Lyon: La Manufacture, 1987.

Raynaud, Gaston, ed. *Les Cent Ballades: Poème du XIVe siècle*. Paris: Firmin Didot (Société des Anciens Textes Français), 1905.

Reed, Thomas L., Jr. *Middle English Debate Poetry and the Aesthetics of Irresolution*. Columbia and London: University of Missouri Press, 1990.

Roy, Maurice, ed. *Œuvres poétiques de Christine de Pizan*. Paris, 1891.

Saïm, Mirela. "Altérité et socialité dans le dialogue médiéval." *Discours social/ Social Discourse* 2 (1989): 83–92.

9

Woman's Cry

Broken Language, Marital Disputes, and the Poetics of Medieval Farce

Christopher Lucken

> Le mary: Saincte sang bieu, quelz motz cuisans,
>   Quel double mors, quelle tranchefille!
>   El desvide plus qu'elle ne fille
>   De babil, sans comparaison.
> Le magister: Femmes ont le bruyt pour parler.
> La femme: Victoire aux femmes, et dehet![1]
>
> to the *belle noiseuse*

Domestic disputes are one of the main features of medieval farce. In keeping with the well-known misogynistic topos, the chattering quarrelsome woman provokes countless squabbles which call into question the union of the two spouses joined together in holy matrimony. She's a burden for her husband, but how could the farce work without her? without her obstreperousness? She rules the stage and proves to be the foundation and the emblem of a poetics that plays on her *noise*—on the sounds and discordances sparked by her excessively loose tongue—in order to deploy a form of language that is severed from intelligibility or any logic of "communication." Before looking at how the authors of such farces played with this misogynistic tradition, making it serve their own comic purposes, I shall begin by considering the origins of the loud-mouthed woman figure—this woman whose cry perturbs man's reason, preventing him from retreating, in the company of his silent double, into the paradisiac garden of a work of art whose harmony echoes that of the spheres.

MAN SPEAKS, WOMAN DANCES

Written toward the end of the thirteenth century and dedicated to "madame Dyonise de Mountechensi pur aprise de langage," to teach French vocabulary to young Englishmen, Walter de Bibbesworth's *Tretiz* contains a feature typical of this kind of book, a section listing the natural *cries* of all sorts of beasts ("la naturele *noise* des toutes manere des bestes"):[2]

Home parle, ourse braie
Ki a demesure se desraie;
Vache mugist, gruue groule,
Leoun rougist, coudre croule,
Chivaule henist, alouwe chaunte,
Columbe gerist e coke chaunte,
Chate mimoune, cerpent cifle,
Asne rezane, cine recifle,
Louwe oule, chein baie . . .
Gopil cleye, thesson traie
Quant li venour li quer praie.
Ouwe jaungle, jars agroile,
Ane en marais jaroile . . .
Crapaut coaule, reyne gaille,
Collure proprement regaille.
Purcel gerist, cengler releie,
Cheverau cherist e tor torreie.
Troye groundile quant drache quert;
Faucoun tercel le plounoun fert.
Ausint diez li geline patile
Quant pouné ad en gardin ou en vile . . .
E ki trop se avaunce sanz resoun
A la geline est compaignoun
Ki plus se avaunce pur un eof
Ki sa arure ne fet li boef.
Berbiz baleie, dame bale. (vv. 248–87)

[Man speaks, the bear growls
And flares up exceedingly;

The cow lows, the crane clatters,
The lion roars, the hazel rustles,
The horse neighs, the lark sings,
The dove coos and the cock crows,
The cat mews, the snake hisses,
The donkey brays, the swan whistles,
The she-wolf howls, the dog bays . . .
The fox yelps, the badger wails
When the hunter tears its skin off.
The goose cackles, the gander honks,
The duck quacks in the marshes . . .
The toad caws, the frog croaks,
The grass snake in truth feasts itself.
The piglet squeals, the boar grumbles,
The kid troats and the bull bellows.
The sow grunts when she searches for grain;
The tiercel falcon strikes the diver.
And you will say that the hen clucks
When she has laid in the garden or in the farm . . .

And whoever puts himself forward without reason
Resembles the hen
Who vaunts herself more for an egg
Than the ox that plows.
The ewe bleats, the lady dances.]

In keeping with the second narrative of the Creation in the book of
Genesis, Walter de Bibbesworth begins his enumeration of animal noises
with that of man. In the beginning, there was silence, until God had his
creatures appear before Adam "to see what he would call them" (Gen.
2:19); this is when Adam first spoke. Man thus manifested his capacity
for reason, both as thought and as language, showing that he had been
created in the image and after the likeness of God (Gen. 1:26). A mosaic in Saint Mark's in Venice shows Adam, who is about to name the
animals, turning his face toward Him from whom all reason flows, the
better to hear His voice—a reminder that the Judeo-Christian tradition
sees human language as the mimetic reflection of the Divine Word
that breathed life into Creation. It is its sonorous, terrestrial version.
Neither corrupted nor shattered by Babel, Adam's speech was one with
the Word of the Father. It was perfect. Which is why Philo of Alexandria

(first century A.D.) asserts that the "giving of names" by the first man was "in no wise incongruous or unsuitable, but bringing out clearly the traits of the creatures who bore them. For the native reasoning power in the soul being still unalloyed, and no infirmity or disease or evil affections having intruded itself, he received the impressions made by bodies and objects in their sheer reality, and the titles he gave were fully apposite, for right well did he divine the character of the creatures he was describing, with the result that their natures were apprehended as soon as their names were uttered."[3] Man at the same time proclaimed his supremacy over creatures that lacked reason. No animal sound can match human language. All the beasts have to offer are their different cries. Similarly, none of the creatures brought before Adam can be compared to him (Gen. 2:20). Man had complete authority over them (Gen. 1:26). Gifted with speech that originated in the Divine Number, he was the King of Creation.[4]

Having enumerated the cries of the animals, and in conformity with the order of the biblical narrative, Walter de Bibbesworth's *Tretiz* continues with woman's "cry"—and after all, wasn't Eve created to put an end to Adam's "bestiary"? But while man speaks, woman dances: "home parle . . . dame bale." Instead of keeping to the vocabulary used to describe the phonic characteristics of the creatures he refers to, Bibbesworth, as soon as he comes to woman, seems to get carried away with the play of the signifier and to abandon his original plan. The woman's "cry," or whatever is used here to represent it, is marked by a deformation of the verb designating the "cry" of man (by the voicing of the initial *p* and the assimilation of the *r*), as if women could only denature his speech and, by preferring the imitation to the reality, call into question the manifestation of reason. Indeed, it would seem that the cries of the animals, which come between them like an inventory of passions, have contributed to the disruption of their mutual understanding. The term used for the "cry" of the "lady" is, more specifically, introduced by the verb that designates the sound of the ewe which bleats ("qui baleie"), mentioned just before. This is not without reason. As can be seen in the farce of *Maître Pathelin*, the bleating of the ewe, or the sheep, stands for a language void of meaning and may function as a parody version of human speech.[5]

In Bibbesworth's *Tretiz*, this shift from one signifier to another marks a deviation in the discourse. From this point on, the list of animal cries turns into a sequence of words that seem to grow out of each other like echoes. Thus, with the presence of woman, the classification of vocabulary describing the "naturele noise" of the animals, introduced by human speech and echoing the naming of the animals by Adam, gives way to the dance of words joined in accordance with their *noise*. The reason that founded the act of naming is swept up into the musical rhythm of signifiers whose *noises* blur any sense of logic. Scholastic classification turns into poetic play:

> Espicer prent ces mers de bale.
> Par trop veiller home baal;
> A sun serjaunt sa chose baille.
> Aprés dormer hom se espreche;
> Le prestre en le eglise preche;
> Li peschour en viver pesche
> Ore de sa rey, ore de son hesche.
> Faily lest sa tere fresche
> Pur achater sa char freische.
> Quant povre femme mene la tresche,
> Plus la vaudrait en mein la besche,
> Car el n'ad ou se abesche
> De payn ne a b[ri]be ne a lesche.
> Soun chael la paele lesche.
> Ore donez a chael a flater,
> Ki lesche la rosé de l'herber.
> Eschuez flatour ki seet flater
> E les genz espeluper.
> E tun chaperoun ne veut lesser
> Un poyton, tant ad cher
> Noun pas tei, mes tun aveir
> Ke desire de tei aver. (vv. 288–309)

[The grocer takes these bales of goods.
From staying up too late, man yawns;
He yields his goods to his servant.
Having slept, man stretches and yawns;
The priest preaches in the church;
The fisherman fishes in the fish pond,
Now with a net, now with a hook.
The lazybones leaves his land lying fallow
To go and buy fresh meat.
When a poor woman leads the dance,
She'd better be off spade in hand,

For she has no bread to feed herself
Not even a chunk or slice.
Her puppy licks the pan.
Give the little animal something to lap,
Who licks the dew on the grass.
Avoid the flatterer who is skilled at flattering
And despoiling people,
And who will not leave even a thread
Of your hood, so strongly he cares
Not for you, but for your possessions
Which he desires to take from you.]

This play on the signifier introduced by the "dame" (whose dance is taken up here by the "povre femme," thus sketching out the typical situation of the fabliau or farce), and the subversion of the grammatical utterance that follows, can be considered perfectly emblematic of the role generally attributed to woman with regard to man's speech—which is constantly in danger of lapsing into the diabolic rhetoric of the "lescheors," the lechers and other flatterers.

EVE, OR THE GENESIS OF NOISE

In the second narrative of the Creation, as we know, God creates the animals and brings them before Adam so that he might find a companion similar to himself, for "It is not good that the man should be alone" (Gen. 2:18–19). Since no animal is suitable, God takes one of his ribs and makes a woman from it (2:20–23). Adam names her from the word used for his own gender, placing her in the order of discourse. "Therefore shall man . . . cleave unto his wife; and they shall be one flesh" (2:24). Woman's raison d'être is the reflection of man's. If man is made in the image of God, then woman is first of all created in the image of man.[6] And that is why she must remain united with her husband and obey him, as the body does the head (Eph. 5:22–24), submitting to the authority of him through whom she is attached to God.[7]

According to Philo of Alexandria, it is the fact that woman was separated from the body of man that caused the misfortune that befell him. "For so long as he was by himself, as accorded with such solitude, he went on growing like to the world and like to God." If love "brings together and fits into one the divided halves," at the same time it engenders "bodily pleasure, that pleasure which is the beginning of wrongs and violation of law, the pleasure for the sake of which men bring on themselves the life of mortality and wretchedness in lieu of that of immortality and bliss"—which pleasure Philo identifies with the serpent.[8] At the heart of the division of the sexes, within the cleft that separates man and woman, instead of the amorous relation that should unite them, there exist passions born of physical pleasure which are like so many animals over which man has lost all power and which now threaten his very reason.

For Augustine, the Fall was not due simply to the creation of woman and the separation of the sexes.[9] It was the work of the Devil, acting through the serpent. Whereas God brought the animals before Adam under the effect of an impulse felt directly in their souls,[10] and while he spoke to Adam's intellect—and *still speaks* to the angels—"without the noise of syllables" (*sine strepitu syllabarum*) as was the case for the Creation of the world,[11] the Devil spoke to woman through the intermediary of an "instrument":[12] a kind of phonatory apparatus that took the form of a beast not endowed with reason and which served to produce words perceptible to the senses. For, as Augustine points out, "The serpent did not understand the meaning of the words which were spoken through him to the woman, for we cannot suppose that its soul was changed into a rational soul."[13] The serpent embodies speech severed from reason, and the Devil is the origin of its capture through the senses. If we follow Augustine's logic here, it is not so much sexual division as such that brings about the Fall as the seductive power of language reduced to its "acoustic image," that is to say, in Saussurian terms, the play of the signifier detached from the signified that founds its legitimacy and authority.

It was the woman whom the serpent chose to persuade to disobey the order not to eat of the fruit of the knowledge of good and evil, an order that God had made known to the man. According to *Le Blasme des Fames*, a misogynous text composed toward the end of the thirteenth century:

> Pur ceo qe femme out fieble sens
> L'enginnat primes li serpens; . . .
> Puis lui donna une dowarie
> Ke fust unfant en toute sa vie;
> Otriat lui en gereisoun
> Que tus tens fust encontre reison.[14]

> [Because of woman's weaker wit
> She fell into the snake's gambit; . . .
> The dowry bestowed upon the wife

Was childishness throughout her life;
He granted her as remedy
A loathing for rationality.]

As we know, ever since antiquity it was common to think of woman as a fundamentally irrational being. Whereas man was given the attributes of reason and intelligence, she was associated with sensibility.[15] According to Saint Bonaventure, "woman, by giving ear to the suggestion of the serpent in the exterior book, did not turn back to the interior book which is evidenced by an upright decision of reason, but yielded to the sensual in the exterior book and began to negotiate for the exterior good."[16] Here, woman is a perfect example of the "illiterate" who responds to the envelope of the letter (the noises of the syllables) without being able to penetrate the meaning (the part of language that is silent, ultimately referring to the Divine Word). Rather than the Divine injunction, she prefers the discourse of the Devil which splits God into a plurality of names. She is more interested in words than in things, and makes the senses prevail over the intellect. She is therefore associated with the colors and figures of rhetoric which provide the—mendacious—finery of speech.[17]

Eve, says Augustine, "took some of the fruit and ate and gave some also to her husband, who was with her, using perhaps some persuasive words which Scripture does not record but leaves to our intelligence to supply."[18] Scripture does record what God said to Adam: "Because thou hast hearkened unto the voice of thy wife . . . cursed is the ground for thy sake" (Gen. 3:17). By preferring to listen to the seductive voice of his wife rather than to that of his Creator, Adam allows a disruptive element, a parasitic noise, to come between him and the Word. His reason is clouded by the hissing of the serpent, to which God's answer will be the curse that drives him and Eve out of paradise. In the Judeo-Christian tradition, it is in memory of this expulsion that the child cries when it comes into the world. According to Peter Comestor, the cry of female newborns forms an *e* and that of males an *a*.[19] Thus the alternating birth cries of women and men (*e vel a*) reproduces the name of their first mother. Man is now forced to use noisy "voices" to communicate. "If the words he utters have to be spoken aloud so that the ear can hear, this is because the world is a deep sea and the flesh is blind: men cannot see thoughts and therefore the truth must be dinned in their ears (*opus sit instrepere in auribus*)."[20] From now on, the idiom of paradise is followed by the tricks of a rhetoric cut off from the veracity of things, a rhetoric that emerges as a consequence of the Fall. And thus language carries within it not only life but also death.[21] In place of truth we have the endless list of all the utterances that belong to adulterated speech: lies, false evidence, perjury, quarrels and disputes, altercations, squabbles, contention, dissent and controversy, blasphemy, oaths, insults, abuse, defamation, slander, mockery, denigration, derision, sarcasm, insolence or, in another register, flattery and insincerity, chatter, gossip, verbal diarrhea, obscenity, coarseness, vulgarity, facetious remarks, pleasantries, and all kinds of idle or wild words, all of them noises born of the passions—sins of language that end up drowning out the Voice of God, finally reducing it to silence, thereby prefiguring the thunderous voices of the Apocalypse and the "wailing and gnashing of teeth" that await the damned in Hell.[22]

"Let your women keep silence in the churches," commands Saint Paul (I Cor. 14:34): they must remain quiet and obey the men for, as Paul insists, "Adam was first formed, then Eve," and it was not Adam who was deceived but the woman who, once deceived, transgressed the divine order (I Tim. 2:11–14). However, such an injunction is only of limited effect when applied to a womankind that can neither be reduced to silence nor brought back under the authority of reason. Haunted by the figure of Eve, behind which hides the hissing of the serpent, woman, in the tradition of medieval misogyny, is generally talkative and quarrelsome.[23] She talks for the sake of talking, or to drown out what others say, and is the source of an endless verbosity that smothers the reason of men. Because she shattered the language of Adam which had its source in the founding silence of the Divine Word, woman thus becomes the very incarnation of *noise*. She is, as the double meaning of this word in Old French indicates, both "noise" and "quarrel."[24] *Les Lamentations de Matheolus*, translated from Latin to French in 1371–72 by Jean Le Fèvre, explain this characteristic by pointing to the matter of which she was first made:

> Pourquoy sont femmes plus noiseuses,
> Plaines de paroles oiseuses
> Et plus jangleuses que les hommes?
> Car elles sont d'os et nous sommes
> Fais de terre en nostre personne:
> L'os plus haut que la terre sonne.[25]

> [Why are women more noisy,
> Full of idle words
> And more garrulous than men?

Because they are made of bones and we
Ourselves are made of earth
And bone sounds louder than earth.]

The *silence* of a person made of *earth* ("taire," to be silent, is the homo-phone of "terre," earth) by the hand of God—the masculine as mask—is followed by the *noise* of *bones*, or a *mouth* (if we take the Latin meaning of the word "os") which raises the voice to the point that it resembles a serpentine flute, the flute that devilishly disfigures the face when it forms the slit that blows behind its "persona," its mask. Eve turns the world into a stage with the Devil as prompter. How significant it is, then, that the first play we have in Old French is the *Jeu d'Adam* (*Adam's Play*), which represents the Fall! And no wonder the woman will play the lead role in farce, a genre that seems to repeat the story of the first human couple. Ever since, husband and wife are threatened by the memory of the first tempter, who returns to sow discord disguised in the figure of the lecherous lover.

"It is better to dwell in the wilderness, than with a contentious and an angry woman," advises Proverbs 21:19. The silence and solitude of monastic life dedicated to chastity afford a refuge from marital strife and the clamor of the world (*strepitus mundi*).[26] Farce throws man back into the turbulence of domestic "life."

FARCE: STAGING DOMESTICITY AS NOISE

In the amatory discourse represented by the courtly lyric, the lady is above all a tower of silence. Immured in her reserve, immobile as a mute image painted in the lover's heart, she does not answer his song.[27] In the fabliaux, however, woman is the heiress of Eve, and readily answers her husband back, questioning his reason, his role as master of the house, and indeed her very union with him. In contrast to the musical aesthetic of courtly song, founded as it is on the silence of the lady, there stands "the ill-fitting coat of the fabliaux."[28] For there is no *conjointure* capable of harmoniously tailoring a tale in which marriage is not the culmina-tion of an amorous adventure but, on the contrary, is revealed as the rent in the fabric of Nature.[29]

The theatrical equivalent of the narrative fabliau is farce.[30] But whereas the narrative is structured mainly on a series of incidents, dramatic rep-resentation puts greater emphasis on the speech of the protagonists: the confrontations and misunderstandings of man and wife are thus shifted from a register dominated by sexual adventures to one of linguistic interplay. Quarrels between the two spouses are a mainstay of farce.[31] They theatricalize a conflict that opposes the reason of the husband, which should ensure the smooth functioning of communal life, and the woman's irrepressible desire, which contradicts reason's legitimacy. Without her, there would be no play.

The *noise* to which the marriage is reduced appears, to begin with, as a vital preliminary to the action of the farce itself. It provides the initial situation. For example, the farce *Le Cuvier* (*The Washtub*) begins with the lamentations of the husband:

> Le grant dyable me mena bien
> Quant je me mis en mariage.
> Ce n'est que tempeste et oraige;
> On n'a que soulcy et peine.
> Tousjours ma femme se demaine
> Comme ung saillant; et puis sa mere
> Afferme tousjours la matiere.
> Je n'ay repos, heurt ne arrest;
> Je suis peloté et tourmenté
> De gros cailloux sur ma servelle.
> L'une crye, l'autre grumelle;
> L'une mauldit, l'autre tempeste.[32]

> [The great devil led me well
> When I got married.
> It's all tempest and storm;
> It's only worry and grief.
> My wife always behaves
> Like a hopping creature; and then her mother
> Always backs her up.
> I have no rest, halt or interruption;
> I'm pelted and tormented
> With big stones on my brain.
> One cries, the other growls;
> One curses, the other rages.]

This farce then continues by showing how the husband recovers the mastery that the woman contested. It ends when he finally manages to reestablish the rule of his own reason in the household, but it lasts as long as the woman keeps shouting—and we can be certain she won't wait long before starting to shout again: there is no end to her noise and there will always be a new farce to play.

The farce called *L'Obstination des femmes* (*Women's Obstinacy*) begins with a comparable complaint from the husband:

Genz mariez ont assez peine,
A bien considerer leur cas. . . .
A besongner ne fauldray pas;
Car, ce ma femme sourvenoit,
Certainement el me batroit.
Nuyct et jour n'y fait que hongner.
Il me faut aller besongner
Pour eviter son hault langaige.
Je vueil assouvir ceste caige;
Ce sera pour mettre une pie.[33]

[Married people have too much sorrow
To look kindly on their situation. . . .
I will not fail to toil;
For if my wife arrived unexpectedly,
Certainly she would beat me.
Night and day she keeps grumbling.
I must go on working
To avoid her loud speech.
I want to repair this cage;
It will be to put a magpie inside.]

The activity whereby the husband hopes to escape his wife's recriminations is a perfect reflection of his hopes: the *pie* (magpie, also chatterbox) that he tries to lock up in the cage he has repaired is an image of his wife: "Women never shut their beak," he reproaches her at one point ("Femmes n'ont jamais le bec clos": v. 171). But his hopes are vain. In riposte to the babbling bird, the wife comes up with another, this time representing her husband: the cuckoo, i.e., the cuckold ("ung coqu": v. 53), but also his—or another man's—cock. Naturally, it is the *pie* who has the last word. She regains her freedom after locking up the cuckoo in her own "caige" (v. 188). The man is now reduced to silence. And his wife no longer needs to shout at him.

The farce *Colin qui loue et dépite Dieu* (*Colin who praises and spites God*) builds on a common motif of narrative literature: the husband returns, after a long period away from home, to find the household much more wealthy, thanks to the good work of his wife's lover. "But the author of *Colin* seems to have adapted the subject for the stage by developing certain passages in keeping with the principles of farce, using the traditional dispute between the husband and wife, and the dialogue between the lover and the wife."[34] Indeed, the quarrels with his wife are the main factor that prompts Colin to leave. As he repeatedly complains at the beginning of the play, "Tousjours femme demande ou tence, / Sans avoir paix à l'environ" (vv. 40–41) [A woman is always importuning or chiding, / There is never any peace around her] and "Haro, que de br[a] it" or "bruit" (v. 85) [so much braying, or noise].

Il n'est au monde plus grant guerre,
Plus grant tempeste ne tonnerre,
Que d'ouyr ce dyable de femme. (vv. 127–29)

[There's no bigger war on earth,
No bigger tempest or thunder,
Than to hear this devilish woman.]

Colin decides to leave in order to go and "ouyr / L'oysellet par champs et par boys" (vv. 142–43) [hear the little bird in fields and woods]. Meanwhile, the lover calms the "criz" (v. 168) and the "clameur" (v. 206) of the woman who claims to have been abandoned.

The reasons for such discordant behavior on the part of wives is the subject of the farce *Les deux maris et leurs deux femmes* (*The Two Husbands and Their Two Wives*). The wife of the first husband cries, rages, and reprehends ("crye, tempeste et blasme"), while the other wife sings and talks ("chante et devise").[35] One is a stubborn hard-headed woman ("dure de teste": v. 580), the other has a yielding behind ("tendre du derriere": v. 579). The second husband advises the first (v. 117) to hush his wife by giving her a good "clystere" (enema):

Il fault que le bas soit ouvert;
Aultrement la teste se pert.
Car, voys-tu, la challeur qu'elle a,
S'esvacuera par ce lieu là
Incontinent et sans arrest. (vv. 127–31)

[The lower part must be open;
Otherwise the head gets lost.
Because, you see, the heat she possesses
Will escape through this place
Forthwith and without cease.]

And if he were planning to attend to his wife's hindquarters himself by applying some astringent medicine ("restrainctif"), the second husband points out that

... la fumée retournera
Au cerveau, qui la te fera
Incessamment [crier et] braire. (vv. 143–45)

[... the fumes will return
To the brain, which will make her
Endlessly cry and bray.]

Which leads to the following conclusion:

Sans emmoindrir en rien leur fame
Icy nous disons qu'il n'est femme
Qui ne crie, tempeste ou blasme,
Ou à quelc'un le bas ne preste. (vv. 150–53)

[Without diminishing their reputation at all
We'll say here there isn't a woman
Who doesn't cry, rage or reprehend,
Or lend her lower part to someone.]

The sexual significance of such a rule—and of the only remedy possible to cure the woman's cry—will be made clear during the discussion
between the two wives. While the first refuses to give her body to her
husband, the second is happy to offer him her "flower" (v. 258). "And
so it is," she concludes, "that there is no *noise* in our house" ("Et par ce
point jamais de noyse / Nous n'avons en nostre maison": vv. 266–67). In
contrast, the first wife declares:

Nous chantons bien aultre leçon:
"Va, va, villain.—Va, va, villaine.
—Malle bosse!—Fiebvre quartaine!"
Et cent mille aultres mauldissons
[A] chascun coup nous nous disons. (vv. 268–72)

[We recite a very different lesson:
"Go, go, nasty fellow.—Go, go, nasty female.
—Evil hump!—Malaria fever!"
And a hundred thousand other oaths
We say to each other at every blow.]

Domestic rows thus represent the antithesis of woman's sexual pleasure:
they embody its reversal.

In the light of woman's stereotyped insatiability, the domestic peace
enjoyed by the husband of the woman with a yielding behind seems to

be quite exceptional. In both farce and fabliau, the *noise* of the stubborn hard-headed woman is the general rule. Such is the conclusion drawn by the character of the fool that the author of *Le Pauvre Jouhan* (*Poor John*) added to the trio formed by husband, wife, and lover. Acting as the tutelary figure of the noise that farce is constantly seeking and engendering ("Je suis partout pour avoir bruit" [I am everywhere to have noise]—"Je suis partout pour faire bruit" [I am everywhere to make noise]),[36] the fool interlards Jouhan's monologue at the end of the play with an aphoristic refrain whose emphatic repetition, at the end of each couplet pronounced by the husband, underlines the inevitability of its message. Indeed this aphorism can be considered one of the main rules of farce:

Jouhan:	Tout beau a esté de me taire
	Et de luy demander qu'elle a.
Fool:	Vela tout: qui femme a, noise a.
Jouhan:	Je me tue pour luy complaire.
	Par bieu, je ne sçay que luy faire,
	Et de pis en pis elle va.
Fool:	Vela tout: qui femme a, noise a.
Jouhan:	Je la cuide tousjours atraire
	Par beau parler et debonnaire;
	Mais sans cesser el tensera.
Fool:	Vela tout: qui femme a, noise a.
Jouhan:	Et quant je la voy ainsi braire,
	Je me tais et m'en voys retraire
	En ung coing, et la laisse la.
Fool:	Vela tout: qui femme a, noise a. (vv. 410–24)

[Jouhan:	In vain have I kept silent
	And asked her what's the matter.
Fool:	The fact is, who has a wife has noise.
Jouhan:	I'm killing myself to please her.
	By Gosh, I don't know what I can do for her
	And she's getting worse and worse.
Fool:	The fact is, who has a wife has noise.
Jouhan:	I always hope to attract her
	With sweet and gentle talk,
	But constantly she will slang me.
Fool:	The fact is, who has a wife has noise.
Jouhan:	And when I see her braying so,

I keep quiet and I withdraw
In a corner, and leave her there.
Fool: The fact is, who has a wife has noise.]

A NOISE MACHINE

In farce, woman's *noise* plays more than a thematic or narrative role. It has major consequences in terms of the actual discourse. For instead of offering a simple realistic representation of married life, or a misogynistic satire of women and society, or support for some traditional moral, the domestic quarrels lead to what Robert Garapon has called a "verbal fantasia"—that is to say, to repartee in which linguistic play is more important than the strict desire to communicate or signify (inside the couple as well as toward the public).[37] Here, I shall limit myself to only one mode: repetition. A good example can be found in *Colin qui loue et dépite Dieu*, after the husband has complained of having to work while his wife (who, as is usually the case, has no name) spends all the money he earns:

The woman: Colin!
Colin: Hau!
The woman: Muez ce langaige.
Colin: Comme quoy?
The woman: Il fault l'argent.
Colin: C'est au propos de mon courage.
The woman: Colin!
Colin: Hau!
The woman: Muez le language.
Colin: Parlez de faire bon potaige;
            Car ce parler n'est beau ne gent.
The woman: Colin!
Colin: Hau!
The woman: Muez ce language.
Colin: Comme quoy?
The woman: Il fault de l'argent.
Colin: Et pour quoy? (vv. 12–20)

[The woman: Colin!
Colin: Ay!
The woman: Change this language.
Colin: How so?

The woman: We need money.
Colin: That's what I was thinking.
The woman: Colin!
Colin: Ay!
The woman: Change this language.
Colin: Say you'll make a good soup;
            Because this talk is not nice nor gentle.
The woman: Colin!
Colin: Ay!
The woman: Change this language.
Colin: How so?
The woman: We need money.
Colin: And what for?]

This passage consists of a triolet (ABaAabAB), followed here by the beginning of a new verse which suggests the endless repetition of the same dialogue.[38] The regular reiteration of the refrain, characteristic of this fixed-form close to the rondeau and frequently used in the farce, breaks with the dramatic action and introduces a lyrical structure that marks a suspension of time favorable to the play of language. It is clear that this is more important here than the actual story. The text organizes the couple's dispute which tends to burst language into meaningless pieces, containing the overflow of their dialogue within a formal arrangement, but it does so using a mechanical procedure that tends to remove any signifying value from the words and to assimilate them to the grating cogs of a machine: a noise machine fueled by the shattered leftovers of a language incapable of establishing any basis for understanding between the spouses. The laughter it provokes would be the echo of this shattering.[39]

This procedure is amplified in *L'Obstination des femmes*, when the husband and wife fall to arguing about the kind of bird to be locked up in the cage:

Rifflart: Et, belle dame, taisez-vous;
            Paix!
The woman: Pour [qui]?
Rifflart: Taisez-vous meshuy.
The woman: Pour ung loudier, pour ung yvrongne.
Rifflart: Encores!
The woman: Fy, fy, fy!

Rifflart:	C'est trop dit;
	Paix!
The woman:	Pour qui?
Rifflart:	Taisez-vous meshuy.
The woman:	Me tayrai-ge pour ung yvrongne?
Rifflart:	Avoir pourriés sus vostre trongne.
The woman:	De qui? de vous?
Rifflart:	Et de qui doncques?
The woman:	Faictes, faictes vostre besongne.
Rifflart:	Avoir pourriés sus vostre trongne.
The woman:	Par Nostre Dame de Boulongne,
	Je ne vous crains en rien quelconques.
Rifflart:	Avoir pourriés sus vostre trongne.
The woman:	De qui? de vous?
Rifflart:	Et de qui doncques?
	Par la mort bieu, je ne vis oncques
	Femme qui eust telle caboche.
	Mais que j'aye mis cy une broche,
	Ma caige sera assouvie.
The woman:	Et qu'i mettra l'en?
Rifflart:	Une pie.
The woman:	Mais ung coqu.
Rifflart:	Mais ung estronc.
	Laissez moy faire.
The woman:	Quel follie!
	Mais qu'i mettra l'en?
Rifflart:	Une pie.
	Elle sera cointe et jolie,
	Et si sera à demy ront.
The woman:	Mais qu'i mettra l'en?
Rifflart:	Une pie.
The woman:	Mais ung coqu.
Rifflart:	Mais ung estronc.
	Aussi tost que les gens l'orront
	Appeller macquereau, siffler,
	Par mon ame, ce sera f[er]!
	Il n'en fault point parler du pris.
The woman:	Ung coqu dedans sera mis,
	Qui est ung oyseau de grant bien.

Rifflart: Par my foy, je n'en feray rien;
   Et ne m'en parlés plus, Finette.
   Aussi tost qu'elle sera faicte,
   G'iray une pie achepter.

The woman: Pourquoy faire?

Rifflart: Pour y bouter.

The woman: Sainct Jehan, mais ung coqu jolis.

Rifflart: Se sur vous je gette mes gris,
   Vous dirés une pie.

The woman: Feray?
   Par Dieu, ennuyct ne me tairay
   [D'ung coqu;] oués-vous?

Rifflart: La chair bieu, vous aurés des coups.
   Tenés, dictes la pie. Ferés.

The woman: Mais ung coqu.

Rifflart: Vous en aurés.

The woman: C'est pour neant; avant me tueriés.

Rifflart: Dictes une pie, je vous prie.

The woman: Non feray, par saincte Marie,
   Mais ung coqu.

Rifflart: Vous en aurés
   Plus de cent coups, n'en doubtés mye. (vv. 75–124)

[Rifflart: And, good lady, shut up;
   Peace!

The woman: For whom?

Rifflart: Shut up at once.

The woman: For a rotter, for a drunkard.

Rifflart: More!

The woman: Fie, fie, fie!

Rifflart: Too much talk;
   Peace!

The woman: For whom?

Rifflart: Shut up at once.

The woman: Shall I keep quiet for a drunkard?

Rifflart: You could get it in your bloated face.

The woman: Who from? From you?

Rifflart: And who else, then?

The woman: Go on, do your work.

Rifflart: You could get it in your bloated face.

The woman: By Our Lady of Boulogne,
          I don't fear you in any thing.

Rifflart: You could get it in your bloated face.

The woman: Who from? From you?

Rifflart: And who else, then?
          By 'Sdeath, I've never seen
          A wife with such a nut.
          But when I manage to put a pin here,
          My cage will be mended.

The woman: And what shall we put in it?

Rifflart: A magpie.

The woman: But a cuckoo.

Rifflart: But a turd.
          Let me do it.

The woman: What madness!
          But what shall we put in it?

Rifflart: A magpie.
          It'll be sweet and pretty,
          And it will be half-round.

The woman: But what shall we put in it?

Rifflart: A magpie.

The woman: But a cuckoo.

Rifflart: But a turd.
          As soon as the people hear it
          Call mackerel, whistle,
          By my soul, it will be fine!
          No need to talk of the price.

The woman: A cuckoo will be put inside,
          Which is a bird of great worth.

Rifflart: By my faith, I won't do such a thing;
          And don't say more to me, Foxy.
          As soon as it's done,
          I will buy a magpie.

The woman: What for?

Rifflart: To put it inside.

The woman: Saint John, but a pretty cuckoo.

Rifflart: If I put my claws on you,
          You will say a magpie.

The woman: Shall I?
            By God, I'll never stop saying
            A cuckoo, can you hear?
Rifflart: Odds bodkins, you'll get a beating.
            Here, say magpie. Go on.
The woman: But a cuckoo.
Rifflart: You'll get it.
The woman: It's for nought; you'll have to kill me first.
Rifflart: Say a magpie, I beg you.
The woman: I shan't, by the Virgin Mary,
            But a cuckoo.
Rifflart: You'll get
            More than a hundred blows, be sure of that.]

The metrical structure of this long passage is rather complicated: after the first line it starts with a kind of triolet whose central couplet would be reduced (ABaAB), followed by a normal one, four lines and another triolet; then after thirteen lines with no special type of metrical structure (but not without repetition) we have two other couplets that can also be associated to the triolet, delimitated by a refrain (AabbA). Once again, the repetitive movement that constitutes this scene is more like a machinery for producing sound than a real dialogue. The language is constantly turning back on itself, giving no sign of any thought process that might enable the two characters to reach an understanding or progress toward the termination of their conflict. It goes nowhere.

The conjugal quarrels depicted in these farces generally develop into verbal games that bring about a complete break with the process of signification usually associated with the exchange of words. They thus shift from the level of the story—the opposition between husband and wife—to that of its representation in the theatrical space of language. Having nothing to do with the transmission of any message or any form of communication, leading to no agreement that would allow for the return of a silence synonymous with conjugal harmony, these domestic quarrels serve to introduce *noise* into the farce itself. This is the *noise* of language which, since it has nothing meaningful to say, deliberately makes a *charivari*, creates that turbulent confusion in which, amidst an ear-splitting racket, the wild hordes of an archaic world return to the civilization of the city to call into question the law that underlies the union of man and wife.[40]

This deviation of language—and the faltering of meaning that affects both the protagonists of the farce and the audience, or readers—reaches a climax at the very moment the couple comes to blows.[41] This indeed is the solution offered to the husband of the farce *Le pont aux ânes* (*The Asses' Bridge*) as a way of vanquishing his wife. Compared to the donkey because of her stubborn, intractable character, but also because of her bray (*brait*), the woman is assumed to require the same treatment as the quadruped to make her see sense. But the woman's return to silence at the same time marks the defeat of a language whose *noise* has condemned it to being only an incoherent sequence of sounds bound to yield to "stage games."[42] As the farce draws to an end, instead of speech, all we have is the clatter of blows traded between the man and the woman.

If it can be said that the *dame* of the courtly lyric is its specular image, then the chattering, quarrelsome woman is the incarnation of farce. Not only is she one of its characters, she is the very principle of the poetics deployed in the form itself. The fracture that her *noise* introduces into the marital relation can be seen as the pivot of a language that, having freed itself of the constraints of reason at the moment the woman challenges the authority of her husband, gives itself up to its own sound without trying to establish the slightest harmonic relation between the protagonists.[43] Woman's cry, which marks the opening of so many farces, becomes the "cry" of the farce, thus echoing the call usually placed at the beginning of *sotties* in the manner of the cries uttered on the streets by barkers selling their wares or town criers proclaiming important events.[44] It initiates and announces the farce whose generative principle it contains. The authors of these farces are not concerned either to vindicate or to condemn the descendant of Eve. Using the figure of the shrew in pursuit of their own artistic purposes, using her in accordance with a rhetorical pattern rather than a simple expression of a misogynistic tradition, as a means to contradict the need for intelligibility represented by man and the theory of signs that goes with it, these farces play with their characters in order to play their own game, that of a language left to its sensuous fantasy in a world where the Fall has put an end to the Word of God[45]—a language whose sounds drown out not only reason but also the ideal, silent beauty of the courtly *dame*, vanished in the broken dream of a *conjointure*, a conjoining based on that love which is generated by the divine Number—leaving us with the *belle noiseuse*.[46]

NOTES

Author's note: This article was originally published in French, in a slightly different form, under the title "Le cri de la femme: Bris de langue, scènes de ménage et poétique de la farce médiévale" in *Equinoxe* 14, *Bruits* (1995): 83–98. The English version has been translated with the invaluable help of Charles Penwarden; if not otherwise stated, the translations of medieval French and Latin texts are ours.

1. These three rejoinders are taken from three farces found in Tissier, *Recueil de farces:* the husband's ("'Sblood, such biting words, / What a double jaw, what a hatchet face! / She reels off more than she spins / Her prattling, beyond compare") is from *Le Pont aux ânes,* 6:92–93, vv. 100–103; the master's ("Women are famous for speaking" or equally "Women have noise to speak with") is from *Maître Mimin Étudiant,* 3:271, v. 409; and the wife's ("Victory to women, by Gosh!") is from *Le Chaudronnier,* 3:101, v. 61.

2. de Bibbesworth, *Le Tretiz,* 3. See also Rothwell's introduction and bibliography, 1–2. Verse references on the two long quotes are to this edition.

3. Philo of Alexandria, *De Opificio Mundi,* 149–50. On the naming of animals by Adam, see Muratova, "Adam donne leurs noms."

4. Augustine, *Genesis,* IX:xiv.25.

5. This analogy is already manifest in classical Latin with the word *balare* (to bleat).

6. See I Cor. 11:7. On this question, see Aubert, *Les Femmes: Antiféminisme et christianisme,* 86–92.

7. "The woman with her husband is the image of God in such a way that the whole of that substance is one image, but when she is assigned her function of being an assistant, which is her concern alone, she is not the image of God; whereas in what concerns the man alone he is the image of God as fully and completely as when the woman is joined to him in one whole" (Augustine, *The Trinity,* XII:iii.10). On the position of woman and the tradition of misogyny in the Christian church in the Middle Ages, see the essays in Ruether, *Religion and Sexism;* d'Alverny, "Comment les théologiens et les philosophes voient la femme"; and Bloch, *Medieval Misogyny,* esp. 22–27.

8. Philo of Alexandria, *De Opificio Mundi,* 151–52; see also *Legum allegoriae,* 72, and Gregory of Nyssa, *The Creation of Man,* chaps. 17 and 18.

9. On the consequences of this concept, see Clark, "Adam's Only Companion."

10. Augustine, *Genesis,* IX:xiv.24–25.

11. Augustine, *Confessions,* XI:iii.5 and XIII:xv.18.

12. "In the serpent it was the Devil who spoke, using that creature as an *instrument,* moving it as he was able to move it and as it was capable of being moved, to produce the sounds of words and the bodily signs by which the woman would understand the will of the tempter" (*Genesis,* XI:xxvii.34, italics mine). See also Jager, *The Tempter's Voice.*

13. Augustine, *Genesis*, XI:xxviii.35.

14. *Le Blasme des Fames*, vv. 21–28; this text is in Fiero, Pfeffer, and Allain, *Three Medieval Views*.

15. Philo of Alexandria, *De Opificio mundi*, 165, and *Legum allegoriae*, 2:38; and Lloyd, *The Man of Reason*.

16. Bonaventure, *Breviloquium*, III:iii.2.

17. Quintilian's animadversions on "feminine" verbal excess (e.g., in his *Institutio oratoria*, VIII:proemium.20 and VIII.iii.6) can be compared with those of Tertullian in *On the Apparel of Woman*.

18. Augustine, *Genesis*, XI:xxx.39.

19. Peter Comestor, *Historia Scholastica*, Patrologia Latina 198, col. 1071.

20. Augustine, *Confessions*, III:xxii.34.

21. James 3:5–10.

22. Casagrande and Vecchio, *I Peccati della lingua*.

23. Ibid., and Bloch, *Medieval Misogyny*, 14–22. The abundance of this misogynistic discourse is such that it invites parallels with its subject, as if these commentators themselves took on the volubility they condemned in women. To give a few examples, Proverbs compares "a woman's quarrelling" to "an endless guttering" (19:13 and 27:15). "She floods his house with constant nagging and daily chatter, and ousts him from his own home, that is church," says Jerome in his treatise *Adversus Jovinianum* (I:28, translated in *A Select Library of Nicene and Post-Nicene Fathers of the Christian Church*, 2d ser., eds. Philipp Schaff and Henry Wace [Grand Rapids, Mich.: Eerdmans, 1890–1900]), 6:367. In the third book of his *De amore*, Andreas Capellanus states that "all woman are . . . free with their tongues, for not one of them can restrain her tongue from reviling people, or from crying out all day long like a barking dog over the loss of a single egg, disturbing the whole neighborhood for a trifle. A woman gossiping with other women would never willingly give another a chance to speak; she always tries to dominate the conversation with her own opinions, and to go on talking longest. Her tongue or breath could never be exhausted by talking. We see, too, numerous women on many occasions who are so keen to talk that when they are alone they break into speech, and speak out aloud to themselves. Then too a woman recklessly contradicts everyone, and could never agree with anyone's opinion, but always strives to put her own view first on every topic" (*Andreas Capellanus on Love*, ed. and trans. P. G. Walsh [London: Duckworth, 1982], 317). The *Contenance des Fames* warns, "Ja de parlier ne cessera" (v. 89) [She'll talk your head off]; the text is in Fiero, Pfeffer, and Allain, *Three Medieval Views*. Also in that volume, the *Blasme des Fames* ends in Latin with a line (v. 147) that describes woman as "verbosum vas sine clave"—in other words, as a vessel full of words but without any kind of lid or plug. This misogynistic discourse can also be found in the classical tradition: in his famous sixth satire, Juvenal compares the "learned woman," whose flow of speech no one is able to halt, to "a din of cauldrons and bells" (v. 441).

24. See Andrieux-Reix, "Les bruits et la rumeur," 89–99, and especially, on the meaning of this word in medieval French, 89–93.

25. *Lamentations de Matheolus*, vv. 241–46.

26. This is the main argument of Jerome's *Adversius Jovinianum*, which was followed, in the Middle Ages, by a whole series of opuscules against marriage, such as the *Dissuasio ad Ruffinum philosophum ne uxorem ducat*, fictitiously attributed by Walter Map to a certain Valerius and included in his *De Nugis curialium*, or the *Lamentations de Matheolus*, Eustache Deschamps's *Miroir de mariage* and *Les XV Joies de mariage*, written circa 1400, not to mention *Le Roman de la Rose* by Jean de Meun. On the importance of silence and virginity, see Gehl, *"Competens Silentium,"* and Brown, *The Body and Society.*

27. See Lucken, "L'imagination de la dame."

28. See Bloch, *Scandal of the Fabliaux*, esp. 22–58.

29. According to the *De Planctu Naturae* written by Alan of Lille (late twelfth century).

30. On the relation between farce and fabliau, albeit in a different perspective from the one considered here, see B. Rey-Flaud, *La Farce*, esp. 35–143.

31. According, for example, to André Tissier, the kinds of situations shown in farce "are not very varied: husband and wife at loggerheads (in which case it is the subject of the debate or quarrel that provides diversity); or the husband, the wife and the lover (the personality of the lover is what provides diversity . . .)" (introduction to his *Recueil de farces*, 1:38). The fact that quarrels are an essential part of farce was already noted by Gustave Lanson, "Molière et la farce," *Revue de Paris*, 1 May 1901, 150; Bowen, *Caractéristiques essentielles*, 31, 46; and Aubailly, *Théâtre médiéval*, 115.

32. *Le Cuvier*, vv. 1–12, in Tissier, *Recueil de farces*, vol. 3.

33. *L'Obstination des femmes*, vv. 1–16, in Tissier, *Recueil de farces*, vol. 4.

34. Tissier, *Recueil de farces*, 1:116; on the narrative tradition, see 109–16.

35. *Les Deux maris et leurs deux femmes*, vv. 11 and 10, in Tissier, *Recueil de farces*, vol. 1.

36. *Le Pauvre Jouhan*, vv. 10 and 13, in Tissier, *Recueil de farces*, vol. 10 (1996).

37. "We know that quarrels occur frequently in our medieval farces," notes Robert Garapon. "But do these quarrels always have the realistic quality we often attribute to them? Often, the altercations in our old plays are embellished with sumptuous accumulations of insults and, as a result, become an almost pure verbal fantasia: often, the antagonists achieve an abundance in their invectives whose very form is amusing, independently of the irreducible opposition it is supposed to express. This is particularly true of certain marital scenes" (*Fantaisie verbale*, 83). Occurring "as soon as language is diverted from its usual function of communication," such "verbal fantasia can," says Garapon, "be defined as that which, in a given text, constitutes a game that is liberated from the concern of signification and set under the sign of gratuitousness" (10). On the different forms of "verbal fantasia" in fifteenth-century medieval theater, see

36–114. In an article called "Le réalisme de la farce" (*Cahiers de l'Association Internationale des Études Françaises* 26 [1974], 18), Garapon stresses again the importance of linguistic play over any sociological point of view: "What we call realism in the medieval farce may well just be a deliberate esthetical purpose, the will to retain from everyday life only some base, disgusting and laughable aspects." Halina Lewicka has also studied the language of the farce, but from an essentially lexical and descriptive point of view, in her book *La Langue et le style du théâtre comique* and in two papers on miscomprehension and the use of dialects published in *Études sur l'ancienne farce*, 57–72. See also Bowen, "Le théâtre du cliché."

38. I must thank Graham A. Runnals here for calling my attention to the precise poetic structure of the triolet in this and the following passage, which were not described accurately in the French version of this article.

39. Farce, which Bernadette Rey-Flaud calls a *machine à rire*, a laughter machine, could just as well be called a *machine à bruire*, a noise machine.

40. See H. Rey-Flaud, *Le Charivari*.

41. Concerning quarrels, Barbara C. Bowen observes that "the author [of farces] usually shows consummate skill in leading them adroitly to a crescendo. They start with reasonable, mild words, leading gradually to jocose or coarse insults, and then to threats of brutality and, finally, blows" (*Caractéristiques essentielles*, 46).

42. As defined by Bowen, "the term stage games designates physical comic games" (*Caractéristiques essentielles*, 35). "At the forefront of these stage games we of course find *blows*. . . . They are usually dealt by the husband to the wife, by the wife to the husband, or are reciprocal, and form the logical climax of a row, a vital feature of the depiction of a marriage" (37).

43. In *Bodytalk*, E. Jane Burns attempts to establish the anatomical-discursive components that characterize the subjectivity of the feminine voice and its alterity with regard to masculine reason in French medieval literature. The book has a chapter on farces and fabliaux, and particularly the farce *Les Deux maris et leurs deux femmes* (31–70). But are we really "listening" to "women's bodies" talking through the text, and not to a text playing with the stereotyped image of women? Can we understand these literary productions without taking into account their poetics? See also Solterer, *The Master and Minerva*.

44. On the function of the "cry" in the *sottie* form (satirical farce), see Dull, *Folie et rhétorique*, 104–32.

45. As Garapon points out, "the comic effect of verbal fantasia, far from belonging to the category of verbal sanctions masterfully brought to light by Bergson, often induces a state of euphoria and implicit admiration in the spectator—in a word, a happy mood—which is markedly different" (*Fantaisie verbale*, 24).

46. On the *belle noiseuse* in Balzac's *Chef-d'oeuvre inconnu*, see Michel Serres, *Genèse* (Paris: Grasset, 1982).

Selected Bibliography

d'Alverny, Marie-Thérèse. "Comment les théologiens et les philosophes voient la femme." *Cahiers de Civilisations Médiévales* 20 (1977): 105–29.

Andrieux-Reix, Nelly. "Les Bruits et la rumeur: *noise* au moyen âge." In *Et c'est la fin pour quoy sommes ensemble: Hommage à Jean Dufournet*, 1:89–98. Paris: Champion; Geneva: Slatkine, 1993.

Aubailly, Jean-Claude. *Le Théâtre médiéval profane et comique*. Paris: Larousse, 1975.

Aubert, Jean-Marie. *Les Femmes: Antiféminisme et christianisme*. Paris: Cerf/ Desclée, 1975.

Augustine, Saint. *Confessions*. Translated by R. S. Pine-Coffin. London: Penguin Books, 1961.

———. *The Literal Meaning of Genesis*. Translated by John Hammond Taylor, S.J. Vol. 11. New York: Newman Press, 1982.

———. *The Trinity*. Vol. 5 of *The Works of Saint Augustine*. Translated by Edmund Hill, O.P. Brooklyn, N.Y.: New City Press, 1990.

de Bibbesworth, Walter. *Le Tretiz*. Edited by William Rothwell. London: Anglo-Norman Text Society, 1990.

Bloch, R. Howard. *The Scandal of the Fabliaux*. Chicago: University of Chicago Press, 1986.

———. *Medieval Misogyny and the Invention of Western Romantic Love*. Chicago and London: Chicago University Press, 1991.

Bonaventure, Saint. *Breviloquium*. Translated by Erwin E. Nemmers. St. Louis: B. Herder, 1946.

Bowen, Barbara C. *Les Caractéristiques essentielles de la farce française et leur survivance dans les années 1550–1620*. Urbana: University of Illinois Press, 1964.

———. "Le théâtre du cliché." *Cahiers de l'Association Internationale des Études Françaises* 26 (1974): 33–74.

Brown, Peter. *The Body and Society: Men, Women and Sexual Renunciation in Early Christianity*. New York: Columbia University Press, 1988.

Burns, E. Jane. *Bodytalk: When Women Speak in Old French Literature*. Philadelphia: University of Pennsylvania Press, 1993.

Casagrande, Carla, and Silvana Vecchio. *I Peccati della Lingua: Disciplina ed Etica della Parole nella Cultura Medievale*. Rome: Istituto della Enciclopedia Italiana, 1987.

Clark, Elisabeth A. "Adam's Only Companion: Augustine and the Early Christian Debate on Marriage." *Recherches Augustiniennes* 21 (1986): 139–62.

Dull, Olga A. *Folie et rhétorique dans la sottie*. Geneva: Droz, 1994.

Fiero, Gloria K., Wendy Pfeffer, and Mathé Allain, eds. and trans. *Three Medieval Views of Women*. New Haven and London: Yale University Press, 1989.

Garapon, Robert. *La Fantaisie verbale et le comique dans le théâtre français: Du Moyen Âge à la fin du XVIIIe siècle.* Paris: Armand Colin, 1957.

Gehl, Paul F. "*Competens Silentium:* Varieties of Monastic Silence in the Medieval West." *Viator* 18 (1987): 125–60.

Gregory of Nyssa. *On the Creation of Man.* Vol. 5 of *Nicene and Post-Nicene Fathers.* 2d ser. Edited by Philip Schaff and Henry Wace. Peabody, Mass.: Hendrickson Publishers, 1994.

Jager, Eric. *The Tempter's Voice: Language and the Fall in Medieval Literature.* Ithaca and London: Cornell University Press, 1987.

Legum allegoriae.

Les Lamentations de Matheolus et le Livre de leesce de Jehan Le Fèvre de Resson. Edited by A. G. van Hamel. 2 vols. Paris, 1892–1905.

Lewicka, Halina. *La Langue et le style du théâtre comique des XVe et XVIe siècles.* 2 vols. Paris: Klincksieck; Warsaw: PWN (Éditions scientifiques de Pologne), 1960, 1968.

———. *Études sur l'ancienne farce.* Paris: Klincksieck; Warsaw: PWN (Éditions scientifiques de Pologne), 1974.

Lloyd, Genevieve. *The Man of Reason: "Male" and "Female" in Western Philosophy.* London: Methuen, 1984.

Lucken, Christopher. "L'imagination de la dame: Fantasmes amoureux et poésie courtoise." *Micrologus* 6 (1998). *La Visione e lo sguardo nel Medio Evo / View and Vision in the Middle Ages,* 2:201–23.

Muratova, Xenia. "Adam donne leurs noms aux animaux: L'iconographie de la scène dans l'art du Moyen Âge: les manuscrits des bestiaires enluminés du XIIe et du XIIIe siècles." *Studi Medievali* 16 (1975): 367–94.

Philo of Alexandria. *The Works of Philo: Complete and Unabridged.* Translated by C. D. Yonge. New updated ed. Peabody, Mass.: Hendrickson Publishers, 1993.

Rey-Flaud, Bernadette. *La Farce ou la machine à rire: Théorie d'un genre dramatique, 1450–1550.* Geneva: Droz, 1984.

Rey-Flaud, Henri. *Le Charivari: Les rituels fondamentaux de la sexualité.* Paris: Payot, 1985.

Ruether, Rosemary R., ed. *Religion and Sexism: Images of Woman in the Jewish and Christian Traditions.* New York: Simon and Schuster, 1974.

Solterer, Helen. *The Master and Minerva: Disputing Women in French Medieval Culture.* Berkeley, Los Angeles, and London: University of California Press, 1995.

Tissier, André, ed. *Recueil de farces (1450–1550).* 13 vols. Geneva: Droz, 1986–2000.

Contributors

Nadine Bordessoule teaches at the Collège de l'Aubépine in Geneva, Switzerland. She is the author of several articles on late medieval French literature, including "La Voix engloutie: Représentations de l'avalement du narrateur chez Christine de Pizan et François Rabelais," in *Constructions* (1994). Her book on images of the hunt in fourteenth-century literature is forthcoming from Lang.

Sally Tartline Carden was assistant professor of French at the University of Missouri–Rolla from 1996 to 1999. She has recently published articles on the works of René d'Anjou, Christine de Pizan, and Oton de Grandson in *Les Lettres Romanes, Le Moyen Français*, and the *Dictionary of Literary Biography*. She is currently taking a leave from teaching.

Joan Tasker Grimbert is professor of modern languages at the Catholic University of America, where she teaches French and medieval studies. Her publications include *"Yvain" dans le Miroir: Une poétique de la réflexion dans le "Chevalier au lion" de Chrétien de Troyes* (1988), *Tristan and Isolde: A Casebook* (1995), and *Songs of the Women Trouvères* (2000). She is preparing a second book on the Tristan legend.

Kathy M. Krause, professor of French at the University of Missouri-Kansas City, is the author of numerous articles on medieval literature and culture, and coeditor with Alison Stones of *Gautier de Coinci: Miracles, Music, and Manuscripts*. Her most recent articles appear in *Arizona Medieval and Renaissance Studies, English Language Notes*, and *Manuscripta*.

Christopher Lucken is *maître de conférences* at the University of Paris 8 (Vincennes/Saint-Denis) and *chargé de cours* at the University of Geneva. He has recently coedited "Paul Zumthor ou l'invention permanente" and "L'orgueil de la littérature: Autour de Roger Dragonetti" and is presently completing a monograph titled "Les Portes de la mémoire: Richard de Fournival ou l'Ariereban de l'amour."

William D. Paden is professor of French at Northwestern University. He is the author of *Introduction to Old Occitan* (Modern Language Association, 1998) and the editor of *Medieval Lyric: Genres in Historical Context* (University of Illinois Press, 2000). In 1995 he directed an NEH institute on medieval lyric.

Ana Pairet is assistant professor of French at Rutgers University. She has published articles on translation, historical writing, and medieval romance and is completing a book on myths and tales of metamorphosis in Medieval French literature.

Duncan Robertson is professor of French and Spanish at Augusta State University (Georgia). His studies, focused in recent years on Old French hagiographical writings, include *The Medieval Saints' Lives: Spiritual Renewal and Old French Literature* (French Forum, 1995) and "The Anglo-Norman Verse Life of St. Mary the Egyptian," in *Romance Philology* (1998). He is coediting, with Renate Blumenfeld-Kosinski and Nancy Warren, a volume of essays titled *The Vernacular Spirit*.

David J. Wrisley is assistant professor of French at the College of Staten Island (City University of New York). His research areas include Old French romance and hagiography in the thirteenth century, Burgundian prosification, and the literature of the Crusades. He is the author of "Narrating and Performing the Saintly in Romance: Philippe de Remi's *La Manekine*," in *Essays on the Literary and Legal Writings of Philippe de Remy/Beaumanoir* (Beaumanoir, 2000), and is preparing a monograph on Philippe de Remi.

Except for Kathy Krause, all biographies are current as of 2001.

Index

www.ingramcontent.com/pod-product-compliance
Lightning Source LLC
Chambersburg PA
CBHW021401090426
42742CB00009B/955